THE BIOGRAPHY OF A NEW CANADIAN FAMILY

THE BIOGRAPHY OF A NEW CANADIAN FAMILY

Volume IV

Pierre L. Delva
and
Joan Campbell-Delva

To order additional copies of this book, contact:
Xlibris Corporation
1-888-795-4274
www.Xlibris.com
Orders@Xlibris.com
110285

CONTENTS

CHAPTER 41

My first two years at the University of Montréal, (1974-1976).

Montréal was founded in 1642. The present campus of the **University of Montréal** was built between 1928 and 1943. Its tower can be seen for miles around, the centre of a large campus that spans three subway stops and three kilometers on the north-east slope of Mount-Royal.

The main building was designed by a world-famous architect trained in Paris (1908-1918), *Ernest Cormier* (Montréal, 1885-1980), the largest of his works and the best of his generation. He designed the Supreme Court of Canada in Ottawa amongst others and taught at the University of Montréal from 1925 to 1954.

It is the largest French-speaking University in the world outside Paris in France, with, **in 2006,** over 37,000 full-time and 18,000 part-time students in 237 undergraduate and 288 graduate programs. During the academic year 2004-2005, it received more than $430 million in research funding. It is the second largest in Canada after the University of Toronto, with a strong focus on the Sciences.

In retrospect, I consider myself very lucky to have been chosen in 1974 to work there at a crucial moment in its development and at an appropriate time for my career. I remained there for over fifteen years until I retired. In 1980-81, there were over 1800 professors on staff.

As of to-day (March 2006), *l'Université of Montréal* medical students have led the country for the past six years in the results of the Licence to Practice Medicine National Examinations (Licence Medical Colleges Canada).

An excellent history of *la faculté de Médecine de l'Université de Montréal* (500 pages) was published in **1993** to coincide with the one hundred and fiftieth anniversary of its founding, written by *Dennis Goulet.*

Guy Lamarche, an old acquaintance, had become associate dean in the Faculty of Medicine at *l'universite de Montréal* having moved from the *CHUS* where he, a basic scientist, was professor and head of the department of Physiology and Pharmacology.

He was a graduate of *l'UdeM,* had started working at *le CHUS* in July 1967 two years before I arrived. He returned to his Alma Mater perhaps a year or two after I had started work in Montréal and after a year at the ACMC (Association of Canadian Medical Colleges) in Ottawa where he was unhappy. I believe this was his only Canadian sojourn outside Quebec.

His roots in Quebec are quite old. Two of his brothers are also consultant physicians. We met fairly often, in Sherbrooke and in Montreal, and we agreed in lots of ways.

At Dean Bois' request, he became responsible for moving forward my successful demand to become a *Professeur Titulaire, département de médecine sociale et préventive,* (full Professor) in 1978, quite a headache in such a large institution.

The best way to give the reader a brief overview of the history of my new work-place is to translate the first half of the *'préface'* of the book *'histoire de la faculté de médecine de l'université de Montréal';* it was written by *Guy Lamarche* and is quite typical of his personality:

> *The first law for writing a history is not to lie;*
> *The second is not to be scared of telling the truth.*

> *Pope Léon XIII*, 1883.

The history of the Faculty of Medicine of the University of Montréal parallels that of French Canadians who, in 1843, failed to

---

*   **Leon XIII** (1810-1903) was Pope from 1878 to 1903. He recommended Catholics in France to support the Republic, and in a series of encyclicals on modern society *(rerum novarum, 1891)* encouraged a more social Catholicism and the evangelization of workers as well as more Biblical, Historical and Theological studies, thus attempting to modernize the thinking of the Church.

constitute a people or a nation, not even a society: perhaps to-day it might be referred to as just an ethnic group.

The defeat in 1759 skimmed them of their élites. After the brutal repressions of 1837-38 and after the Durham report, they are poor; their health is also poor; they are poorly educated, without government, without a University, dominated by a Church that fails to distinguish its pastoral mission from its cooperative interests, just busily administering its lands and possessions. It is itself divided in doctrinaire ways, Ultramontanism and Gallicisme**, each wanting to dominate the other. Impotent and without vision, the Quebec Church keeps referring to the Sacred Congregation of Propaganda in Rome for arbitration of debates and for the settlement of conflicts.

The above is even truer in Montréal where French Canadians are even poorer in this rich town where businesses are English, the Church Spires and Towers mainly Protestant, and the University Anglophone.

It is hardly surprising that the first medical school accessible for their children is not francophone but bilingual, founded by five Anglophone physicians, upset at not being able to be part of the only medical school in Canada at the time, English speaking McGill. The five founders start a medical school, conscious of its potential for professional growth, and, let's face it, for financial contributions from student clients and numerous French speaking patients.

That day in 1843 starts the history of a school which had only one objective during its first fifty years, mere survival.

Ignatius Bourget (1799-1885), the new young Bishop of Montréal appointed in 1840, became the rallying link. His message in 1848 was repeated in the schools and the parish churches for over a century: *Catholiques et Français toujours;* those two words became inseparable from then on.

The new *ecole de médecine et de chirurgie de Montréal* rapidly became unilingual *Catholique et Canadienne-française*, with the wholehearted support of *Monseigneur Bourget***, and, through him, the support of the nuns of the Hotel-Dieu Hospital, the Grey Sisters and the Sisters of Providence who opened the doors of their hospitals and dispensaries to the professors and their students.

** **Ultramontanisme:** theological doctrines favorable to the absolute power of the Pope

It was a victory over McGill, because McGill had nearly succeeded in assimilating the new school by offering help based at the Montréal General Hospital.

The laws in Quebec required University affiliation, but all efforts to obtain a cooperative partner in the Province of Quebec as well as in Kingston and Ottawa failed.

In 1866, Victoria College in Cobourg, Ontario, unexpectedly came to the rescue although no formal demand had been made.

Able now to grant diplomas through affiliation *ad practicandum,* the new school had to face an even tougher and powerful adversary, *l'université Laval* in Quebec City.

Through a papal *bulle* (an apostolic letter of general interest with a papal seal) **'Inter varias sollitudines'** in 1876, *l'université Laval* became a provincial University.

It decided to open a branch in Montréal, confident that it would be able to assimilate the new medical school and incorporate it in its own Faculty of Medicine.

Bishop Bourget resigned and the new School dug in its heels. The Quebec Church threatened the professors and their students with Excommunication. The Laval branch opened in 1878, but *l'École* did not close.

'Suspende omnia, schola continuet anno proximo' cabled cardinal Simeoni from Rome in 1883. Excommunication was thus avoided. The school continued to give its courses, the Laval branch also. The quarrel continued.

Rome and the Government of Quebec finally decide to fuse the two institutions; just at the same time Victoria College in Cobourg joined the University of Toronto; thus affiliation was discontinued. But the fusion marks the end of the hegemony of *l'université Laval:* apart from signing diplomas, it fails to retain power over its own Montreal branch.

'L'école de medecine et de chirurgie' keeps its name, its autonomy and its regulations.

Just up till **1920**. Up till then, *l'école* adjusts as much as possible to imported medical knowledge from France and continues to form good physicians who settled throughout Quebec. It then became the Faculty of Medicine of the University of Montreal. With the new direction, a kind of morose and delectable dreaming of the creation of a new University Medical Centre took over. Neglect ensued.

Still inspired by French medicine which promotes the art of medicine first rather than being primarily a science, the faculty is severely criticized and even threatened in 1955 by the American evaluation organizations particularly the Rockefeller Foundation and the American Medical Association. Finally the suggested changes are implemented.

In **1970**, a full-time Dean is appointed, paid clinical professors are hired and research initiated.

During the past two decades (1973-1993), the faculty has gradually reached its cruising speed, approaching the excellence of the best and largest of the North-American Medical Schools.

Guy Lamarche, MD

Gallicanisme: a more liberal approach, starting during the 16th and 17th centuries under Louis XIV and under Napoleon (Concordat, 1801) in France. It was finally squashed by the dogma of Infallibility of the Pope (1870) and the separation of Church and State (1905).

Bishop Bourget was *Ultramontain,* insisting that the state should be linked to and dominated by the Church. He had a vast diocese, from James Bay to the American border, 79 parishes, 34 mission churches and four Indian missions, over 186,000 people.

Under his leadership, religious orders became increasingly involved in education and health care.

His zeal inspired the raising of **507 'Zouaves'** from his diocese, all sent to Rome in 1868 to help defend the papal state. A Zouave was also the name of an infantry corps in the French Army originally formed of Algerians and retaining their oriental uniform between 1830 and 1962.

The **Flexner** report (1911) had errors which had to be corrected. Apologies were received.

The Creation of the Departments of Social and Preventive Medicine and of Family Medicine at l'UdeM.

The birth of both the Department of Social and Preventive Medicine and the Department of Family Medicine at the Faculty of Medicine of the University of Montréal was extremely laborious. **However, it did occur,** whereas at Queen's University John Read's efforts (Chapter 36) to create such a department, even after his appointment to do just that, had completely failed.

I had joined that new Department of Epidemiology and Preventive Medicine at Queen's in 1965. After just three years, John Read, who had arrived just a year before by invitation, joined the new faculty of the University of Calgary in 1968 to found the Department; I left in 1969, also by invitation, to join the new Medical School in Sherbrook.

The traditionally trained departmental epidemiologist became the next Head of Department at Queen's. The main reason the process failed in Kingston was the opposition of the Department of Internal Medicine, the big power-house.

The other main clinical departments, Surgery, Pediatrics, Obstetrics and Gynaecology just followed suit. Change at Queen's, founded in 1854, has often been difficult. The Unit of Family Medicine there was led by a young internist from Sudbury, his appointment consented by the Department of Internal Medicine at the suggestion of the Dean, an older person with whom I got on very well. Both were helpful and pleasant, unaware, as I was when I went to Queen's in 1965, of the complexity of the situation.

A proper Department of Family Medicine was only created at Queen's in 1973. Dr Ernie Haynes, a Family Physician, became head of the department. A new Family Practice building opened in 1977 down town, next to the Hotel-Dieu Hospital which now has no beds, half a mile away from the University Hospital, the Kingston General.

The **opposition was just the same** *à l'UdeM*, but the dean there was a younger anatomist who saw Medicine in a different light. At Queen's the dean was a neuro-surgeon, and surgeons are, as a group, quite obsessive, facing day-in day-out black and white questions. He had little respect for general practitioners, and failed to understand much about the new Community Medicine or the new Family Medicine. Do I cut or not cut, that was his question. Surgeons have to be by nature somewhat rigid. They have little time to hesitate.

Surgery has become an advanced scientific technique. In the old days, surgeons had to think in detail in advance exactly what they would have to do and what the variations might be to their original plans should unexpected complications arise. They had to be fast, as anesthesia was a problem that most often no longer exists. They have little patience in administrative matters. Decisions were made quickly and decisively.

Surgeons are rarely humanists. They are individualists. I only ever met two of them personally who were humanists, Henry Souttar at the London Hospital and José Trueta (Ch.40) of WWII fame. Others are mentioned in this book, Ambroise Paré, the Master Barber Surgeon in the sixteenth century (Ch.10) who had a great sense of humor, and Norman Bethune, a historically important physician/surgeon, known by over a billion people, more than any other doctor ever in the whole world.

L'histoire du département de médecine sociale et préventive de la faculté de médecine de l'Université de Montréal, 1970-1993, (Georges Desrosiers, 1996, published by the Department of Social and Preventive Medicine, University of Montréal), is an excellent introduction to what happened, well-documented, factual information, exactly what was needed. Much of what follows comes from that document. I am grateful to the author for his arduous work: it has saved me many hours!

- In response to the advice of accreditation bodies, **a Department of Social and Preventive Medicine** was created officially at *l'UdeM* in **1965,** but it remained a paper decision, an **empty shell, until 1970.**
- The Faculty of the old *École de Médecine* and that of the new one since 1920 had taught its students Public Health without interruption for **94** years until <u>**1967**</u> when **the course was cancelled.**

    There was also an independent School of Public Health at *l'UdeM* that granted a **diploma in Public Health,** equivalent to a professional Master's degree, and had been doing so for **24** years, the only one in the Province of Quebec to do so. In **October 1970,** the University decided to attach this School to the Faculty of Medicine, which had never made such a request and showed no interest in it. It was an undesired gift. **This Diploma granting program was also indefinitely cancelled.**

- In <u>**1969.**</u> a young pediatrician, ***docteur Paul Landry*** from Ste Justine Hospital went to Harvard and returned a year later with a Master's degree in Public Health.

    That same year, students were doing unsupervised medical work in a street clinic that would become a *CLSC,* and the Quebec College of Physicians and Surgeons complained about it in a letter to the Dean.

- In <u>**1970,**</u> Paul Landry on his return was asked to supervise those students mentioned above. It was then realized that the Federal Government had made funds available for just that kind of situation, with the stipulation that the program would be under the umbrella of a Department of Community Health/Medicine.

    Paul Landry thus became the **sole first member** of a department which had no Head. That first year, Paul prepared a course to be offered in **1971,** *'Introduction à la médecine sociale, préventive et communautaire'.*

- *Pierre Bois,* a Professor of Anatomy at *l'UdeM,* became the **first full-time fully salaried dean** of the Faculty of Medicine at the University of Montréal in that same year, **1970**. Luckily he was a Humanist, seeking solely rational ways of solving human problems (OED). He remained Dean until 1981.

  In North America, deans are now quite powerful people, whereas at my old teaching hospital with its old traditions, the part-time Dean was just a director/administrator of a teaching program for prospective doctors. Deans played perhaps just a small role in the running of Voluntary Hospitals, and Universities were for many years only very marginally involved.

  The first quality in choosing a Dean to-day in North America must be to find out if the candidate is a humanist. Outstanding deans are humanists. The second quality must be an understanding of the workings of the faculty he has to lead; it is preferable that he be promoted from the professors of that same faculty, or at least from the same province/country. The third lot of qualities is toughness, guts, and patience, all necessary if one has a vision of things to come.

  Dean Bois, a humanist, claimed at the end of his mandate that his most important achievement was the creation of a well-funded and well-staffed Institute of Nutrition.

- In **1971,** in response to a demand of the **Canadian College of Family Physicians,** the faculty formed a committee to choose a director for the department of Family Medicine. There were two difficulties:

  = finding a general practitioner who had the necessary University qualifications (a PhD, a Masters degree, or a specialist certificate).
  = the University location of such a unit: just two possibilities, the Department of Medicine, the majority of Internists being opposed to even talking about such a dreadful possibility and the Department of Social and Preventive Medicine which still had no Head.

Thus, this request by the Canadian College of Family Physicians became the **principal motivation** for finally finding a director for the Department of Social and Preventive Medicine. It would take another fourteen years for the Department of Family Medicine to become fully established.

- In **1973, Dr Georges Desrosiers***, medical director of *l'hopital Maisonneuve-Rosemont,* with previous experience as a general practitioner plus the required training in the Sciences of Public Health finally became **the first Head of** *'le département de médecine sociale et préventive'.*

He and Dean Bois had met several times, and, as a condition for accepting the nomination, the dean accepted that the first priority would be to develop as fast as possible the specialized training in the area of *la santé publique* while accepting to set up simultaneously a program of *la médecine familiale.*

- In the spring of **1974, Dr Desrosiers and I** participated in the activities of a meeting of the Quebec branch of the Canadian Medical Association in Sherbrooke. He asked me to join his new Department with the specific mandate of starting a family practice teaching unit at *l'Hopital du Sacré-Coeur de Cartierville,* on the North Shore of the Island of Montréal. I accepted shortly afterwards after having thought about it and discussed the matter with Joan. I would officially start in September 1975.

A half of a whole **fifth floor** of the old School of Nursing was empty, and a government grant of $35,000 was available for transforming the area into a teaching/caring area. It was the only space available but it was as far away as possible from the main entrance. I would go to Montréal several times a month from September 1974 for planning purposes. I thought this might just be a tremendous once in a life-time opportunity to do something that was needed, useful and creative. I sincerely felt I had the past academic and practical experiences that were needed.

---

* **Georges Desrosiers** was born in August 1927, trained at the University of Montréal, qualifying in 1954. He became a general practitioner, settling in a poorer area of Montréal near *l'hopital général de Fleury.* He then studied the Sciences of Public Health at *l'University of Montréal,* ending, as part of his training, as *directeur médical adjoint de l'hopital du Sacré-Coeur de Cartierville* (September 1967 to February 1968).

- By **1979,** four such teaching units had been created. *Docteur Desrosiers* knew that he would have to proceed in stages. He was in favor of having an associate co-director in the department of social and preventive medicine who would be responsible for family medicine.

I succeeded *Nadine St Pierre, (vide infra)* in that position in **1980** after her sudden death in 1979. By that time, there were 60 residents in the program with six full-time and six part-time professors.

La fédération des médecins omnipractiticiens du Quebec (FMOQ) as well as the Canadian College of family Physicians (CFPC) clamored for autonomous departments in all medical schools. By then, most Canadian universities had complied.

A department of Family Medicine was actually on the books in **1980** at *l'Universite of Montréal,* but it was a paper decision, the Clinical Departments not having given their approval. But I, the sole full-Professor of the University Department of Social and Preventive Medicine, had to chose the department to which I would belong, cross-appointments not being allowed at *l'UdeM.*

I chose to be based in Family Medicine, thus becoming **the first full-professor of Family Medicine in an official but phantom Department.**

- In **1981,** dean Bois suggested that the post of Assistant Dean in Family Medicine be created as an interim measure, with an office next to his in the main building. I became an <u>assistant dean</u> on June 1st. I felt I fitted the bill, but the whole environment was for me totally new.

I remained in that position <u>for exactly three years until May the 31st 1984</u>. This simple action put Family Medicine on the faculty map, as every visitor to the Dean's office had to pass the door with a large label of the new headquarters of Family Medicine, with a suitably qualified assistant Dean as director.

That was a **master stroke.** The Department of Social and Preventive Medicine, off the beaten track, had been our University headquarters until then. Many of the University staff had never heard of Family Medicine. All the Faculty Heads of Department were uniformly welcoming. Some felt sorry for me!

When I met Dean Bois before my appointment, he said he knew nothing about Family Medicine, just insisting that, at the end of every month, he receive reports of two meetings, the department and the program committees. Dr Bois' term expired at the end of 1981.

He went to Ontario during that later period and heard that physicians in that province were contemplating making family medicine optional as an academic subject. The next morning, we had a two minute talk, and I asked him what he would think if surgery were optional as an academic pursuit. And that was that.

-   eighteen months after my departure, on **October 29ᵗʰ 1985, the Department of Family Medicine was officially created,** all the clinical departments having finally agreed.

He is now retired and lives in a condominium overlooking *l'hopital du Sacré-Coeur* from the north side of *rivière-des-Prairies* on the Island of Laval. Over the years, we talked together quite a lot. He suggested very nicely on one occasion when I was leaving the province to live on the Fundy coast in New Brunswick that perhaps I should have settled in Quebec and stopped emigrating! This is so typical of Quebec thinking.

His family settled in Quebec in the mid 17th century. One of his ancestors had married a surgeon who obtained a government job in Detroit in the 1670s. With their young child, they had travelled up the St Lawrence in one of those large *'voyageurs'* canoes, crossed the whole length of Lake Ontario, spending a few days rest at Fort Frontenac in Cataraqui, (now Kingston), the ruins of which I can see as I type this sheet looking out of my window! We last met yesterday, Friday May 5th 2006, in Montréal. He is quiet, intelligent and non-assuming, a perfect boss! I had known him for thirty years before he told me of his ancestor's trip to Cataraqui!

The Clinical Teaching Institutions of l'Université de Montréal in 2006.

The following *centres hospitaliers, hopitaux affiliés, les instituts* and other organizations are to-day the main teaching components of the Medical School of the University of Montréal:

-   *Two CHU (Centre Hospitalier Universitaire):*

Le CHUM incorporates three old hospitals, all close together down-town: *l'Hotel-Dieu*, *l'hopital Notre-Dame*, (with its own Family Practice Unit in the large basement of a large Church close-by with off-the-street access), *et l'hopital St Luc.*

Le CHUME est le centre hospitalier universitaire **Mère Enfant**, *l'hopital Sainte-Justine*, 4,000 births a year and **no Family Practice Unit.**

- Two *CAU (centres affililiés universitaires):* in the north of the island, *l'hopital du Sacré-Coeur de Montréal*, and in the east, *l'hopital Maisonneuve-Rosemont*, both with Family Practice teaching units dating from the early years.
- Two *IU (instituts universitaires): l'institut de cardiologie de Montréal, et l'institut universitaire de gériatrie de Montréal* (with many of our Family Medicine graduates on the staff).
- Eight *CHA centres hospitaliers affiliés)* including *la Cité de la Santé* in Laval, mainly staffed by family physicians, and *l'hopital général de Verdun*, with its family practice teaching unit.
- One *IRCM (institut de recherches cliniques de Montréal)*, founded by **_Jacques Genest_**, the physician of vision of the 20th century at the University, a real humanist, succeeded by *Michel Chrétien*, the brother of *Jean*, head of the Liberal Party and past Prime Minister of Canada.

It was Jacques Genest who told me all about Norman Bethune's refusal as a staff member of l'Hotel-Dieu after Dr Archibald, one of the two North American founders of thoracic surgery from the Royal Victoria Hospital just next door, dissuaded the Reverend Mother in charge from appointing him. That is why Dr Norman Bethune 'ended up' at *l'Hopital du Sacré-Coeur.*

- In addition to the five Family Practice Units mentioned above, there are four teaching *CLSCs* in the *Montréal/Laval* area, and eleven *CH/CLSCs* in the outbacks as they would say in Australia, northern Quebec, Gaspésie, and the north-eastern shore of *le Fleuve.* Since 1986, all residents in Family Medicine have to spend some time in those far away regions. They look forward to it and enjoy the experience.

<u>*L'hopital du Sacré-Coeur* in the year 2006.</u>

L'hopital du Sacré-Coeur(HSCM) has been mentioned in preceding chapters (Ch 2, 4 & 8). To-day, it has reached an excellent level of care in terms of width, depth, integration of primary, secondary and tertiary care services and excellence in research.

Its has a big advantage of being out of Montréal's down-town area, far enough from university and provincial politics, yet responsible for the care of a large, mixed, local population living on the north-west of *l'Isle de Montréal* north of autoroute 40, and because it is situated on the south side of the bridge over *Rivière des Prairies* on the western end of *l'Isle Laval*. The City of Laval houses 365,000 people (2004) and is rapidly expanding, now the second largest town in Quebec.

L'HSCM also serves as the most important **referral centre** for the whole of north-western Quebec, *Laurentides-Lanaudière, l'Abitibi-Temiscamingue, et l'Outaouais*. Consultants regularly visit out-of-town locations, and there is continuous television contact with outlying stations for urgent consultations.

Although ultra-specialized, *l'HSCM* offers the population **primary care** of a high quality, dispensing care to the population with or without appointment, and ensuring continuity of care for patients in need of specialized care. In the context of controlling costs, specialized care and primary care must complement each other.

L'HSCM is an important centre for teaching future family doctors, with eleven professors and a lovely, large, well-situated teaching unit. It has the largest and best emergency department in Quebec. All emergency physicians-in-training from *l'UdeM* get their training there and the orthopedic department is first-class: it is the nearest university hospital that will look after those who break bones skiing in the Laurentians! Family Medicine is responsible for the care of around **30% of the hospitalized patients.**

As of the spring 2009, the Department of Family Medicine has become the Department of Family Medicine and Emergency Medicine, as they both deal with primary care. Over forty% of students chose it for their future career, as opposed to 30% or less elsewhere in Canada.

At *l'HSC*, the two departments now have entrances opposite each other and there is a continuing relationship between the two.

Le département de psychosomatique is very sophisticated, with seven full-time psychiatrists, the most in any general hospital in Montréal. *Le Pavilion Albert Prevost*, founded in 1921, was the first French Canadian Psychiatric Hospital, just around the corner, now an integral part of *l'HSC*.

As examples of **ultraspecialised care and research,** the **HSCM** is the only centre in Quebec where the surgical treatment of arrhythmia is performed, where there is the only hyper-baric chamber in eastern Canada, where there is a program for renal dialysis with a night-time service, where autloguous (from the patient) and allogenic (from a donor) marrow transplants are performed (over 100 cases to date).

It is a hospital with a fully functional helicopter pad to ensure rapid and safe transportation of patients. <u>It is a cohesive institution with faithful and trusting staff</u>. In the front hall of the doctors's entrance there are rows of photographs of all the physicians with fifteen years or more of service.

The New Teaching Unit, the first two years (1974-1976).

The first part-time year (1974-75)

I commuted from Lennoxville to Montréal every Monday, arriving at ten and returning in the late afternoon. Four Family Practice teaching units were being established, one in Verdun with *le docteur Robert Bourret,* who would become President of the College of Family Physicians (1983-84).

He was a pleasant and cooperative person, and his unit was based in a *private group-practice setting* on a street in Verdun, a very useful experience which later proved to be unsustainable. The Verdun Hospital, a future *CHA,* was close-by and took it over. We became quite friendly, ending up in China together in 1983.

The second was a new set-up like mine at *l'hopital Maisonneuve-Rosemont,* on the east side of the City. The hospital there also had an empty wing on the top floor of their defunct Nursing School, and had received the same grant for transformations, $35,000. The head of that unit was an active, intelligent, and remarkable lady, *docteur Nadine St Pierre. Nadine Schertenlieb* and her widowed mother had emigrated from Switzerland during the 1960s. She graduated in Medicine at *l'UdeM* during the early 1970s and married a fellow-student, *Antoine St Pierre,* who worked as a physician for Air Canada.

She could stand up to any man, telling him exactly what she thought in quite colorful language, a quality that was very useful in her new position! I had never met anybody like her before. People in authority at her hospital were quite intimidated. She was of great help, as she had been involved in the same process as I but had started a year earlier.

We were both immigrants and we both had similar administrative problems. For instance, she had made lists of medical instruments that would be needed in her new unit, gave me copies, saving me a lot of drudgery. She used to say that she was the doer and I the thinker. Unfortunately she suddenly died in 1978, very sad.

Guy Lamarche and I attended her funeral as University representatives. She was sorely missed. The College of Family Physicians named a yearly prize in her memory.

A fourth Family Practice Unit on the island of Laval remained somewhat embryonic for a while, awaiting the construction of a new hospital on the island itself: *La Cité de la Santé de Laval* was one of the eight *Centres Hospitaliers Affiliés (CHA)*, **staffed by all the general practitioners on the Island.** Specialists act as Consultants only. <u>*Docteur Bernard Millette*</u>, who became a good friend, led the teaching program. *La Cité de la Santé* finally opened in 1979. It replaced a small 'cottage type hospital'.

At *l'hopital du Sacré-Coeur* my neighbor on the sixth floor was *docteur* **Marcel Cantin,** director of the Public Health Unit, renamed Department of Community Health (DSC, *Département de Santé Communautaire*) all of which were now incorporated in hospitals. He was a very charming and affable person with whom I had interesting conversations. He qualified in 1950 and knew many members of the hospital staff, who did what and so forth. Many of them were old friends. He made me realize that most of the medical staff working in *l'HSC* had trained at the University of Montréal.

Everybody seemed to know each other, what kind of background they had, who their professors in medical school had been, and so on. They all had these jokes about their old professors. It was a very chummy place, the atmosphere reminding me of the London Hospital where I had trained. I tried to imagine the impact a family practice unit would have at the London: it would have been laughed at beyond bounds!

Marcel understood very little of my motivation for starting this general practitioner training program. He never stated he did not really approve of all this new stuff, but neither did he ever say he approved either. I always felt he was not a person with whom one could open one's heart. He was cagey. He respected authority but never seemed to judge it.

On several occasions he introduced me to staff members, suggesting afterwards they would be excellent colleagues who would be willing to work there to help me in my endeavors. They were all functioned mostly as older internists. As far as I was concerned, mum was the word. I rarely openly disagreed with him. It would serve no purpose.

He had known my new boss *Georges Desrosiers* for years but never mentioned him once. To me, retrospectively, he seemed like a caricature of a senior civil servant as seen in the English TV series **'Yes Minister'**.

Mme Rachel Parent was his Head Nurse, and she was just a delightful person. I think she took pity of me, poor fellow! But she was never condescending. She knew about Dr Norman Bethune, and told me about people who had known him. She had been working with *Marcel Cantin* for many years, and told me on the quiet that his decisions used to be better in the past.

She helped me with recruiting staff and introduced me to people who would come to the DSC for some reason or other. The young *administrative assistant* there was very bright and cooperative. She knew all about the health statistics of the people living in the area, and would give me photocopies of documents that would be helpful without my even asking.

Monsieur Martin was the director of the hospital. He was quite charming with a good sense of humor. We established a good working relationship right from the beginning. He was and remained very supportive. He understood the motives of the whole exercise. I could talk about my problems and he always listened. He was a great help. He gave me good advice. His high-powered staff was uniformly enthusiastic and equally helpful.

This part-time preparatory year proved to be extremely useful: *Georges Desrosiers* had insisted on it. I started by being somewhat skeptical, but I soon changed my mind. I also made up my mind at that time that I would only ask for colleagues who had obtained by examination their Canadian qualifications in Family Medicine to help in teaching in our unit on a permanent basis. It meant in practice that my future helpers would have trained at one of the units at *l'UdeM*, mostly at *l'HSC*.

It also meant that within ten years a group of young physicians at *l'HSC* would all have been trained in the same way, and would form a core of family physicians/teachers that would function as a cohesive group, able to survive and prosper during the next century. The only exception to this rule were to follow suggestions by *Georges Desrosiers*. He suggested for instance that *docteur Louise Séguin* amongst others would be helpful, and she indeed proved to be. She had gone to Berkeley in California for a year to obtain a Master's degree in Maternal and Child Health with Dr Helen Wallace, one of the few world authorities.

My First Year Full-Time, (1975-76).

The space for the new Family Medicine Teaching Unit was excellent. We transformed (winter of **1976**) small bedrooms for nursing students on the sixth floor of the ex-School of Nursing into rooms of different dimensions: three were large rooms,

- = the first as a waiting/meeting room, with small tables that could be joined to form a circle for meetings,
- = the second a treatment room with kitchen-type cabinets on two sides, a quite well-equipped laboratory, a couch/operating table, a comfortable padded chair to recline in when blood was taken, a microscope, a centrifuge and so on, where doctors, young and old, could obtain samples from their patients or do minor procedures,

= the third a room with desks and chairs and pertinent texts, in which **each resident had his own desk.**

Taking blood for laboratory tests from one's own patient increases bonding in addition to the acquisition of practical skills. It also saves the patient a lot of time.

There were smaller offices for the staff and for consulting rooms. Each consulting room had the usual instruments and its own professional weighing scales. I was quite proud of the end result. I thought of it as the best to be seen!

We started functioning in a small way, one new patient at a time, that spring, preparing for September! But access was so difficult. Our really attractive quarters were such a long way from the bus-stop, certainly a fifteen minute walk, a quarter of it out of doors, as far from the front door as possible. The elevator was the smallest and most rickety/fragile in the hospital.

After my experiences first as a young house-physician/surgeon in one of the top teaching hospitals in the UK, then as a mature Canadian pediatric resident and instructor in a large modern American medical school, one of the best in the USA, for four years altogether, let alone my experiences as a principal in a large general practice and in different milieus for over twenty years, plus my four years at Queen's, I was very conscious of **the need for a supportive team** in our new program.

I was conscious of the horrible possible outcomes following failure of professional examinations, and the need for the success of our new program right from the start. I thought we had a lovely, well-equipped unit. We had the support of the administration and many of the non-medical departments but we were totally ignored by the medical staff. In fact, they thought I was totally out of my mind!

I had to be interviewed by a committee to be nominated as a member of the hospital staff. The only question I was asked by the Chairman, the very charming, efficient, suave Head of Cardiology, was 'why, as a well-qualified physician, had I accepted such a job'?

I implied in my answer that a well-qualified person had a greater chance of succeeding, and that I felt it was an extremely important issue that would bring immense benefits to the Hospital and to Society.

Rachel Parent was a great help in finding a **secretary,** *Claudette Richer,* a young, petite, attractive, blond and efficient bomb-shell.

The **nurse** was more difficult to find. I had decided that she should be well-qualified, so that she would be considered by our residents and by the staff of *l'HSC* as a caring member of an academic teaching team, as well as an expert in nursing, her academic qualifications at least equal to that of young physicians. *Marielle Beauger* was the answer, with two young children, her husband a mathematics teacher in a public high-school in Laval. She had a *BNSc* plus an *MSc* in administration.

La famille Beauger were fairly recent immigrants from *Haiti,* and *Marielle* suffered a great deal from the incapacity of her beloved country to extract itself from what seemed to be a permanent disability, similar to the birth of a severely handicapped child that remains handicapped for all his life, perhaps 75 years.

Immigrants from Western Europe never have to think about such horrible things. But we both also shared the similar problems that all immigrants have, associated with sudden transplantation to an entirely different milieu, similar to transplanting trees to a different climate over an ocean. There are many Haitians living in Montréal, a closely knit, caring part of the Montréal landscape, one of which has now become Governor General of Canada (2006).

Marielle became interested in one of my pet projects, a <u>medical record that belongs to the patient</u>. She elaborated with little help from me a booklet of about thirty pages. The beauty of her project was an attempt to demonstrate the efficacy of the booklet. She successfully obtained a PhD by elaborating a long-term follow-up with grills that she had to complete over the telephone over a period of several years.

At the start, we had planned to develop a conjoined teaching program with the University Faculty of Nursing in the field of primary care. We soon abandoned this part of the project as we had so much to do.

Our **social worker** proved to be the icing on the cake, *Yolande St Germain,* around my age, a faithful follower of **Virginia Satir** (1916-1988), a therapist and author in California, known as **'The Mother of Family System Therapy'**. She emphasized personal growth rather than focusing on illness:

> **'Problems are not the problem; coping is the problem. Coping is the outcome of self-worth, rules of the family systems, and links to the outside world'.**

In working, Virginia Satir would always try to be on the same level as her client, with eye contact, physical touching and a sense of humour. She sat on low stools when talking to children.

> **'I am Me. I own my fantasies, my dreams, my hopes, my fears. I own my triumphs and other successes, all my failures and mistakes . . . I have the tools to survive, to be close to others, to be productive . . . I am me, and I am OK'.**

Yolande must have been a perfect student, because the lines above apply to her to a tee. She used to go to Califonia at least once a year to recharge her batteries. She happened to be looking for a challenging job at that time, and what she found was just that. *Le département des services sociaux de l'HSC* had known her for a long time, and was delighted that she had accepted the position. I realized after a while that <u>Virginia Satir and Hilliard Jason complemented each other</u>.

Michel Brouillard MD qualified at *le CHUS* in 1974, and had just completed his internship, thus having the right to practice medicine. I do not remember him as a student. Once upon a time, I gave him a lift from Montréal to Sherbrooke. We stopped on the way to have something to eat. He was a quiet, soft young man, very affable, very polite, somewhat old-fashioned and unassuming.

I learnt that one residency position had been planned for each of the four new family medicine teaching units at *l'UdeM* for the 1975-76 year and, without talking to me about it, *Michel* had applied for the position at *l'HSC*.

I felt badly that I would be unable to help him much during that year, but he reassured me that he would do his best for the future functioning of the new unit! He would cherish the experience. This was quite providential, because he was a native Quebecker, and knew his way around the different parishes, meeting halls, church basements, voluntary organizations of all kinds, disseminating news of the 'new' *médecine familiale*. There is nothing 'new' about family medicine; it is just the setting and quality of its teaching that was changing.

<u>Michel acted as an efficient facilitator, a first class public relations person</u>. At the same time, he met and talked to other interns/residents-in-training at *l'HSC*, most of whom had never heard of *la médecine familiale*. He disappeared at the end of the year, eventually settling down as a country General Practitioner.

I unfortunately totally lost touch with him. I am ashamed to say that I cannot remember thanking him for what he had done. For him, the year must have been like a sabbatical, where one learns a lot by oneself, about the planning of future projects during the coming years. He was free of the usual medical responsibilities, allowed to do as he pleased, do something that was very useful, plan his future, confident that I would never accuse him of sloping off! He was able to provide essential help that I had not even thought of. He obviously felt that I, as a new Quebecker and a new Montrealer, needed help in the area of public relations that he, as a native, could provide. He was quite a guy!

Finally, it was important to seek the help of a physician at l'HSC who would help with the teaching. It would improve the teaching, help with the public relations within the institution. As I did in Kingston at Queen's, I sought the help of a psychiatrist from _le département de médecine psychosomatique de l'HSC._ It took me a while to adapt to Psychosomatic Medicine. I had never been exposed to it. It deals more with the psychological problems of patients. Psychiatry dealing with patients affected by schizophrenia for instance or sever mood disorders, was based in the Psychiatric Institute next door, now part of _l'HSC._

Le docteur Jacques Monday was the perfect answer, a recently qualified psychiatrist/psychosomatician (1975) with a previous quite substantial experience in general practice, qualifying from _l'UdeM_ in 1966; he advised me to purchase plastic covered one inch thick mattresses on which one could lie down on the floor for relaxation exercises, and we purchased a dozen of them. He knew what our problems might be, and proved to be a tower of strength.

I must acknowledge the influence of **John Read** at Queen's in Kingston. In the Child Health Program that he had founded and that I had eventually directed at John's request had the same organization as that of _l'unité de médecine familiale à l'HSC._ The team approach there, nurse/physician/social worker, had been for me a revelation that I was anxious to introduce to our future residents.

John Read was great guy. He was an excellent teacher, particularly to get small groups to work together, very much like Chester Stewart in Halifax who had soon given up lecturing to large classes. Chester would divide the class into groups of ten or so students, and would repeat the process many times rather than give a lecture. He later became a most successful Dean.

At Queen's, things were not that easy to change, and John was less comfortable in the lecture theatre, tending to overwhelm the students with copies of interesting documents they did not have time to read and absorb. He was a quiet non-flamboyant person, always extremely well-prepared.

That first two years had been exciting, unpredictable, and difficult! I looked forward to the next few years: the unit was all new and to my design. I had personally chosen an excellent staff, diverse, keen and full of hope. I had been very lucky and was thankful. Not many people have had such an opportunity. We could not afford to fail and the next few years would be crucial. On the other hand, apart from Jacques Monday not one doctor from _l'HSC_ had visited our new unit! Nobody had even asked me to explain what I was doing.

Until then, during their year's training, interns had shifted from one department to another for relatively short periods, without any chance of belonging to an academic body which assured them a certain security, support, some prestige and respect as well as an academic home.

We wished to give them this support and anchor,

= to demonstrate how a team in primary care could work together,
= to show them how the problem-oriented chart would be helpful in the follow-up of their patients,
= to themselves improve their own skills at interviewing patients by the use of a videocamera,
= to demonstrate how showing affect for your patients improves the relationship one is trying to foster:

all this soft stuff was rarely dealt with in the usual curriculum, using real patients who are in need, patients who are their responsibility from the start. Medical students are bright and willing to take responsibilities provided efficient help is readily accessible.

CHAPTER 42

Politics in la Nouvelle France from the 1940s to the 1980s.

Adélard Godbout (1892-1956), an agronomist and a Liberal, was Prime Minister of Quebec in 1936 and during WWII years from 1939-1944.

Maurice Duplessis (1890-1959), a lawyer, became leader of the Québec Conservatives in 1933, founded *l'Union nationale* in 1935 and became *Premier ministre du Québec* (1936-1939 & 1944-1959).

> He built a powerful political machine, became known as *'le Chef'*, asserted the authority of the state over the Church and undertook enormous public works. In several infamous episodes, he dealt harshly with striking unions and other opposition.

Jean Lesage (1912-1980), a lawyer, became Liberal *Premier ministre du Quebec* (1960-1966) and started *'la révolution tranquille'*.

Daniel Johnson (1915-1968), a lawyer, head of *l'Union nationale* from 1961, became *Premier ministre du Québec* (1966-1968).

Jean-Jacques Bertrand, (1916-1973, an able and successful lawyer, senior minister in *l'Union nationale,* succeeded him (1968-70). He was the last *Premier ministre de l'Union nationale.*

Robert Bourassa (1933-1996), an economist, became the youngest *Premier ministre* ever in the Province (April 19th 1970-Nov 15th 1976 & 1985-1994).

René Lévesque (1922-1987), was born in Edmunston, New Brunswick, raised in anglophone New-Carlyle on the north shore of *la baie des Chaleurs* in *Gaspésie*, becoming comfortable talking English and French at an early age.

>His father, a lawyer, died when René was 14. He started studying Law at Laval University in Quebec City and was sent down, as they say in Oxford and Cambridge, because he was caught smoking (1944).
>
>He became an experienced war-time reporter for the American Forces in Europe, under General Patton. He visited the concentration camp at Dachau.
>
>He then worked for *le Service Internationale de Radio-Canada* and went to Korea as a war correspondant.
>
>By then, he had acquired a wonderful command of language. He returned to Quebec in 1952.
>
>Between 1956 and 1959 he had his own Television show, *Point-de-Mire.*
>
>He joined the Liberal Party, soon becoming a senior member of the Lesage Liberal government. He became responsible for the successful and popular nationalisation of the Hydro-Electric companies, mostly owned by American interests.
>
>He helped to start the new Ministry of Education.
>
>He subsequently founded *le mouvement souveraineté-association (MSA)* which became *le Parti québecois*, devoted at first to the political independence of Quebec, ***séparation,*** with just an economic association with the rest of Canada.
>
>He became <u>*Premier ministre du Quebec*</u> **(1976-1985)**. During his second mandate (1981-1985), he lost a lot of support from his colleagues because he had changed his mind, possibly because of the success of the new language laws that had just been introduced, now suggesting ***souveraineté-association*** once more instead of *séparation.* He resigned in October 1985.

Pierre-Marc Johnson (b 1946), head of the *PQ,* took over temporarily until the election on December 3rd when Robert Bourassa returned to power.

Thus, René Lévesque's employers for at least a decade had been two neighbouring countries with a Federal organisation, the American Armed Forces and the Canadian Broadcasting Corporation. Both had helped him immensely in launching his successful political career, becoming a senior member of the Liberal Party before the age of forty. Of all the politicians of his generation, **René Lévesque** was perhaps the one who was the most open-minded, well-travelled, and mature.

He had witnessed at close quarters the horrors of WWII, and appreciated the efforts of the allies in their fight in Europe, the cooperation of different nationalities and cultures to attain a final result.

At the end, he had become able to appreciate the advantages of *souveraineté-association* for Quebec. Of his many political friends, René Lévesque seemed the nearest to the people, just like the family physician is compared with the specialist, or the South American parish priest with his Bishop, or Norman Bethune with the medical and political systems of his time.

René Lévesque was a rebel, able to make tough decisions and to stick with it because he felt it was the right thing to do, whatever his colleagues thought.

He might often have thought about the many advantages his colleagues had had in life, all this advanced university education with, perhaps, a lack of understanding of the difficulties ordinary people faced and that he himself had faced. He must have felt immense pressures but he stuck to his guns. His private life suffered as a consequence.

**There were four physicians that I knew** and occasionally talked to who became influential in Québec political life: in alphabetical order, Pierre-Marc Johnson, Camille L̲aurin, Marc L̲avallée and Denis L̲azure. They all joined *le Parti Québecois* as soon as it was founded:

Pierre-Marc Johnson was born with the silver spoon in 1946, the youngest of the two sons of Daniel Johnson. He obtained a law degree then entered medical school at the *CHUS* in 1971, qualifying in 1975. I got to know him well as a student, a very pleasant, cooperative, sensible and sensitive young man. He joined the Parti Quebecois as soon as it came into being, and, as head of the *PQ*, succeeded René Lévesque temporarily when he resigned as *Premier ministre* on October 3rd 1985. Robert Bourassa returned as *Premier ministre* on December 3rd.

Pierre-Marc officially abandoned ideas of independance in 2005 because he thought that the economy should now be the no 1 priority in Quebec. He teaches law at McGill and has become involved at a very senior level with two large international issues, the World Environment and the Development of Nations, both World Priorities. On the rare occasions when we met, he would welcome me with open arms and introduce me by name as one of his teachers in Medical School. He always wears the most perfect clothes.

Camille Laurin was born on May the 6th 1922 in Charlemagne, a small village on the North Shore of *le fleuve* just off the eastern point of the Island of Montréal, the fourth of 13 children. As was so common at that time, Dr Laurin chose Medicine as a career rather than entering the Priesthood as was his original intention. He qualified at *l'UdeM* in 1950, always remaining a true catholic, devoted to his faith.

<u>Academically</u>, in 1958, just one year after completing his postdoctoral studies in Psychiatry and Psychoanalysis in Boston and Paris, he became Head of the Department of Psychiatry at *l'UdeM*.

Within three years, he had totally revamped the undergraduate curriculum in Psychiatry and Medical Psychology. He had also created a four-year residency program, thus ensuring students could remain in Quebec for post-graduate studies instead of going to Boston or/and Paris.

Also in 1958, he became medical director of *l'institut Albert-Prévost,* and later Head of the Department of Psychiatry à *l'HSC* which became a leading institution for training future Psychiatrists in Quebec. He was a good teacher, able, enthusiastic, with an remarkable capacity for synthesis. He had published over 125 articles in National and International Journals. These reforms were not always easy, but with tenacity and patience he was able to keep the ship on course.

<u>In the area of Social Medicine</u>, Camille Laurin put into place a commission to study the treatment of psychiatric patients which totally changed psychiatric practice in Quebec (cfr Ch38).

He caught public attention in 1957 when he wrote the preface of a best-selling denunciation of *l'hopital Hippolyte-Lafontaine,* the large, old and old-fashioned psychiatric institution in the east end of the island of Montréal. It was written by a patient.

As a result, his contract with *l'institut Albert Prévost* was not renewed when it expired two years later. He got his job back with the help of *Marc Lalonde,* a lawyer friend who later became an important federal minister during the Trudeau years. Amongst other friends were *Gérard Pelletier,* and *Maurice et Jeanne Sauvé,* all future federal ministers.

He could later warmly greet Prime Minister Trudeau, using the familiar *tu*, yet denounce him and his government in the coldest terms a few minutes later.

Clinically and politically, as a psychiatrist, he eventually concluded that his French-speaking patients suffered from 'a feeling of incompleteness and flawed identity' because of the historic experiences of conquest and domination, frustration and insecurity.

Patients who had endorsed Quebec independence seemed healthier. Thus, a 'psychiatrically therapeutic language law' seemed appropriate for *les Québecois*. Politically, he privately broke with federalism in 1961, publicly declaring his political allegiance in 1967 by joining *le mouvement souveraineté association* which later became *le parti québecois*, both founded by *René Lévesque*. When the *PQ* took office, he became the Minister of State for Cultural Development, responsible for developing the new language law, first its white paper, then its charter:

> **'the Quebec we wish to build will be essentialy French. The fact that a majority of its population is French will be clearly visible,—at work, in communications and in the countryside . . . . thus creating a more open and tolerant society . . . . Immigrants would be integrated into the majority'.**

Camille Laurin introduced his new law, Bill 101, on April 27, 1977. Some measures in the law were later struck down by the Supreme Court, but Dr Laurin's success came from pushing the logic of his law as far as he could, challenging his opponents to push it back. He resigned from the *PQ* with other senior colleagues when René Lévesque abandoned *la séparation*, but did not react, and this was criticized by colleagues, when the Supreme Court of Canada struck down some of the more extreme measures of *la loi 101*.

The success of Bill 101 demonstrated that fundamental changes were possible in Canada. Separation might no longer be necessary. Dr Laurin may well have been the savior of Confederation. He returned to *le Pavilion Albert-Prévost* as its medical director. Calm and serene, a great humanist, generous and devoted, always available and wanting to listen, he liked to say 'one judges a tree by its fruit'. This he followed, more than any other. There is more about *le docteur Laurin à l'HSC* later in this auto-biography.

Denis Lazure, (b1925), qualified in 1952 at *l'Ude M*, finishing his psychiatric training in 1957. He became the first Head of the department of Psychiatry at what is now *le CHUME, l'Hopital Ste Justine pour mères et enfants* (1957-1969), then *directeur général (DG) of l'hopital Rivière des Prairies*, a psychiatric institution primarily for children and adolescents, with a large out-patient component (1969-1975). In 1975-76, he had become *DG* of the enormous psychiatric institution in the east end of the town, *l'hopital Hyppolite-Lafontaine,* mentioned above.

Politically, as a student, he was a card-carrying communist. Quite early on, he joined the NDP, and ran for election as an NDP candidate. There were few Quebec candidates in the NDP! He joined René Lévesque right from the start, becoming *ministre d'État au development social,* then Minister of Health in 1976. He promoted the development of the *CLSCs* and the services they provided, such as family planning and the termination of pregnancies.

He firmly supported teaching medical students in *CLSCs,* creating the principle that some of them would be teaching *CLSCs* with a different scale of remuneration to compensate for the time spent on teaching health care personnel.

In 1981, when the *PQ* was returned to power, he became *ministre délégué aux Relations avec les citoyens.* He had to cope with strikes. He never lost his temper, and it must have been quite tough. He resigned on 1984, no longer able to support *souverainté-association.* He still is a separatist. His big interest now is the protection of the rights of the handicapped. There is more about him later on.

In 1973, he accompanied *Pierre Trudeau (1919-2000)* on the first ever official trip to China by a Canadian Prime Minister. Amongst others in the group were *Micheline Letendre,* the first Quebec *marionettist* (1945), and *Jacques Hébert,* a writer and later a liberal senator, who wrote in *la Cité libre et le Devoir.*

The same official Chinese guide remained with them day and night for the whole trip, much to their disgust.

Pierre Trudeau had been to China before after spending some time in Paris studying at la Sorbonne and in London at the London School of Economics. Then, with a rucksack on his back, he visited Eastern Europe, Turkey, Palestine, Pakistan, entering China illegally arriving in Shanghai shortly before Chairman Mao came to power in October 1948, ending in Burma and Vietnam before returning home. He had been away fifteen months.

Our two Psychiatrists of similar age who became senior ministers in the PQ government could not have been more different, one a very catholic humanist and a more traditional politician seeing things in the long term, and the other a left wing politician, also a atheist humanist who dealt quickly and efficiently with difficult issues that most politicians were unwilling to face at that time, both very exceptional and tough. I feel privileged at having met them.

Marc Lavallée was quite different. Born in 1933, he qualified in 1958 at *l'UdeM.* He returned to *l'UdeM* from California in 1963 with a doctorate in biophysics. He is a basic scientist. He also had diplomas in pharmacology and physico-mathematics.

What struck him most in California was the extraordinary feeling of belonging and pride that Americans felt for their country. They felt they owned the place. On one occasion, he was asked to go to Vietnam as an interpreter at a high level meeting. He spoke French without being a Frenchman. While in California, he subscribed to *le Devoir* to keep in touch with what went on at home. It arrived a week late costing him a mint!

That is where he read about *le RASSEMBLEMENT POUR L'INDÉPENDANCE NATIONALE (RIN)*. He liked the idea, feeling the *RIN* was a movement and not a party, joined by mail and was very surprised to receive a letter of thanks from *André d'Allemagne*, *le président général,* dated August 1st 1961. He thought the organization numbered several thousand members. I was never able to find out just how many members there actually were.

He joined the CHUS in 1965 as a basic scientist, head of the Department of Biophysics. He soon became Associate Dean. That is where I met him, and he paid little attention to me throughout my stay in Sherbrooke. He had the nicest office in *le CHUS*, larger than anybody else's, with fitted everything, full book cases, spotlessly clean.

He soon joined *l'union nationale* and became *un conseiller de Daniel Johnson,* while at the same time being elected to the executive of the *RIN*. He subsequently became the first President of the Eastern Township branch of *le mouvement souveraineté–association de René Lévesque,* which became *le parti Québecois (PQ).* He was good administrator, good at raising money for the party, officially going to Paris on one occasion where he obtained $300,000 of French tax-payers money for the coffers of *le PQ,* a strictly illegal operation.

Marc Lavallée returned to live in Montréal, re-oriented his career to direct, amongst other activities, a large CLSC in Pointe-aux-Trembles, a deprived area on the south shore at the eastern extremity of the Island of Montréal. It became a teaching CLSC in the early 1980s. We cooperated on that project, ex-residents going there to work full-time.

He quit the *PQ* in disgust when *René Lévesque* gave up on *'souveraineté'* and joined the Liberal Party, working very hard for a couple of months on a book that was published at the end of 1982, *'Adieu la France, Salut l'Amériaue'* (Stanké) where he tries to explain how he wasted twenty years of his life on an impossible dream. That book, knowing Marc Lavallée quite well by then, is factually correct, and well-worth reading. It is not popular. He talks about

---

* *André d'Allemagne* qualified at *l'UdeM* in linguistics and political science, and taught at the secondary school and *CEGEP (collège d'éducation générale et professionel)* level. He died of cancer in 2001, aged 71.

- *Mme Gravelin (1907-2004)* and her influential *salon* in Paris, *administratrice de l'association France-Quebec,* her brother-in-law being the permanent correspondant of the *Radiodiffusion-Television Française (RTF)* in Montréal,
- how the 60,000 original *colons* of *la Nouvelle France* suffered when their élites returned to their native land, *la Nouvelle France* as a territory now restricted just to the area around *le Fleuve,*
- *Bourget's* motto *'Catholiques et Français toujours'* having become just *'Français toujours',*
- the contrast between the visit to Montréal of Queen Elizabeth at the opening of EXPO 1967, arranged completely by Ottawa, and the arrival of *General de Gaulle* by battleship to Quebec City a couple or so of weeks later, the whole visit carefully orchestrated by *le premier ministre Daniel Johnson.*

Le *général* drove triumphantly in an open car to Montréal on *la route royale,* the oldest long road in North America (1750) between Quebec City and Montréal through old villages and towns, each entrance carefully decorated, with arches covered with millions of flowers and thousands of spectators lining the old road.

It set the stage for de Gaulle's *'Vive le Quebec, Vive le Quebec libre!' du Balcon de l'Hotel-de-Ville* a couple of days later, that visit coinciding with the onset of the PQ's rise to power.

Ottawa had insisted that General de Gaulle's visit would include Ottawa, trying to arrange for him to get there before going to Quebec. Marc talked about this visit as crucial to the creation of the Parti Quebecois. It is only then that there seemed the possibility of the creation of a truly independant Quebec: he contrasts the <u>old genetic nationalism,</u> a yearning for the past, that started two centuries ago, to the <u>new nationalism of Jean Lesage that only became fully functional after the visit of General de Gaulle.</u>

He made the point that, for him at the time, English Canada seemed no freer that French Canada, one oriented towards the UK, the other towards France, both still colonies.

I personally felt the same. It took me many years before I truly felt allegiance to Canada as a separate entity, probably a quarter of a century. Neither as a young adult did I feel true allegiance to Belgium or England. I was subconsciously exposed to quite an apprenticeship.

I was quite horrified by the French government giving the Quebec government a gift, a propaganda truck to travel around within Quebec to efficiently disseminate whatever information with screens and projectors for showing films.

Young French adults could chose to do three years military service in Quebec joining a sort of peace corps instead of a compulsory two year's period in the French Army. How patronizing.

The tide finally turned permanently when Pierre Trudeau repatriated the Constitution in 1982. I have difficulty in understanding how anyone could swear allegiance to a province. People emigrate to Canada and not to a province, but they have to chose a province in which to settle.

As a conclusion of this chapter, a list of Canadian Prime Ministers during that period:

- **John Diefenbaker** (1895-1979), Conservative, June 21st 1957 to April 22nd 1963, a lawyer from Prince Albert, Saskatchewan.
- **Lester B Pearson** (1897-1972), Liberal, April 22nd 1963 to April 20th 1968, a Nobel Peace Prize winner, from Ontario. He attended the Highland Games when we lived in Antigonish.
- **Pierre Elliott Trudeau** (1919-2002) Liberal, a Jesuit-educated lawyer *(l'UdeM)*, April 20th 1968 to June 3rd 1979, and from March 3rd 1980 to June 30th 1984, from Outremont, Montréal.
- **Joe Clark** (b1939) from High River, Alberta, his father a journalist who owned a newspaper, Conservative, June 4th 1979 to March 2nd 1980, the youngest ever Prime Minister of Canada
- **John Turner** (b1929), Liberal, June 30th 1984 to September 18th 1985, from Ontario, with a summer house by *l'Isle Ste Croix* in St Andrews where Champlain landed in 1604 and where we also had a summer cottage (1978). We would see him having lunch at the Algonqin Hotel in the summer with his family.
- **Brian Mulroney** (b1939) Conservative, September 18th 1985 to 1993, a Laval-trained lawyer born in Bay Comeau on the North Shore of *le fleuve* in Quebec, his father an electrician.

Chapter 43

Teaching Family Medicine while at l'HSC. Un. of Montréal, 1976-1984.

The Program Itself.

All new Family Medicine residents at the Faculty of Medicine at *l'UdeM* are just finishing an exhausting five year program, as long as any in North America. They are fed-up with formal teaching, dying to start a job, settle down and earn a living. They want to meet real patients for which they would be responsible. They had never done that.

The University of Sherbrook had just a three year course at the start. What follows is a summary of what we offered: at the end of their first year of residency, according to the rules still in place, the residents all had the right to leave the program and work independently in society. Those four residents who started our new program all chose to stay for a second year.

Residents in Family Medicine spend twenty-four months in the program. Their administrative base is the Department of Family Medicine, on the top floor of the same hospital they are attending for most of their rotations. All they have to do is walk from one department to another. Each resident spends at least two months full-time in the Family Practice Unit (FPU) per year. Patients consult them as they would consult any other physician. Each resident thus starts his own practice in the unit:

they visit their patients at home if needed and they participate in the teaching activities of the unit. There are frequent lunch meetings, and once a week there is a round table meeting to which all are invited: the residents and the teachers (medical/psychiatry, nursing and social services) talk about their continuing experiences with their patients. When not full-time in the FPU, a resident can see his patients in the unit or at home at a convenient time during the whole two years. Thus, they learn about continuing care, bonding with their patients, and they experience the team approach to health care. This is the fundamental <u>horizontal element</u> for understanding family medicine. The <u>vertical element</u> consists of the usual rotations in the specialty departments.

Thus, the young family physician is allowed to 'discover' the nature of his calling instead of being trained and examined entirely by bio-scientists who often tend to narrow even further their own individual perspectives. Without family physicians, people can continue to experience discomfort, pain, altered function, changes in behavior they fail to understand without medical help. Illness is culturally defined, help being sought only when the sickness role is deemed officially acceptable.

Thus the family physician can learn to provide continuous, preventive and comprehensive health care, without limitation by age, sex, organ system, or disease entity, in relation to the family unit: healing, counseling, coordinating; as a humanitarian, he can adjust to the needs of his patient. He seeks specialized help when he and/or his patient feel it is needed. This is why a specialist in internal Medicine cannot 'teach' family medicine. This is what internists by and large fail to understand (cfr ch 4).

This in a nutshell is what we tried to expose to our new friends. We did not so much have to 'teach' as just to 'demonstrate' what was going on. They could observe how our team functioned without us having to talk about it. Our meetings were held around a **round table,** so that there was no Head of the Table: thus, everyone was on the same level. We tried to give them the support they needed for the transition from the biosciences, to which they had so-far been exposed, to their new role in society.

The whole exercise involved their personal development. Our own 'patients' soon included our 'students'. Our 'team' soon became aware of some of the personal problems each one had, each senior team member with a little bit different approach. It was a different experience for the teachers themselves. The 'personal problems' our students had became 'our own team's problems'. Our problems became their problems. The 'Us' and 'Them' became one.

The mental health of all of us improved! Our anxieties were allayed. In those first few years, our 'team' was exposed to many happy and unhappy problems our students and their patients had, marriages, births, addictions, deaths, illness and sickness amongst family members, broken relationships, new relationships, problems with older parents/grandparents, moving to a new abode, failure in an examination and the need for taking it again, determination of future career decisions.

What about the further training available to family physicians after their training in family medicine is completed: this had never been talked about before; geriatrics, community medicine, psychiatry, administration, and research in primary care spring to mind. Several of our students took one of those paths.

It is quite a step for a young physician when he leaves the security of the teaching institution to launch his career in the community, more so for the family physician than for a budding specialist who belongs and continues to work in a hospital department similar to the one to which he has bonded as a student but often less sophisticated.

For a family practitioner the leap is greater. It is preferable to settle close to where he will work, close to the problems of his/her community. He has much more difficult choices to make, settling in the countryside, the industrial district, a wealthier area, immigrant district, a slum; one must consider the medical needs of the area, versus the comfort of the area, the needs of the working spouse, of facilities for the education of children. Will he work solo or in a group? He has to have an idea of the working conditions in the factories in his district that may have an impact on the health of his patients.

I soon discovered an area in Montréal with 37,000 people without single doctor's office, a good subject for discussion. The health statistics are totally different between the east and west ends of the island of Montréal, doctors accumulating in the area with the best health statistics. Several of my own student colleagues in the UK settled in areas with lots of old rich people who left them money in their wills! One of them collected old Rolls-Royce cars. My own father might lend money to some of his patients who might be unemployed. All this we had to talk about, areas that cannot be covered by lectures or seminars, just discussed as the situations developed.

What happened in our brand new Family Practice Unit.

We were lucky that first year, not having too many patients and having only four first year residents, each full-time for just two months, the others coming when it was possible according to their time schedule, frequently, for lunch, all of us bringing a sandwich. It was a happy cheerful year for all of us. Our residents seemed to have found a new home.

Just <u>four basic texts</u> were frequently discussed: The **Kerr White** square, **Balint's** description of the doctor as a pill, the **Holmes'** Social Readjustment Rating Scale, and a study concerned with the contents of a syllabus for educating family physicians **(Alpert & Charney):**

In a USA National Census Survey, following answers to pertinent questions, **Kerr-White** demonstrated that for each **1000** adults over the age of sixteen over a four week period:

- **750** had a minor/major health problem,
- **250** visited a physician doing primary care,
- **9** are admitted to hospital,
- **6** are referred to a consultant,
- **1** was admitted to a University affiliated hospital.

This was represented by a large square representing 1,000 adults, within which are five progressively smaller squares, all five starting at the same lower left-hand corner of the largest one. Most of the teaching in medical schools is centered on that one hospitalized patient. **Kerr White** published his conclusions in 1962. Those six squares illustrate the <u>epidemiology of primary care</u>. Coming from a National US Census, the figures did not originate primarily from a medical study, a big advantage.

Michael Balint wrote a short book in 1957, *'The doctor, His Patient and the Illness'*. He describes seminars involving a psychiatrist and a number of general practitioners in England:

> *'the first topic chosen for discussion at one of these seminars happened to be the drugs usually prescribed by practitioners. The discussion quickly revealed—certainly not for the first time in the history of medicine—that by far the most frequently used drug in general practice was the doctor himself, ie, that it was not only the bottle of medicine or the box of pills that mattered, but the way the doctor gave it to his patient—in fact, the whole atmosphere in which the drug was given and taken'.*

As Robert E Taylor[*] puts it, before considering more disease oriented diagnostic and therapeutic methods, it is appropriate to consider the nature

---

[*] **Robert Taylor,** Associate Professor, Department of Family and Community Medicine, Bowman Gray School of Medicine, North Carolina, is the editor of **'Family Medicine, Principles and Practice'**, Springer-Verlag New-York, 1978. It is the first comprehensive complete text on the subject written by Family Physicians

of the family physician himself. What cognitive knowledge and skills does he attain? What are the nature, goals and validation of his training? What are his priorities and objectives?

T.H. Holmes, R.H. Rahe at the University of Washington developed a **Social Readjustment Rating Scale,** derived from responses from 5000 persons, a measure of stressors rather than the response to them by an individual patient. It lists social events associated with the onset of illness. Values exceeding three hundred in one year will result in significant patient illness in 80% of instances. At one end of the scale, death of a spouse (100 points), divorce (73), marital separation (63) all the way down to vacation (13), Christmas (12) and minor violations of the law (11). Forty-three items are listed. This work is on-going.

What follows is a brief description of *the natural history of areas in primary care* according to the time it takes for problems to become detectable, or for symptoms to evolve through critical phases and either stabilize or be resolved: **'The education of physicians for primary care'****, written by two pediatricians, Joel J. Alpert MD (Boston) and Evan Charney MD, (Rochester), was the fourth text we presented. It lists the **Natural History of Areas of Primary Care** according to the time it takes for problems to become detectable, or for symptoms to evolve through critical phases and either stabilize or be resolved. I had visited Joe Alpert with Helen Cave for a week in 1965 (cfr Ch 36). Physicians can classify patients they see in this way:

Short Term (one day to one month):

1) most medical and surgical emergencies;
2) common infections: pharyngitis, otitis media, gastroenteritis, upper-and lower-respiratory tract infections;
3) average acute hospitalization;
4) minor surgical trauma;
5) relationship with the patient: why did he/she come and what does the professional need to meet the demands of the patient.

---

for Family Physicians, over 1300 pages long. I was asked to write chapter 19: The 'Years from Birth to Puberty', which I was thrilled and felt honored to be asked to do, with the help of Louise Séguin while at *l'HSCM*. There are four parts to the new textbook:

** US Department of Health, Education and Welfare, Public Health Service, Health Resource Administration, Bureau of Health Services Research, DHEW Pub. No. (HRA)1974-3113.

Intermediate Term (two to twelve weeks):

1) acute or presenting phase of a chronic disease. Although this does not define the condition's entire 'natural history', it does indicate the length of time it usually takes for the condition to be diagnosed and the initial management pattern established: congenital abnormalities, diabetes, asthma, leukemia;
2) certain behavioral disorders: child rearing conflicts, school adjustment problems, some marital conflicts;
3) recurrent abdominal pain;
4) cardiovascular disorders (acute phase), infarction, hypertension, congestive heart failure;
5) observation of the 'milieu of practice', the life style of the practitioner;
6) learning to work on a hierarchically organized team;
7) observation of the "milieu" of research in patient care: the techniques of the procedures in research;

Long-Term (eight weeks to years and years):

1) the family (the patient) as the focus of care, the disease as the episode, the sociology of the family;
2) most chronic diseases: asthma, cerebral palsy, mental retardation, psychosis and neurosis, diabetes;
3) the growth and development of children;
4) working as a co-professional team member;
5) design and implementation of a patient care project;
6) a working relation that has to be repeated between professional and consumer.

We talked a lot about medical records in primary care, particularly the use of **a problem-oriented record in primary care.** A new resident, with a special aptitude for producing audiovisual aids, produced a slide tape show which was most useful. At their request, copies were sent to the other teaching units.

Residents quickly got used to **seeing themselves on tape,** quite disgusted when seeing themselves sometimes at first: they thought of it as being fun as well as essential. They had to show us a tape of their choice, three or four times a year. How did they feel about the interview, about the patient, about the way they proceeded, eye-contact, ease, decorum, touching the patient, and the substance of the interview, whether they were on track or lost in detail, and so on, too fast, too slow, how the patient felt, anxious, relaxed, hyper, sedated, depressed, stable mentally and so on, the way the interviewee responded.

The contribution of _Jacques Monday_, our psychiatrist/psycho-somatician, was crucial. He came to see us so frequently, much more aware of the potential problems concerning our relationship with the hospital specialists than I, a newcomer, could ever be. He had trained at l'HSC first as a General Practitioner and recently as a Psychiatrist He was a tower of strength, showing us that he cared profoundly in what we were attempting to do. He introduced us all to Jacobson's* relaxation exercises:

> Once or twice a week, we could all be seen lying on our mats on the floor for fifteen minutes doing about eighteen exercises: one tenses each muscle group in sequence from hands to toes for just five seconds, then relax completely to allow the muscles to get entirely limp before going onto the next exercise, an easy technique, lasting fifteen minutes a day, which we could introduce to our patients. He also participated actively in our round-table discussions.

Yolande St Germain and Marielle Beauger, our well-qualified experienced Social Worker and Nurse, were just as excellent. A kind of osmosis linked the four of us together, difficult to describe. I have read about teamwork without ever reading something akin to what happened with our team! The term osmosis seemed to explain best what happened to the four of us.

That first year was a great success: our unit had become a home from home. We soon had many more patients, although they had to walk half a mile to get there! My anxieties were allayed. The residents were so gentle. I always had the cheapest plastic bag to carry my stuff around, and they soon gave me a beautiful leather one! They took care of us. They saw and felt how a team functioned, and we rarely talked about it. They understood things they had never been exposed to before during their five years in medical school. It was like a re-birth.

The proceeds of the 'practice' were re-invested in the occasional parties in the unit, coffee and biscuits for the daily luncheon, an official or unofficial

---

*   **Edmond Jacobso(e)n** was born c.1888 in Chicago, and was educated and worked there at North-Western University. After obtaining a BSc in Physiology, he went to Harvard for his PhD, Once home, he qualified in Medecine in 1915. He worked with the Bell Tel. Co., publishing a book "Electrophysiology of Mental Activities and Introduction to the Physiological Process of Thinking" in 1921. He coined the term **Psychosomatic Medicine;** his second book, published in 1929, "Progressive Muscular Relaxation" (PMR) is based on the premise that an increase in endorphin production, occurring when muscles contract, decreases the level of pain and increases immune activity.

---

meeting, and a get together at the end of the year in a *UdeM* property on the outskirts of town by *'le fleuve'*, with a tennis court, where we had a 'scientific' meeting in the morning, and a relaxing afternoon. They all started to feel secure and enthusiastic about their future career as family physicians. They could relax while learning. The second year, we had our four second year residents, plus five new ones, By the end of the decade, our full complement reached 24 post-graduate students. They all got through their examinations of the Canadian College of Family Physicians, a few on their second attempt.

Of the first four, one took my job over on January 1st 1979, another got a PhD in Community Medicine in 1989, his thesis 'on the Influence of our new Family Medicine on the Conception of Comprehensive Care', a third joined the staff of a CLSC which became a teaching CLSC later on, and the fourth became interested in hospital administration.

But we had plenty of internal problems. Most of the medical staff of *l'HSC* failed to change their minds about our efforts, particularly the internists. Our residents of course soon discovered this reality. They also started to appreciate the need for what we were trying to do: there was nothing offered before we came on the scene for preparing them for their future career. Our residents started to defend us. Thank goodness also that we used the hospital records in our unit with a section adapted for our use. Eventually, the rest of the staff of the hospital might start to read something about what we were doing.

> One of our residents was doing his stint in internal medicine, and one of his patients on that service opted to receive his comprehensive care after being sent home at the Family Practice Unit. This was not unusual. After seeing this particular patient in the unit, the resident felt that a blood test for hypothyroidism would be appropriate, and this proved to be positive proof of the patient's condition. So, after discussing the situation with us he started the proper medication with thyroid tablets. However, the lab report was not inserted in the chart for a few days.
>
> In the meanwhile the patient had returned to see her internist. He exploded when he realized she had been prescribed a thyroid preparation apparently without laboratory proof, wrote utterly disparaging notes in the patient's chart about how incompetent general practitioners were: a totally unacceptable and unethical thing to do. The resident was most upset when he saw the chart; he immediately came to see me to talk about it. I thought about it a couple of days; I went to see the middle aged quite senior internist.
>
> He literally blanched when I showed him his notes and the lab results, which by then had been inserted in the hospital chart.

He offered to resign immediately. I answered that I did not want his resignation but his cooperation: we were both teachers in the same University affiliated hospital with the same residents; we complemented each other. If a problem arose, we could always use the telephone. I noticed that, over the next few weeks, the famous chart had been gradually cleansed of any wrongdoings.

The physical examination is an important item in the armamentarium of the primary care physician. A discomfort/pain/lump/discoloration somewhere must be carefully looked at and felt. The stethoscope must be used: observation, percussion, palpation, and auscultation, are therapeutic as well as diagnostic measures, symbols essential before initiating treatment. It is part of Balint's dictum, 'the doctor is the pill'. It is a serious matter, not to be undertaken flippantly. It is best also to explain quietly what you are doing and its purpose as one goes along. It is a good way of ensuring a satisfactory doctor/patient relationship.

- The Family Physician (140 pages).
- The Patient and the Family (210 pages).
- The Principles in Family Medicine (920 pages).
- Family Practice, to-day and to-morrow (20 pages).

Taylor introduces the Competence Priority (ComPri) Classification of Behavior, Concepts and Skills in Family Medicine:

- ComPri 1, high priority, Definitive Care;
- ComPri 2, intermediate priority, Shared Care;
- ComPri 3, low priority, Supportive Care Problems only.

Every clinical chapter (part 3) follows the ComPri plan.

What about Undergraduate Teaching at l'UdeM.

If we really wanted to educate first-class family physicians, we had to 'invade' the undergraduate program, then five years long. Not one family physician/general practitioner was implicated in teaching in any of those years, and the earlier in curriculum we could start teaching the better. What was actually going on at the time was a selection of the 'best' students for the specialties, the rest of them relegated to academic oblivion, scattered like salt and pepper around the new cathedrals of medical knowledge in the sixteen

Canadian towns that happened to possess one, each with their branch hospitals in the smaller towns near-by, linked by their roots to the central agencies.

Relegated to this academic oblivion with little preparation, the general practitioner had to 'invent' how he would work, doing the best he could, reading his journals written by specialists in their cathedrals. In the circumstances, he achieved a lot, but there was so much more medical schools should feel obligated to offer. Whatever we might achieve in preparing students for primary community care would be better than anything presented to them so far. We had to get away from the dogmatic lectures in a large lecture room and get the students out into the public arena. In 1986, there were 157 students in their first year. I still have rough notes. I tried several approaches:

- **The largest and most important project** was introduced during the first semester of the first year of the curriculum in <u>October 1978</u>: four three hour periods on Monday mornings, all new students, one month after their start, for me the best timing that most teachers were loathe to use because the students were so 'fresh and immature'. The subject matter, **'Child Abuse and Neglect"**, was a dramatic and comparatively new problem. The term-battered child syndrome-was coined in 1961, a dramatic manifestation of family violence, after which the definition was broadened and different factors identified as responsible, <u>child-produced stresses</u> (physically, mentally, temperamentally or behaviorally different), <u>parent-produced stresses</u> (low self-esteem, abused as a child, psychological or psychiatric problems, unrealistic expectations) or/and <u>socio-situational stresses</u> (poverty, isolation, unsatisfactory parental relationship, punitive child rearing, excess or unwanted children). All this leading to injury, inability to provide care, poisoning, psychological maltreatment.

It is estimated that 3-4% of children between 3 and 17 are at risk for physical injury every year, let alone the non-physical insults to which babies and children can be exposed. By 1986, I had the help of two young teachers, a pediatrician, Robert Dubé, a graduate from le CHUS in 1974 when I was there. He had recently written an article about the condition in a provincial medical journal. Gilles Paradis, one of our ex-students at l'HSC who had gone to California to obtain an MSc in an area of Public Health, led the second group for the final session. The four sessions are briefly described below:

---

* <u>An excellent text was provided</u>, **'Pediatric Understanding of Child Abuse and Neglect'** (Bittner and Newberger, Pediatrics in Review, Vol.2, 7th January 1981).

- Two 25 minute lectures each followed by a 15 minute question and answer period, the first explaining primary horizontal care versus secondary (local hospital) and tertiary (university based) care; the second, about the abused/neglected child, the concept of being "at risk", and about primary, secondary and tertiary prevention (before the onset, soon after the onset when the condition is still reversible, and after the condition is fully developed).

- The same format with an overview of what a primary care physician does in his office: taking a history, doing a physical examination, making up a list of problems and a plan for the management of each problem at the level of the individual, the family and the community, frequently involving teamwork, with emphasis on possible diagnoses, one of which is the neglected and abused child.

- Split the 157 students into 15 groups of a maximum of 14 students, each group having to elect a secretary, each group visiting a key person in the community that has had contact with the problem of the abused/neglected child: professionals (teachers, social workers, primary care physicians, pediatricians, radiologists, orthopedists, epidemiologists), representatives of NGOs such as Homes for Battered Women, Children's Aid Society, Centre-Aid (very active in Montréal), and GOs, like CLSCs and departments of Community Health plus implicated lawyers, police, the Corporation of Physicians and Surgeons of Quebec (la corpo to all the doctors in Quebec).

Appointments were made for these visits, and, to my amazement, all contacts with rare exceptions were enthusiastic about the project. Each secretary was responsible for a one page summary of what went on at those individual meetings, the text submitted forty-eight hours prior to the last session for distribution to all participants.

- For the last session, the class was divided in two: each secretary had ten minutes to present what happened to each group followed by a five to ten minute discussion.

A take-home examination followed, stressing the three levels of preventing diseases, an attempt to classify the level of prevention of the work of the different people interviewed. Excellent evaluations by the students followed, with very few exceptions. The problem with this type of teaching is that it takes a lot of preparation. But it is well worth the extra work.

The amazing and wonderful **sequel** was that, by 1982, nine other problems presented in a similar format had been added to my first one, under the banner of Community Medicine and Family Medicine, with an expert in the field responsible for each project:

<u>year one,</u>	2nd semester, **industrial accidents.**
<u>year two,</u>	1st semester, **learning problems at school,** and **road accidents.**
	2nd semester, **alcoholism** and **sexually transmitted diseases.**
<u>year three</u>	1st semester, **loss of autonomy associated with ageing,** and **teen age pregnancy.**
	2nd semester, **depression** and **approaching death.**

By 1982, the curriculum had been shortened to four years to comply with North American norms. <u>A dynamic community medicine/family medicine problem was presented in the teaching program each of the six semesters during the first three years, the fourth year now being an externship year in different mostly hospital-based rotations but including family medicine and community medicine</u>: a big difference in just four years, a cause for celebration.

- **A few other smaller projects** were explored:

= <u>house calls with medical students</u> are a pleasant experience. I have always loved doing house-calls. It is a privilege and an honor to enter somebody's home to look after somebody: I have felt like that ever since I delivered babies at home on the midwifery district at the London Hospital during the winter of 1947. On one of those occasions, with Miss Dear, who had delivered more than 4000 babies at home during WW I and had received a medal for her work, we had just delivered this lovely new baby at home in Whitechapel, a Jewish baker's wife; we might have been there four to five hours, drinking several cups of tea in the process; they lived over the shop in two rooms in a row of small houses. After the event, the happy husband opened a small cupboard and exposed some Grand Marnier, Cointreau and other bottles, and we celebrated briefly, much to my amazement. Such a moment is indeed a privilege.

= At the other extreme, death after a long illness such as cancer of the lung, the course of which you have followed closely, relief at the end of the suffering and caring that you have witnessed is often marked by offering a similar pick-me-up. It is a privilege to assist somebody during their last days. Dying at home is so much more humane than in a hospital. One discovers something new all the time, tragic sometimes as the man who tried to commit suicide, his head in the gas oven as he was kneeling there, discovered by his wife just in time, or the man found dead in his small rented room, flower vases full of smelly old urine, with nobody to care for him. The police had called me in to certify death. He must have been dead for a week, the smell was terrible and nobody in that small house, surprise-surprise, had any idea of what was happening. One has to transmit the enthusiasm one feels for this kind of service.

= You can best do that by having a student accompany you. It is preferable that you travel together in the car so that you can talk about the patient prior to arriving there, and again after departure: an 82 year old diabetic widow, living by herself on a first floor rented apartment, sitting in her wheel-chair with two below knee artificial legs that she put on religiously every morning without ever walking on them, living by herself with her canary that sang all the time and that she loved deeply. She had to be carried downstairs in her wheelchair whenever she had to go to hospital by ambulance for her twice yearly visit. She had long arms, and managed to cook a little, do the washing-up, looking after her-self as best she could.

Her husband had been a purser on the Queen Mary. They lived in Baltimore, and she moved to Montréal when she was widowed. She hated all French Canadians and told everybody about it, including the students. She was on a strict diet, but would phone me up occasionally to ask me whether I could bring her a small ice-cream bar on my next visit. I usually complied! She read Harlequin Romances and Eaton's would send her a regular supply. Quite a few students got to know this lady. Why is she living by herself (this is what she wanted), why on the second floor (more sunshine and light, good for the canary), who visits and helps her, never ending questions.

When I stopped seeing her, one of these newly graduated students was delighted to take her over. I met one of these ex-students earlier this month who told me that once upon a time she had accompanied me on a house-call when I was at le CHUS: it was one of a dozen or so calls to households that had a young child who had fallen and broken some bone, and we wanted to ascertain that, as far as one could tell, it was not caused by violence or neglect: I left le CHUS over thirty-five years ago! The young lady was now well over fifty years old, but to me still looked around thirty! She was not that far off retiring herself.

= sending <u>two young medical students at a time on house-calls with a small portable television camera</u> was a real adventure for them: *à l'UdeM* there was a large, well-equipped and very efficient and helpful audio-visual department and students were encouraged to borrow small television cameras for the purpose of furthering their education. I also submit that retired couples are usually extremely keen to help in this kind of endeavor. It is a welcome change in their often fairly dull day-to-day life. I had a group of eight or so older students on an elective for a few months, and I would send them on house-calls, two at a time, to see patients with a camera: we would discuss the interview together.

Two of the older patients were the parents of the head of the large pharmacy faculty à *l'UdeM;* he had asked me if I could care for his elderly parents at home. They were a charming, helpful and well-educated couple, living in an apartment not far from the university and were delighted and delightful. Some years after they died, their son telephoned me to find out whether I still had the tapes of those interviews as he was collecting documents concerning them both. Of course we never kept such tapes; they were erased immediately after use on principle. I cannot recall a couple that refused such kind of experience. Patients unanimously enjoyed it and so did the students. Life in a government institution for an older retired person is the last possible choice to end one's days. On my first visit to one of them, I asked one of the older patients, walking with difficulty with a stick, what he was doing there: *j'attend la mort* was the reply. This is not an unusual response.

- <u>starting a small clinic in the damp basement of a tenement house in *le quartier St Michel*, 37,000 people without a doctor's office or green spaces of any kind</u>, with a resident intent on studying psychiatry after a year with us in family medicine at *l'HSC*. I would do two clinics a week there. We had a very good secretary from around the corner, and an excellent nurse, an RC Nun, who volunteered her services.

We soon organized a special morning once a week to collect laboratory specimens that a volunteer would take to the laboratories at *l'HSC* in his car. We did house calls. For residents it was not a satisfactory experience because of the absence of regular supervision, legally necessary; but for medical students it was excellent. I wrote an article that was published in the Journal of the

Canadian Medical Association, with photographs, comparing East Ham with *St Michel (Paroisse René Goupil),* not so different after all, except that in East Ham a general practitioner could not use hospital laboratories at that time. He also was paid a capitation fee! There was more misery in *St Michel,* but the area was well organized as far as volunteers were concerned. There is a large *CLSC* there now.

The local TV station came around one day to accompany us on house-call: it was a total disaster because it had not been prepared. We met for the first time on the patient's door-step. I had all sorts of patients, a young lesbian couple who danced on tables in night-clubs, Haitian taxi drivers, many older retirees of all sorts of background. I convinced a lady with an extraordinary story to write it all down; I referred her to an editor who helped her a lot. *'Sylvie B. une fille comme moi'* was published in 1982, published by *les éditions héritage, inc, Montréal.* It proved also to be good therapy. I have an autographed copy. The story of the district was the subject for a book by a health professional with photographs published in 1983: *'au coin de la quarante-septième',* by *Andrée Pilon Quiviger* (Léméac), full of hope and looking forward to a brighter future.

Glitches occurred as one can imagine:

An old patient was sent home without anyone at the small local hospital near St Michel finding out whether there were adequate facilities available at his home address to care for him: this is strictly against the law. I tried talking about the problem at the hospital without success. I ended up by telling his wife to visit a relative for a few days so that the house would be locked and empty, and sent the patient back in an ambulance with an appropriate curt note: this was not appreciated. I received telephone threats of complaints at the highest level from the hospital administration!

Although a qualified pediatrician with the Canadian Royal College degree with a lot of experience looking after the new-born, I was never encouraged to even visit the maternity/pediatric wards at *l'HSC.* I might not even exist as far as my colleagues were concerned. I later realized that the reason was that few of the physicians there were qualified specialists and they were concerned about their future.

The same was true of the Department of Human Genetics at *le CHUMME (hospital St Justine,* maternity and children), the only one at the UdeM. The obstetricians at *l'HSC* with whom I got on well, sent me patients for genetic counseling, the only specialists to do so. However, I became one of the twenty-five or so founding members of the Canadian Society of Human Genetics.

I would meet Dr Bois, Dean of the Medical School, at the local Shell gas station. We always went to the same one. The owner, an efficient man who ran his own clean well decorated garage, with a little lobby where you could actually sit down, was very worried about his son, a resident at the time in the oto-rhino-laryngology (ear, nose and throat) department at *l'UdeM*, and kept talking to the dean about it at the gas pump. The young man had developed a brain tumor six months or so before from which he was recovering, but the university department to which he was attached refused to have him back as a resident, although he had been very satisfactory in his studies until his health had broken down. He had lost most of his hair after radiation. He was just dropped like a hot brick from the program without support of any kind. He was under the care of the Montréal Neurological Institute (MNI), as good as any in the world. After a month or so, the dean told me about it one morning by the pumps, and asked me what I thought might be done. The dean was very apologetic about this oral request. I told dean Bois I would think about it for a couple of days.

Had this happened at the *CHUS*, I would have received a written note from the dean's office stating that the transfer to family medicine would take place immediately without any spoken word. There was a very nice quiet and sensible student at the *CHUS* who had difficulties with his 'studies' but who would undoubtedly be suitable for family medicine: this kind of behavior always made me see red. This student at the *CHUS* later became an excellent family physician.

I saw the Professor of Surgery first: he knew all about it of course, was adamant about the decision: he might develop an epileptic fit during an operation, and there was simply no question of his being reinstated. I had talked to him before. He was so stubborn. He felt women had no place in surgery; they could not possibly work at night, their place was in the home with their children, and they might just cope with part-time general practice one or two afternoons a week. I was amused and barely surprised. That was that. I then sat down with the young man and took a detailed history *à la* London Hospital. Much to my surprise, he had not been referred to Dr Brenda Milner, a basic scientist at the MNI with a world-class reputation in diagnostic neurology.

I got to know quite a lot about the MNI at about that time, and Dr Milner was for me a real model of a basic scientist. She is still working there to-day although in her early eighties. Dr Milner accepted to see the patient at very short notice. I got a detailed report stating that there was a serious hearing memory loss, but that the visual memory was practically normal. In other words, he should read rather than listen. The ultimate prognosis seemed excellent: rather than attending conferences and lectures, it was preferable to read and see movies. I then prepared for him a gradual return to a residency program in Family Medicine. I thought it would be easier for him to be based in a *CLSC*. By that time, the one in *Pointe-aux-Trembles*, at the eastern end of the Island of Montréal, was working very efficiently. He would feel much more at home and welcome in a comparatively small teaching unit with colleagues of his own age, two afternoons a week for a month, extending to full-time employment in six-nine months.

I telephoned *Augustin (Roy)* as everybody called him, *président et secrétaire générale de la Corpo,* to find out about the amount of time the new resident would have to spend in the program, and that was that. Dean Bois was quite delighted. By that time our young friend had consulted a toupee specialist who advised him to shave off the remaining tuft of hair he had on his forehead. This he insisted he would not do: that was the remains of his own hair, and he would keep it. Thus the toupee was a more expensive undertaking. Color matching had become a consideration. It reminded me of Mona, my dear young friend with leukemia from my days in Sherbrook, who also wore a wig on my advice; she would rip it off when too warm in the school bus, much to everyone's consternation!

Lots of <u>mistakes</u>, <u>errors of judgment</u>, occur in medicine, at all levels. The first doctor consulted by a patient is so often a physician in primary care working by himself, with little immediate access to laboratory, radiological and other professional help, confronted by many problems of many patients of different age and sex, culture and background, very much at risk for making mistakes. He himself is subject to the same common problems, discomforts, chronic diseases, addiction and worries of all kinds. Sitting in his chair listening to his patients, some of whom he has known for years, he may become desensitized regarding some of their problems.

Some patients lead you to form a wrong impression. Others always remain a special challenge. The physician is only told what the patient wants to talk about. Mistakes are difficult to avoid. What is inexcusable is missing the diagnosis of an acute disease, in young people in particular, who might die as a consequence, such as meningitis, acute epiglottitis in young children, acute appendicitis, acute osteomyelitis or a ruptured spleen.

The primary physician has a far more difficult job than a catholic priest in his confessional, who just gives a benediction and a penance at the end of the consultation from behind a grill. Alphonse Daudet's *'Les Trois Messes Basses'* is worth re-reading! Some patients are more difficult than others. Psychological problems and certain life-styles are difficult to fathom, such as homosexuality, disease of the mind, habits and addictions of all kinds. The more senior you are as a professional in the health care system, the more protected from mistakes you become.

Specialists, by definition, limit their work to the diseases of a certain organ, the heart, the kidney, the eye, and so on, an easier task. Primary care is their portal. The senior physician in an institution has a tremendous advantage, being the ultimate judge. All the information has been collected and classified. The crossword is complete apart from the last clue. In any case, in primary care, the patient comes to see you for an opinion, an opinion that is not necessarily accepted, or to the patient necessarily acceptable. What the primary care physician must do first is rule out emergencies.

Working with a team makes it easier, as one can share responsibilities by supporting one another. One can practically guarantee that every patient does not have anything medically serious by excessive use of the laboratory and radiology, and some patients are quite delighted that their doctor 'never leaves a stone unturned'! But this is poor medicine and too expensive to sustain. To feel secure does not depend on the quantity of the investigations requested. Here is where the quality of a judgment comes in, essential for success, and for this, the quality of teaching and the teaching milieu itself is all important. One gets better at it with experience, but the challenge always remains. This is what we tried <u>to demonstrate</u>.

<u>Coping is the Everyone's Problem,</u> whether one is a patient or a physician.

<u>Postscript</u> (January **2010**):

At the Level of the University of Montréal:

=   there are now 286 students a year starting their medical studies at the University of Montreal.

=   the Department of Family Medicine has become the Department of Family and Emergency Medicine (primary care). Over half the physicians in Emergency Medicine are certified Family Physicians.

= **half the teaching of clinical medicine during the first three years is the responsibility of the Department of Family and Emergency Medicine.**

= 41% of the students chose primary care as a career; the Canadian average is under 30%.

= the model I had proposed in 1978 for problem teaching in Community and Family Medicine is still in place.

= two of our old residents played a very active part in the development of the new Institute of Geriatrics. After their two years in Family Medicine they chose to study Social and Community Medicine for a further two years.

At the Sacré-Coeur Hospital:

= Family Medicine and Emergency Medicine occupy adjoining spaces on the first floor; there is much communication between them; there is ample parking space. The same Round Table, somewhat worn out, is still in use in Family Medicine; a helicopter pad is on the site.

= The Emergency Department is now the only fully accredited Teaching Unit in French Quebec. It includes about 100 emergency beds.

= **Family Medicine is responsible for the care of 40-50% of the hospitalized patients at the Sacré-Coeur Hospital.**

= The clinical record, that includes hospital and family medicine, has remained largely unchanged.

At a Personal Level:

= In 1988, I was given the W. Victor Johnston Oration Award by the College of Family Medicine. It is their highest honor and is granted once a year.

= In 1996, on the 25th anniversary of the Foundation of the Department of Social and Community Medicine at the *UdM*, I was chosen by the Professors of the department to be one of two recipients of a plaque recognizing an *outstanding contribution to the development of Community and Family Medicine*.

= In 2008, Joan and I were invited to join the Head Table to celebrate the 25th anniversary of the Department of Family Medicine, with the present Head of Department, Francois Lehmann, the Dean and the ex-Dean and their wives, plus 300 staff members, a very enjoyable occasion, at the prestigious Mount St Stephen Club in Montréal (George Stephen, 1829-1921, Scots/Quebecker, Railway Executive).

CHAPTER 44

The Canada China Connection: Doctor Norman Bethune, an important link.

SETTING THE SCENE:

Two stamps of Dr Bethune were issued in China on November 20th **1960,** the 21st anniversary of his death, **the next two** on November 12th **1979,** the 40th anniversary. What follows in this section is a survey of some of the events that occurred in Canada between those two dates that concerned his memory.

The Peking Opera Company visited Montréal in **1961**; it included a performance at the **Royal Victoria Hospital**. Dr Ronald Christie (1*) was then physician-in-chief.

As a direct outcome, **an exchange professorship** between McGill University and the Peking **Academy** of Medical Science was organized to honor Dr Bethune.

> **Dr Alan Elliott** became the first exchange professor to go to China during the era of Chairman Mao. Alan died on Monday 28th of April 1986 at the age of 82. He was a founder of neuro-biochemistry, a South African. He became director of the neuro-chemical laboratory at the Montréal Neurological Institute (MNI) in 1944.

1* Dr Christie, as part of his medical studies, had had the exact same house-jobs at The London Hospital as I had, with Sir Alun Rowlands and Mr Clive Butler.

He was a founding member of the Bethune Memorial Committee.

Joan and I were quite close to him during the latter part of his life. He became a real friend. He was a prolific writer, his last book **(Common Sense Revolution, and other essays about Life and the World),** sixteen short essays published as late as 1980 are well-worth reading, the second essay entitled Violence and Creativity.

We would drive him home where he lived by himself, and we would visit him there. He introduced us to Unitarianism.

He would go to New York for a couple of days to participate in a Peace March when he was over 80 years old. He was a most intelligent, loving and creative person, one of my last three 'Canadian' models, all from the MNI, with **Francis McNaughton**, a fantastic neurologist who had worked with Dr Bethune on various projects in the thirties. We got to know him well. **Brenda Milner**, a neurophysiologist whom I had never met, was the third. There was absolutely no pretense in any of those three real experts.

Dr Maurice McGregor, also a South African, who later became senior physician at the Royal Victoria Hospital and Dean of the Medical school, also subsequently went to China as a Bethune Exchange Professor in Beijing.

The Ottawa bureau of the New China News Agency was opened in Ottawa in **1964,** and its directors visited the Royal Victoria Hospital to present a book of photographs of Dr Bethune while he was in China.

Marc Lalonde was born in 1929, schooled by the Jesuits, then obtaining his Law degree in 1955 at *l'Université de Montréal.*

From the 22nd of April 1963 to the 19th of April 1968 he had become Special Advisor to the new Prime Minister of Canada, *Lester Bowles Pearson.* Most people considered Marc Lalonde as Mr Pearson's Chief of Staff, but he always considered himself to be just a special advisor.

When *Pierre Elliott Trudeau* became Prime Minister, Marc Lalonde became his Principal Secretary, Chief of Staff and Main Political Advisor, his right-hand man. He remained in this position until 1972. He then became Minister of Health, publishing his now world famous working document on Health Care, a New Perspective on the Health of Canadians (April 1974).

Marc Lalonde visited China prior to **1970** when diplomatic relations between the two countries were established, the first country on the north American continent to do so. During that exploratory visit, the Chinese kept mentioning a Dr Bethune, much to his surprise as he had never heard of him.

He had never heard of this doctor! His ignorance is hardly surprising considering that he was ten years old when Bethune died. His war-time education, although academically excellent, was warped by religious intolerance, his Jesuit schooling and its curriculum identical to mine, and his University education at *l'UdeM,* with a *Monseigneur* as it's Head at that time, just as stilted.

Ted Allen's biography of Dr Bethune had not yet been translated into French. A translation by Jean Pare, *"Docteur Bethune"* was only published in the early seventies.

Les Soeurs de la Providence had founded *l'Hopital du Sacre-Coeur* in 1926, and someone in Ottawa told Marc Lalonde on his return of Dr Bethune's three and a half years' stay there (January 1933-June 1936).

A few remaining surgical instruments that were developed by Dr Bethune were promptly collected from somewhere in the dusty basement of *l'HSC.*

Pierre Trudeau flew to Beijing on his first official visit **(October 10th-16th, 1973):** Canada was the first North-American country to recognize China officially and exchange ambassadors.

He was not, however, invited to meet Chairman Mao, as were President Nixon, and *monsieur Pompidou.* The instruments were presented. The present location of these instruments in China remains unknown, probably deposited in another dusty basement.

A **Chinese Embassy** was built in Ottawa at great cost with a great deal of secret electronic gadgetry.

The Chinese had one look at it and opted to purchase an **old convent** instead, more in tune with their needs, at 515 Patrick Street, with many rooms, large enough to house all the embassy staff-members for years to come who all had to live-in, like at boarding school, with the head-master/ambassador in the principal suite. A beautiful large building belonging to an autocratic religious community had been taken over by another autocratic but communist government, both with similar domiciliary/working requirements.

Chang Wen-Chin, one of China's most able and likeable diplomats, was assigned to be the first Ambassador to Canada just prior to the Prime Minister

Trudeau's visit to Beijing. He was succeeded by **Wang Tung,** Ambassador Extraordinary and Plenipotentiary of the People's Republic of China to Canada, and his wife, **Liu Feng,** both very charming, intelligent and affable. Joan and I met them both several times.

The Bethune Memorial Committee was announced at a day-long symposium at <u>McGill University</u> in honor of Dr Norman Bethune during the fall of **1971.**

<u>Dr Wilder Penfield</u> was elected Honorary Chairman, <u>Hazen Sise</u> (Dr Bethune's ambulance driver in Spain) Chairman, <u>Dr Gérard Rolland</u> (Dr Bethune's surgical assistant at *l'HSC*) and <u>Mrs Mary Weil</u> (Public Relations Director at the Royal Victoria Hospital), Vice-Chairpersons, plus eleven other members.

The Bethune Memorial Committee was renamed **The Bethune Foundation** in 1974, and **The Norman Bethune Foundation** in 1981. The priority of the Foundation at the beginning was fund-raising to encourage exchanges between the Chinese and Canadian people.

Six members of The Bethune Memorial Committee, a more appropriate name, were invited to visit China during the fall of 1973 for three weeks, led by Hazen Sise and Mary Weil; Wendell McLeod was included.

Unfortunately Hazen Sise died in 1974. His last essay about Dr Bethune was read at that first meeting of the Committee, but was only published posthumously, a wonderful, thoughtful, sincere seven-page memoir (2*).

A perplexed editorialist in the Montréal Gazette (5) in 1972 wrote:**

'What is so odd is that it required mounting visits by Chinese, who invariably made a pilgrimage to Gravenhurst, to educate Canadians about the unusual character of Dr Bethune' .... *'Bethune, it happened, went to work to save lives on the Loyalist side in the Spanish Civil War and later on the Communist side in the Chinese struggle against the Japanese. But fundamentally no ideological tag fits him. He might be called an iconoclast who opposed entrenched ideas, even of hospitals in*

2* **The Vivid Air Signed with his Honour: In Memory of Norman Bethune',** in 'NORMAN BETHUNE, his times and his legacy', proceedings of a conference published by The Canadian Public Health Association, 1982.

5** Stanley Ryerson, in <u>Bethune. The Montréal Years,</u> James Lorimer & Co, Toronto, 1978, p 165.

---

*Montréal; he may be called a non-conformist who believed that he was his own man, and no one else's. **Essentially, however, he was a humanitarian—with daring, imagination and flair in rare combination—and it is for this, fittingly, that he deserves to be remembered'.***

At *l'HSC*, visitors from China would sometimes come to look at and perhaps visit the hospital where Dr Bethune had worked before going to Spain and China, usually an official or two visiting Montréal or members of a visiting group of artists, (ballet dancers, circus performers, actors, acrobats).

There was nothing at *l'HSC* itself to indicate that Dr Bethune had actually worked there, no photograph or plaque of any kind. Visitors were then shown his office on the fourth floor, a room in use with bare walls, a desk, chairs, a book-case, and a view of the beautiful grounds.

The fiftieth anniversary of the hospital was fast approaching, and the suggested **program** by a committee made up mainly of members of the very conservative and mostly Roman Catholic pastoral service (a week-long celebration, meetings, conferences, celebratory lunches and dinners, with well-known guests) was sent to the various departments for information early in the year. It was to take place **during the fall of 1976.**

I received a copy and was quite horrified that there was no mention whatsoever of Dr Bethune. I thought about it during the next few days: I had enough on my plate without a new burden, yet felt I could not just ignore the situation.

So I ended up by going to see the Hospital *directeur general,* **monsieur Jean-Claude Martin**. Prior to working at *l'HSC,* he had worked at the Montréal Children's Hospital. He may well have heard of Dr Bethune.

What followed proved to be an extraordinary experience that Joan and I never expected. It would occupy an important part of our lives for the next twenty years.

Monsieur Martin told me he would think about it for a couple of days, after which he asked me whether I would agree to arrange some kind of exhibit in the hospital and think of other possible activities. He provided me with a $4000 expense account.

I thought about it with Joan, and accepted the mandate. He also told me about the Bethun Foundation, based at the Royal Victoria Hospital, the present President of which was Mrs Mary Weil who worked there and was in charge of Public Relations.

All this was news for me. I soon met **Mrs Weil**. She was a smart and good-looking older lady with a lot of charm and with a severe limp, married to Paul Weil, mentioned earlier in Chapter 11.

> They were both retired or near retirement. Mrs Weil had developed a severe affliction of a hip as a young child and was sent to Liverpool in the UK for treatment under the care of Sir Robert Jones (cfr Ch 13). She was very tough, always refusing help when she would trip and nearly fall in the street, very embarrassing when you walked with her. We became friends. Paul was also quite a sociablel person. A Hematologist, he had been involved in blood banks since WW II at the Royal Victoria Hospital.
>
> They lived just around the corner from the Royal Vic in an old stone house, and had a lovely large lake-side property, designed and built by the famous Montreal architect, **Edward Maxwell,** at the turn of the Century. It was situated on the extreme north-west shore of the island of Montréal in *Senneville* on *le Lac des Deux Montagnes*, at the junction of the Ottawa and St Lawrence rivers, such a historical house in a historical location, with a large original Emily Carr oil painting amongst others hanging in the living-room, the only one I had ever seen up to that time. Devoted Catholics, they had seven children, some of whom were very successful in their careers.

We spent the month of August that summer on a small island on *Lac des Isles,* but I returned unexpectedly to *l'HSC* on Saturday 28th to attend a reception for ten Chinese guests who had been invited by the Canadian Government to attend the **opening of Bethune House** in **Gravenhurst.** Norman Bethune was born there. It was arranged at the last minute, thus the lack of notice:

> three were from the Ministry of Public Health, three from the Ministry of Foreign Affairs, two from Peoples' Liberation Army Hospitals (one in Beijing and one from the Bethune International Peace Hospital in Shijiazhuang, the new capital of Hebei province), and one each from the Association for Friendship with Foreign Countries and the Capital Hospital no1 in Beijing (3*).

3*   cfr Ch-3: the most Americanized of all Chinese medical schools, originally started by the Methodist Church, then supported and caught in the net for over half a century by American funds following the Flexner report of 1911.

Because of delays, the guests were divided into two groups that afternoon, so that five of them came to *l'HSC*. I remember very little about that first meeting, but it was important for the direction of *l'HSC* which had from then on to adapt to a new kind of front-line situations. The Chinese spent two nights in Ottawa, one in Montréal, three in Toronto, and three in Vancouver.

Mary Weil and I agreed that we could organize a <u>photograph exhibit</u> in the large front hall of the hospital: anyone who came to the hospital could not miss seeing it, thus ensuring that many people would be exposed to Dr Bethune. The Bethune Memorial Committee, during their trip to China in 1973, had received a beautiful set of photographs, at least half of which involved Dr Bethune's final year and a half in China.

> The story of what happened to those photographs is interesting: it was easy enough to take the 35mm photographs with a Leica camera (inherited from a German advisor), but there were no facilities available for processing them in Northern China at that time. So they were sent to Russia for development and printing. It took six months before they were returned. People were naturally worried about a possible loss.

The **carpenters at *l'HSC*** built two three-sided towers with six sheets of good quality plywood. They did a beautifully smooth job, and we attached the photographs to our wooden triangular towers. Each photograph had its caption.

Our second major activity was centered on the participation of members of the Chinese embassy to **the celebration dinner for the staff of *l'HSC***. Few people believed they would even attend. The Chinese Embassy was delighted with the invitation.

> Over two hundred members of the hospital staff were invited that evening, floor cleaners, secretaries, archivists, technicians of all branches, plumbers and carpenters, nurses, nursing aids, a few physicians, most with some seniority. Next to the Head Table was an extra one for just six people from outside, three from the Chinese Embassy, Mary Weil, myself, and a younger assistant-hospital administrator.
>
> It was a great success. The food was typical, beautifully prepared Quebec food, pigs' trotters, delicious *tourtières,* plenty of red wine, salads and all sorts of desserts, *tartes au sucre, gateaux carottes* etc . . . . An *apéritif* had been served beforehand in an adjoining conference room.

It was typical of a Chinese organized dinner with all sections of the hospital staff represented, with typical Quebec food, beautifully and generously prepared and served! The noise level was incredible. The service was excellent.

The Chinese were absolutely enchanted, as rare an occasion for them as it was for me. What an experience for the three of them: a great surgeon works in that very hospital during the thirties for over three years, going off immediately to fight fascism in both Spain and China to looking after the wounded.

In their own country he dies of septicemia after cutting his finger with a scalpel without having rubber gloves and without the help of even sulpha drugs. Nearly forty years later, those three Chinese representatives are present at the 50th anniversary dinner of that same Canadian Hospital where he had started to practice at the end of his training! Fantastic!

Interestingly for me, not one of my colleagues at *l'HSC* ever approached me to talk about what was going on!

Bethune Park gets funds, a headline in The Gazette on Wednesday April 20th 1977, where a beautiful white marble statue was to end up on a fifteen-foot pedestal, donated by the PRC, sculpted by four artists in Beijing, received and put on display at the Montréal Museum of Fine Arts the day before. It had been exhibited in the Chinese Pavilion that summer at the Man and his World Exhibition and finally was to be located in Place Norman Bethune that fall at the corner of Guy Street and de Maisonnneuve Boulevard, surrounded by a few trees in a small park. The Foundation visited the site on the Anniversary of his death that year with a bunch of flowers, and this became an annual event.

All these events were happening in the middle of ___La Revolution Tranquille officially initiated by Jean Lesage___ but started in a small way by Duplessis himself and Adélard Godbout during the war years.

For many Quebec Politicians, including Marc Lalonde and Pierre Trudeau, the changes in their relationship with the Quebec Catholic Church were difficult to face, particularly if they had been to school at Jesuit Institutions which many Quebec leading politicians had attended in their youth. Give me a child for five years, and they will remain faithful the rest of their lives, the Jesuits used to say.

I got to know very well Gérard Rolland and Georges Cousineau, and both refused to believe that the most important of their models, Norman Bethune, whom they both worshipped, could possibly have become a Communist. *Cela ne se pout pas.*

The women, just as religious, were to my mind far less rigid. For them, how the individual performed in society was far more important:

> On one occasion in **1966 a meeting was organized at *l'HSC* to**
> reminisce about Norman Bethune, and many francophone Montréal
> communists attended (4'). It was a free, well-publicized meeting.
> The nuns never worried about it, perhaps not even realizing what
> was going on, just as they did not worry when Dr Bethune slept in
> his tent in the hospital grounds decades before with a girlfriend. This
> could never have happened in a male Roman Catholic Institution.

The **Bethune Foundation** itself had very rigid rules about membership, and prominent Canadians, one of which would later receive the Order of Canada, was not invited to join at the start. Political affiliation was important. Membership, never numbering much over twenty-four members, had to be suggested by two members filling-in and signing a one page document that then had to be approved by the committee of three. Thus, prominent Anglophones, often just as religious, were also handicapped by bigotry.

Norman Bethune would have laughed his head off. By that time, he had become the physician/surgeon known by more people in the world than ever before: so many schools in China, a country with over a billion people, teaching about him, distributing millions of little linen-made children's books to most of them. One cannot do that in Canada because of our Federal system of Government, school programs being a provincial responsibility. All Chinese children grew up knowing him.

DR NORMAN BETHUNE'S DEATH FORTY YEARS AGO:
a **Commemoration in Montreal, November 1979.**

In retrospect, commemorating the fortieth anniversary of Dr Bethune's death in November 1979 proved to be the most important task for the Bethune Foundation during the twenty-two years of its existence.

Shortly after the events described above, Joan and I were both asked to join the Foundation, **Joan** soon replacing Mary Weil as the secretary. Mary Weil had replaced Hazen Sise as President in 1974; thus she had two functions in the Foundation for six years. Mary Weil had done all the work.

4*   Organized by **Dr Yves Duchastel**, a young neurologist who had just started
      to work at l'HSC. My boss, Dr Georges Desrosiers, was doing his six-months'
      internship in Hospital Administration there at that time. They both started to
      talk about this event voluntarily and independantly.

In February 1980, I became the third President.

Five Canadians were invited to go to China on an official visit lasting three weeks during that fall, at the invitation of the Chinese People's Association for Friendship with Foreign Countries.

I had never really seen myself doing that kind of work, had no experience in that line of events and was an entire newcomer to the Montréal scene.

I was a francophone by birth working in French in a francophone university-affiliated hospital where Dr Norman Bethune had worked, a full-time *Professeur Titulaire* of Social and Preventive Medicine in the foremost French-speaking University in the world outside Paris. I was truly bilingual. I had been a salaried professor in both anglophone and francophone medical schools in Canada, finally starting to feel truly Canadian.

The Foundation was an anglophone creation, few francophone Quebecers chosen to become members. It was time for change and I might have been a suitable compromise. All these thoughts ran through my mind at the time. I felt very sorry never to have met Hazen Sise. But I met and got to know well his Polish-born wife Jola, Wendell McLeod, Gérard Rolland (surgeon, *HSC*), Georges Cousineau (anesthetist, *HSC*), Francis McNaughton amongst others who had all known well and worked with Dr Bethune, so I was able to establish a link with the past.

Dr J. Wendell MacLeod, born in 1906, started the eight year course in Arts and Medicine at McGill University in 1922. This is what he wrote (1") about seeing Dr Bethune for the first time in the winter or early spring of 1930:

> 'On a Sunday morning, while still a student, I passed on the McGill campus near the Roddick Gates the dashing surgeon with beret and a colourful scarf, accompanied by his stylish and very good-looking wife—the only time I saw Frances'.
>
> When Dr Bethune was sent by Dr Archibald to provide surgical advice,
>
> 'he was like a breath of fresh air. He was informal, outgoing, dynamic in speech and body movements, cheerful and sometimes even gay'.

In discussions with interns and residents, he would sit on a stretcher and ask them what they would like to talk about, unusual at that time. He got to know Dr Bethune well during six years until June 1936, when Bethune decided to go to Spain.

1** 'Bethune The Montréal Years', by Wendell Mac Leod, Libbie Park, and Stanley Ryerson, published by James Lorimer & Co, Toronto, 1978.

After helping with the publication of Bethune's plan for a Canadian National Health Service, Wendell settled as an internist in Montréal, joined the Royal Canadian Navy during WW II as a destroyer's medical officer on the Canadian half of the Trans-Atlantic run, became the first Dean of the new Medical School in Saskatoon, supporting Tommy Douglas and the NDP, which did not endear him to the medical fraternity. He then became the first director of the Association of Canadian Medical Colleges (ACMC) in Ottawa, becoming comfortable with the politics prevalent there during the seventies. He knew personally many of the Anglophones involved in Dr Bethune's life during the barely <u>eight years of his stay in Montréal, such a short period</u>.

Wendell insisted that a conference take place, thus becoming the ideal person to lead and guide us through our biggest project: **the conference on the fortieth anniversary of Dr Bethune's death.** He believed in what he was doing, and became our beacon. He was not invited to join the Bethune Memorial Committee at its start in 1971, becoming a member in 1973 when he went to China with Hazen Sise.

His father, a Methodist Minister, had worked in the pastoral service of the famous Bordeaux jail, not far from l'HSC on the north shore of the island of Montréal, and, when he was a teenager, Wendell would accompany him on his rounds.

Before going to McGill, he also spent three months during that summer earning some money in St Stephen, Charlotte County, New Brunswick, not far from where we had just bought a cottage in St Andrews in September 1978, selling brushes from door to door for the Fuller Brush Company (personal communication).

I had met him for the first time during my Kingston days, when he helped us start the Canadian Association of Teachers of Social and Preventive Medicine (CATSPM) at Chaffeys' Lock, on the Rideau Canal, in October 1965, the same kind of job as he was doing with and for us in early 1979. He knew the Mott family, Dr Mott being deputy Minister of Health in Saskatchewan when he was Dean of Medicine there, but they never really did get on although they both went to McGill. The medical world remains a relatively small world. Wendell was a modest, honest and unassuming highly principled person, not born with a silver spoon, remaining on the defensive regarding the Quebec Catholic Church and French Canadians in general. We got on very well together, and he coached me the best he could without me understanding totally what really he was doing at the time!

The two and a half days conference itself attempted to cover most of the fields of interest of Norman Bethune:

his poetry, paintings, medicals writings, the management of tuberculosis, his interest for looking after the unemployed, his creativity of new and improved surgical instruments, his articles in the medical press, his love of children, his choice of patients for surgical interventions, his medical teaching, his participation in medical meetings, his interest in the different methods for providing medical care to populations.

This all culminated in the plans for a National Health Service written by a multidisciplinary team, published and sent to the authorities.

It was Wendell who insisted that the bilingual <u>proceedings of the conference</u> be published (2*); he also suggested an excellent editor, **Dr David AE Shephard,** an anesthetist by training, former scientific editor of the Canadian Medical Association Journal (CMAJ), and former editor for CIBA medical publications in New York. David also wrote an excellent chapter for us

'Creativity in Norman Bethune: His Medical Writings and Innovations'.

He promptly sought a francophone co-editor, **Mme Andrée Lévesque,** from the history department of the University of Ottawa at the time, responsible for editing the French manuscripts and with whom editorial decisions were taken. Every article had a shortened summary in the other language.

He was also very strict: all presentations had to have suitable references, with a deadline as to their delivery to his office. I was baptized Chairman of the Board. This sounds easy, but is'nt necessarily, particularly with two Chinese guest speakers Lu Wan-Ru, and Ma Hai-teh, a Lebanese-American physician (Georges Hatem) who had helped Bethune in Yenan. Their presentations had no references; I had to ask them to send me some: both mentioned Chairman Mao's little red book.

Wendell was assisted by **<u>Hilary Russell,</u>** an excellent historian from Parks Canada living in Ottawa, much involved in the Bethune House project in Gravenhurst. Hilary was also an expert on the Bethune family, writing a quite detailed account published in <u>'The Beaver'</u> on one of Dr Bethune's great-great uncles who had travelled twice to China on business.

2*　'Norman Bethune, his times and his legacy, *son époque et son message'*, published by the Canadian Public Health Association, 1982—ISBN 0-919245-11-0.

Many years later, David Sheppard told me that getting that book together was his best endeavor as an editor.

It was Wendell and MaryWeil who suggested the <u>Conference and Special Events Office of McGill University</u> should be responsible for the whole organization of the conference, including

=   the design and printing of a magnificent poster and a beautiful program folder,
=   transportation in special buses to and from various sites,
=   a reception by the maire of Montréal, Jean Drapeau,
=   a dinner at l'HSC given by the Minister of Health which the Chinese Ambassador and his wife attended,
=   a conference on present-day health issues that I organized including Denis Lazure, Quebec Minister of Health, talking about the achievements and gaps in present-day services, during which workers on strike were just outside with banners flying.

This last round table discussion on Sunday morning was entitled '<u>Beyond Bethune: Controversy in to-day's health care—the Quebec experience</u>'. Thus our conference ended.

There were four cessions on the previous two days, conferences and round table discussions, with about three hundred paying participants, over forty speakers of over fifteen different disciplines, attempting to cover all aspects of **"Norman Bethune, 'his times and his legacy'** *'son époque et son message'"*.

Looking back, it was a complex and difficult undertaking. We did not realize it at the time.

Some of the half dozen reviews of the conference and later of the book talked about hagiography, others found it a stimulating and very fair exercise, nobody expressing too much enthusiasm. The conference and the publication cost over $75,000, which the Foundation managed to collect within the next three years or so, with the help of the Federal government, corporations and many individual gifts.

Two thousand copies of our book were printed and distributed ($11.50). The Foundation sent free copies to many public libraries throughout the country. I personally thought it was a tremendous achievement, considering the negative attitudes of so many physicians, Anglophone and Francophone, towards our hero. It would never have happened without Wendell MacLeod. He was so persevering and tough. It attempted to be a truly bilingual effort.

Joan and I were both truly exhausted after those few days.

We both received an invitation to join the celebration of the 30th anniversary of the PRC at the Joy Inn Restaurant, 1017, St Laurent, Ottawa, on September 28th 1979, at 7.30 pm, ($10 each). Our host was the First Secretary, Liu Ching-Hua, and there could not have been more than thirty or forty guests present. It was a pleasant but in no way a big occasion.

Two years later, the occasion was celebrated in a much more cheerful environment at the Embassy, with masses of delicious foods and drink, a couple of hundred guests, with Ambassador Wang Tung and his wife in attendance. By that time, the cook there was rated the best of all embassy cooks in Ottawa, and I had become president of the Foundation.

There were unpredictable snags to that job, such as the monitoring of telephone calls to places outside Montréal, and occasional questions by duty RCMP officers when we visited the Embassy in Ottawa. What are you doing here? One of their cars was always stationed close-by.

CHAPTER 45

The Peoples' Republic of China invites five Canadians to visit their Country, from Canton back to Canton. September 8th to 26th 1980.

We were very busy that summer; our son Nicholas married Dianne Smith, a physician, in September, my mother crossing the pond from London for the celebrations. We were starting to get familiar with our little summer house and its town, St Andrews, New Brunswick.

We were invited to attend a reception at the Chinese Embassy on August the 26th to meet the Vice-Premier of the State Council of the PRC, **Mr Bo Yibo,** very impressive, but unfortunately we could not attend. I felt quite guilty about it.

That same year, **Dr Wendell Mac Leod** became an Officer of the Order of Canada.

I received a letter from **Dr Ho Yun Qing,** president of the Bethune Medical University in Changchun, Jilin Province. Changchun used to be the Japanese Manchurian Capital.

He had learned that we would be going there: I had been asked whether we would rather go there or go to Xian, and we thought we should visit this new medical school with such a famous name! He wrote to welcome us in anticipation of our visit. He proved to be a very impressive person, a survivor of the Long March, present when Dr Bethune actually died.

Never in our wildest dreams did Joan and I ever think that we would be invited to spend eighteen days travelling in China, **the oldest surviving civilisation** (Ch 15), as guests of the Chinese Government. What excitement and what a privilege.

I received a lovely letter from our Dean, Pierre Bois, always positive, never directive. He also gave me a cheque for $500, regretting that it was such a small amount, to help us on our way. He sent me the copy of a letter he had received from the University's *Attaché de Coopération* suggesting liaison with a University medical school as being preferable to association with a Military hospital, indicating his lack of knowledge about the background of the visit. What a nerve!

I also received an encouraging letter from the new **directeur général de l'HSC, Guy St Onge.** I was sorry that *monsieur Martin* had left. A staunch federalist, he had joined the Canadian Hospital Association or some such National organization in Ottawa at the end of his first term at *l'HSC*.

Immediately after our return, Joan wrote a thirty-one page quite detailed account of our exciting trip; what follows largely reflects her document.

On **Thursday September 4th 1980,** with **Irene Kon** (Ch 8), we caught the 7:45 train to Toronto from Windsor station. At the airport we joined **Hilary Russell,** wearing a beautiful orchid, a gift from Wendell, and **Maryellen Corcelli** and we were soon on our way to San Francisco.

Hilary and Maryellen treated us with some champagne on that first leg of our trip together! Maryellen lived in Gravenhurst: she worked half-time for Parks Canada at Bethune House and seemed to be the stabilizing influence there, establishing continuity in the administration every time a new full-time staff change occurred. Her husband was a local business man and they had two daughters.

Irene Kon's father and Dr Bethune knew each other very well from 1933/1934 onwards. Irene was born in 1911 in Winnipeg. She had gone to New York to meet Dr Bethune on his return from Spain in 1937, coming back home with him. She was very proud and open about her political orientation although her father had never joined the communist party. Her grandchildren attended private schools. Only in January 1981 did she become a member by invitation of the Foundation. Our two other new friends represented Parks Canada, and Joan and I the Bethune Foundation.

We arrived in San Francisco at 7pm, took a taxi, had a tram-drive to Powell and Hyde, visited Fishermen's warf, had delicious hot chocolate at the St Francis Hotel before boarding a brand new **Singapore Airlines Boeing 747** to Hong-Kong with a short stop in Honolulu. By that short time, the five of us had bonded, the plane trip without doubt the most comfortable ever, the staff perfect, the attractive hostesses with their Pierre Balmain designed Singapore Airline clothes invariably courteous and helpful, the food excellent.

We crossed the date-line for the first time, arriving at **Kai Tak Airport, Kowloon,** with its one runway by the sea, at 0730h on Saturday, September **6th,** 36 hours after leaving home, half-way around the world. Landing there is an experience by itself, the sea on both sides of the runway, with tall buildings on both sides just beyond it's edges: thus, the plane has to bank just before landing to fit into the gap. Yet, there has never been a serious accident at Kai-Tak.

We felt exhilarated and disoriented more than tired. We took a taxi to our hotel that morning, the **'New World',** luxurious, excellent service, with very comfortable though small rooms with a view of a central patio full of plants, much cheaper than the North-American chains and patronized largely by Chinese. We had a welcome shower, followed by a drink and lunch by the pool, reveling in the sunshine, the exotic surroundings, and the thought of our wonderful trip yet to come. We slept until 9pm, walked around Kowloon, had an omelet for supper, and went to bed just after midnight on our first night on the Asian continent.

On Sunday morning, I got up early to catch the **Star Ferry** to the Island of Hong Kong: I wanted to take photographs with the early morning sun. The ride takes just fifteen minutes to cross the old Victoria Harbor, full of boats and junks, an enchanting sight. Unfortunately, in my haste, I forgot to load my camera!

We then thought we would have breakfast at the **Peninsula Hotel,** Kowloon, "the best hotel east of Suez", with a fleet of identical green Rolls-Royces waiting outside. It was so comfortable and welcoming, the service so impeccable, and the food tasted so good.

Cary Grant (b 1904) was there with his attractive wife. We must have remained a couple of hours. Maryellen, Hilary and I then went to the station to get our tickets for Canton/Guangzhou, our last expense before our free trip, while Joan and Irene returned to the hotel before taking the Star Ferry. We all had supper together and were in bed by 9pm.

On **Monday the 8th** we arrived at the station at 0730h for the 0820h train ride to Guangzhou (Canton), one hundred and ten miles away: this line is the last section of the Trans-Siberian Express (started in 1891), Moscow to Hong Kong via Omsk, Lake Baikal, Ulan Bator, Beijing and Canton, reminding me of Jules Verne's Michel Strogoff (1876), one of my favorite novels during my schooldays. In fact, that trip was just as magical.

There were two parts to our trip that morning, the first to the Chinese border where one had to leave our modern suburban electric train to walk across a narrow river via a small bridge that delineates it. There was lots of wire-netting to prevent illegal crossings.

One then passes the Chinese customs, pause to have a snack at the PRC station restaurant, and boards the second train.

The first modern part of the trip was very lovely, with several stops from the outskirts of Kowloon itself, through lush and busy countryside lined with flowering trees and plants for perhaps thirty miles,

The second was spectacular, with a diesel engine pulling comfortable air-conditioned older cars on a single continuously curving slow track, with headrests and pale blue velvet side curtains, curiously quaint and comfortable, with masses of tea in mugs with lids served by a young lady going around with enormous thermos flasks of hot water, also keeping the carriage tidy, sweeping and moping the floor as necessary.

The scenery was just beautiful, peaceful lush fields, rice paddies, people everywhere carrying those two baskets hanging from a pole carried over their shoulders, carts and buffaloes, the villages shabby but so neat and tidy, and a striking absence of cars and trucks, a picture hundreds of years old.

All of a sudden, a grinding stop: a worker had got too near the train and had been hit. Luckily, he just had just a few abrasions on the back of his hand, and the train started off within ten minutes.

Looking out of the window reminded us of watching a beautiful ever-changing movie about a foreign land, but this was real, something that one remembers all one's life.

We arrived in **Canton** at 1135h, and were met by **Mr Shi,** from the Friendship Association, with two interpreters. They took us on a quick tour of the city, its new part with parks and wide boulevards, its old city with narrow streets, teeming with people and bicycles.

Canton, 'the conqueror of the sea', is a very old port, incorporated in the Chinese Empire by the Chin dynasty (221-207 BC). Throughout its history it has often been on the verge of rebellion, called by Europeans the "Ulster" or the "Catalonia" of China.

It produced the Kuomintang, or the People's Party, founded by Dr Sun Yat Sen in 1911. He is buried there in the **Sun Yat Sen Memorial,** a huge building in large grounds with a lovely deep vibrant blue tiled roof.

We then visited the **Zhenhai Tower,** built around 1380 AD, five stories high, originally and for many centuries a kind of gentlemen's club from the top floor of which one could see boats approaching on the sea; it became a museum. We drank some tea on its top floor, after having seen the exhibits on our way up.

We then had **dinner in a private room in an old tea house,** full of antique furniture made of lychee and mulberry wood with fine stained glass windows in deep rich colors. We were told many legends about the city. The food was absolutely delicious. Canton is supposed to have the best restaurants in China: it certainly would be difficult to surpass. Let us see! The people were charming. It was surprising that, even with interpreters, it was so easy to communicate with our Chinese hosts and friends. But then, Canton has been for a log time an important far-eastern stop-over port.

We already started to feel at home. We said thank you and good-by to our hosts at the airport, and caught the plane to Beijing at 1945h for the three hour flight.

It was a new 747 barely a week old. It was sitting on the tarmac quite a way from the terminal, and we were driven there by bus. We walked up the stairs, entered the plane, and were amazed by what we saw: the hot cabin was lit by candle-light: there was no electric light or air-conditioning. We were given lovely paper fans as well as the usual candy and chewing-gum.

The electricians had not yet completed their assignment of arranging the electric hook-up, and the electric lights and air-conditioning only started when the pilot came aboard just a few minutes before leaving. So we were sitting in this new 747 all fanning ourselves vigorously under candle-light! Only in China could this happen and how marvelous it seemed. The plane was 100% full, the comfortable seats quite close to each other, Mr and Mrs Cary Grant just ahead of us. It was a comfortable trip.

From then on, we never had to worry about our luggage: it all disappeared and reappeared magically at the appropriate moments. And the waiting, when necessary, was so comfortable, around a table talking with our hosts sipping a mug with a lid and kept full of delicious tea sitting in an armchair.

We arrived on time in Beijing (the northern capital). **Lu Wan-Ru,** whom we had met in Montréal, and **Ma Hui Yun,** both from the Friendship Association, were there to meet us, and they remained with us during the rest of our trip, both delightful companions. We all became very fond of one another.

Wan-ru had two sons, aged 20 and 16. Her husband had something to do with the official written Press. During the Cultural Revolution, Wan-Ru had been separated from her family and forced to live on a farm in a small village for two years. The separation was a terrible blow; but she got to know and appreciate farming people, their closely knit families, the way they lived, and particularly their judgment. She knew all about farming and crops and animal care. She much appreciated this beneficial part of her experiences at that difficult time of her life.

She also appreciated classical music, both Chinese and Western.

Ma Hui Yun (Cioma, a term of endearment meaning little young Ma) was 27 years old, had married a photographer and had a little boy of three. She had been one of the first Chinese students in Canada at Carleton University in Ottawa (1973-76). She had been recalled suddenly the week before her final examinations we later found out. Thus her university training had never been recognized, now limiting her capacity for finding a better-paying job in the Chinese capital.

There was absolutely nothing Wan-Ru and Cioma could have done for us that they didn't do. With them both at the airport was another charming lady, Mary Sun, PhD, the first secretary, Canadian Embassy, who told us not to hesitate to contact her if ever we needed help or just some information. **Mr Arthur Menzies** was the Canadian Ambassador at that time.

Right in front of us at the airport was Mr and Mrs Cary Grant who both spoke to us, but our hosts were not impressed: "just some Holliwood film star, we heard"!

Two cars were waiting to drive us to our hotel, the old Peking Palace (now, the Peking Hotel), the best hotel in China, built in 1911, at the end of the Empire, just off Tian an Men Square and on the Tian an Men Avenue itself, right next to the walls of the old Imperial Palace.

We walked through a large very tall hall with stairs and enormous dark red pillars to the reception area: two of our rooms overlooked the square, and one of them was a back room: we tossed and lost.

Still, we had a lovely view of an old Pagoda in the distance! All the rooms were similar, very comfortably furnished with attached bathrooms.

That hotel complex is enormous, the old part dwarfed by a large new concrete wing just next door with sixteen floors, mainly for foreign tourists, particularly from the USA. The old part where we were was the original old historic classical wing. So, to bed and we slept like logs. What an exciting day it had been. How could anybody in the whole world be exposed to so much that was so gorgeous and unexpected in one single day!

On **Tuesday September 9th** after choosing a Chinese breakfast in the large classical wood-lined dining room down stairs, with comfortable chairs and older experienced staff, we explored our hotel with its own post office, buying lovely stamps, and its gift-shop, selling beautiful table linens, scrolls, silk scarves, old second-hand jade bracelets and so many other items.

Wan-Ru and Cioma arrived at 10am to drive us to the *Forbidden City*, quite close-by, just a ten minute walk up the road, a rectangular complex with its own <u>two and a quarter miles long</u>, high, wide and purple-colored brick wall flanked by towers. It included the *Imperial Palace*. The *Forbidden City* was all that remained of the many original old buildings included within <u>thirty miles of walls</u>, containing the *Forbidden City* at its centre.

Entry to the *Imperial Palace* was forbidden to all except the imperial family and their servants. Thus, the emperor and his family seemed imprisoned in a beautiful palace, leaving it only for summer holidays in the hills close-by and for official trips. How sad.

Huge paved courtyards lead from pavilion to pavilion, magnificent carved marble balustrades, wide flights of steps centered by huge slabs of marble carved intricately with dragons and lotuses, the pavilions containing exquisitely carved and gilded wood, all somehow permeated by ghosts from the past. And there are huge bronze lions, imagined as there were no lions in China, standing guard over the peasants as they did over the emperors, enormous brass bells without too much gilding after a British raid. Great urns stood around formerly containing water in case of fire.

During the following years, I returned there several times, arriving at when it open8:30 am: there were very few people around at that time. I would go straight to the *imperial gardens,* a superb, quiet and relaxing place for the past emperors to spend their time, surrounded by beautiful plants, flowers, trees and the sounds of birds. There, in the middle of this big city, the emperor and family could relate to nature and relax.

This seems the most human component of this incredible building complex in this fantastic place, founded by Kublai Khan (1216-1294) of the Mongol Yuan dynasty (1271-1368). He came to power in 1260. He was a tolerant leader who tried twice to conquer Japan and failed. He also failed to conquer what is now Vietnam. He admitted foreigners to his court, Tibetan lamas,

Nestorian priests, and Marco Polo (1254-1324) from Venice, who became an important government official.

Chairman Mao took office on October the 1st 1949. He sought the advice of the best Chinese experts regarding the future development of the City. In unison they recommended building a new administrative capital to incorporate a new much more sophisticated modem administrative complex on the City's outskirts, thus preserving all the old walls.

He took this personally as an effort to relegate him to the sidelines in a new suburb: he ordered the destruction of all the old walls, part of an inheritance for which he had no more time, thus demolishing a historical heritage seven hundred years old. All that is left now is the *Forbidden City* plus here and there, small important bits of the old walls that survived. Thus, Chairman Mao chose to continue to administer the whole of China from the middle of the Northern Capital, Beijing, as it always had been.

We returned to our hotel for lunch (very good food) and a two hour rest. We spent the afternoon at *the National Museum,* viewing fascinating relics from the past 5000 years: Peking man, breathtaking finds from Xian with its ranks of ceramic soldiers and horses from the hundreds that have been unearthed there, Ming and Tang horses, the exquisite Jade burial suit now in the Shijiazhuang museum, room after room of marvelous treasures that one can only sample briefly, such a multitude of beautiful things.

That evening, we were guests of honor at a <u>reception</u> given by the Friendship Association at their headquarters in the old Italian Embassy, a lovely large old building not far from the hotel. The President, **<u>Mr Wang Ping-nan,</u>** welcomed us nicely, encouraging us to work hard to foster China-Canada relations! He was a senior, multilingual, suave, polite, cultured and tough ex-diplomat, deserving nearly a page-long biography in Edgar Snow's 'Red Star over China', (cfr Ch15).

> Born in 1906, he helped to bring about Chiang Kai-shek's captivity in 1936, and became China's senior diplomat in Europe, Chinese ambassador to Warsaw (1955-1964). The only political contacts between China and the USA during that period took place in Warsaw. Wang Ping-nan had had a very impressive career, but lost a lot of influence during the Great Proletariat Cultural Revolution (GPCR) as Snow (1*) calls it (1966-1976).

1*   As *"the GPCR took foreign political experts on China as a complete surprise, so China's explosion of a hydrogen bomb* (1967)—*twenty-six months after atomic fission was achieved—nonplused foreign military and scientific savants. The same step had taken*

He did not accompany us to the banquet because he had to attend a meeting of the People's Congress that evening. Snow mentions one hundred or so names in the biographical notes at the end of 'Red Star' (60 pages), and also that Mao had told him in 1960 that China *"would be run for some years by those eight hundred survivors"* of the hard times, one quarter of which were then members or alternate members of the Central Committee. Only in 1969 were sixteen new members elected from outside those eight hundred.

We then all moved to **Generalissimo Chiang Kai-shek's** former spacious mansion in lovely grounds surrounded by its own big wall and controlled entry for a delicious dinner, with our own name tags written in Chinese. **Mr Hou Tong, vice-president of the Friendship Association** was our host, with **Dr and Mrs Ma Hai-deh** (also mentioned in the biographical section of 'Red Star') who had both come to Canada a year before, **Madame Lu Chia,** an older lady who had come to Canada to raise funds for China during the 1930s, and **Mr Duan,** a senior member of the Association, twelve of us altogether. As Joan wrote in her journal:

> *"as always, we ate at a round table with Peter on our host's right, and myself on his left, We had a fabulous banquet with more than twelve courses: all the guests signed the menu, written in beautiful calligraphy: we always ate with chopsticks, although we were usually provided with knives and forks too. The hosts will help the guests with the choicest morsels and keep replenishing your plate if you do not leave something on it! The dinner was simply delicious, one mouthwatering dish following another, washed down by little glasses of sweet wine, Mao-Tai (very strong liquor made of sorghum), beer or lemonade. Tea is not served at meals, but drunk in between them, and soup is eaten at the end of the meal. At the beginning, middle and end of the meal hot or chilled facecloths are passed around to wipe your hands (and face too if you wish). Many toasts are drunk to the guests, Canada, friendship, and of course Dr Bethune. Glasses are clinked and 'Gambay' means no heeltaps! A dangerous procedure with 70 percent proof Mao-Tai: a wonderful evening".*

On **Wednesday September 10th** we opted for a Western breakfast. This included all sorts of things, an omelette, fruit juice, bacon and eggs, blintzes,

---

the USA more than seven years; France after eight years of effort, had yet to test its first H-bomb".

French toast, doughnuts, toast and marmalade, etc . . . We did enjoy our coffee, especially Irene.

We left early by car for the **Great Wall**, a beautiful drive, 50 kms, a wide two lane road, with myriads of bicycles, trucks, army vehicles, carts. On arrival, we had a drink of lemonade, glanced in passing at the arrival of **Mrs Flora Macdonald**, <u>our Minister of Foreign Affairs</u>, Conservative MP for Kingston and the Isles. She preceded us for sections of our trip, a true successor of John A Macdonald, our first Prime Minister.

> We proceeded to climb to the first look-out tower. What a thrill to see that famous wall snaking up and down over mountains on and on! It is wide enough to take five horses abreast, although they must be very sure-footed to negotiate the steep ascents and flights of steps. At the top we had a wonderful view of the surroundings, far in the distance the Mongolian plains and beyond that the Gobi desert, from where in winter great clouds of dust blow into Peking filling the eyes and throat with grit. But that day, the sun was shining gloriously and we could imagine it as it was in the days when soldiers paced the ramparts guarding the empire.

On our way back to Beijing, we visited the famous **Summer Palace**—riches on riches!—and had lunch in one of the beautiful pavilions, again a lovely meal. We explored some of it, walking through the covered wooden colonnade, one km long, marvelously painted and gilded, at the end of which we had a ride in a small boat for just the seven of us, watching other visitors drift calmly over the serene surfaces admiring the many beautiful pavilions, beautiful bridges, pagodas, each entrancing view after another. We saw the famous marble boat, built by the Empress Dowager with the money allotted for the Chinese Navy. As usual, many people stopped and stared at us, and an old lady, a peasant, very chatty and interested, asking questions about us to our interpreters who did not seem too keen to encourage the conversation!

Then, back in our hotel, Joan had her hair washed. This always included a wonderful massage which Joan much appreciated. We had dinner all together before going to see a ballet, *"The Silk Road"*, a marvelous performance with glorious costumes, colors, a classical ballet of the Chinese school. At the theatre, Wanru and Cioma would sit behind us and explain what was going on. The audience never seemed to mind, although we would not have appreciated it, too noisy for us. On our return, Dr Ma Hai-deh called to see us briefly. He was very busy with the People's Congress. We slept like logs after another wonderful day, only the seventh night of our trip!

Thursday September 11th was just as fascinating. After an early breakfast, we visited the *13th Middle School*, (a High School in Canada). We drove through parts of the old town with narrow streets, and were welcomed by the Headmaster in an attractive garden tended by pupils; they had painted a large welcoming board for us, decorated with flowers (2').

=   <u>We talked to the Headmaster</u> over a cup of tea. There is a five year program, a staff of 200 for 1300 students.

The objectives are focused on intellectual, moral and physical development according to Chairman Mao. Great stress is laid on correct moral standards and high expectations, with two political education classes a week, plus a school and a class meeting.

There are Young Pioneers and other Youth Organizations. During vacations, the students are organized to take part in 'beneficial activities'. The Bethune story is stressed, an important part of the curriculum. The emphasis is on the fundamentals for integrating theory and practice in the analysis and solution of problems.

Most students study English as a second language and have six to eight courses a year.

A small factory is attached to the school; students work there in order to understand the laborer's point of view, again integrating theory and practice. There are links with a factory and a commune where students work at fixed intervals.

Two forty minutes long Phys-Ed classes are held per week, and every day at eleven o'clock at the sound of a bell, there is a five to ten minute silent period during which students sit silently at their desks massaging their eyes with both hands, otherwise relaxing. We witnessed this, arriving in a classroom at exactly eleven.

The students play basketball, soccer etc . . . , inter and extra-mural.

We were very impressed with this teacher/principal who had majored in philosophy. He seemed very devoted to and fond of his students: the school obtained the best examination results in the city. He claimed the education was still suffering from the results of the Cultural Revolution when students were encouraged to abuse teachers, running wild, losing respect for intellectuals and authority. Intellectuals, such as Lu Wanru, really suffered during that time.

=   <u>We visited</u> the biology museum, an English class, and the physics laboratory. There were about 55 pupils in each class; the atmosphere was peaceful and controlled. The teachers can participate in post-graduate activities by televison courses and by university courses. They teach for 12-14 hours per week.

The school day begins at 7:30; there are four forty minute classes with a ten minute break between them, plus the eye/relaxation exercises. In the afternoons there are two classes and then sports. It is a six day week, with one half day off and Saturday afternoons devoted to self-study.

In a year, nine months are devoted to school-work, one month for physical work in a commune or factory, and two for holidays. A meeting with parents is held at least once each term.

= The notes that follow are from a discussion we had with the principal and one another teacher after our class-room visits:

Term exams are set by the school to evaluate both pupils and teachers. The emphasis is on the cause of a student's problems. There is no physical punishment. University enrolment is limited, and this results in considerable stress for the students.

There are again the three standards for University entrance, moral, decided by the school, intellectual by the school exams, and physical by a clinical check-up.

In Political Education, socialist morality, socialist revolution and the best socialist principles are stressed. Special teachers give lectures on special topics. Younger students do not remember capitalist exploitation, and may follow the extreme ideas of the Gang of four (2*). Slogans are written on blackboards to correct this ideology: *"Be Patriotic, Aim High beginning Now and with Oneself"*.

The school Clinic has a staff of three, and their work is mainly preventive, a yearly check-up with an X-ray. There is no tuberculosis.

Most teachers specialize, forming a group with a teaching research program. They also work in factories and communes. There is some apprehension about the influence of tourists, but friendship and international understanding are

---

2*   Arthur Cotterell (cfr Ch 15) talks about the three periods in the history of China, *Pre-Imperial* (down to 221 BC), *Imperial* for over two millenia, (221 BC to AD 1912) and *Post-Imperial* (from 1912 onwards). "THE CHINESE PEOPLE HAVE STOOD UP!" Thus, Mao Zedong explained the establishment of the Peoples' Republic on 1 October 1949.

stressed: *"we try and draw distinction between a healthy desire for beauty and an unhealthy one such as long hair, pornography, etc . . . ".*

English is compulsory from grades 1 to 5. German, Spanish, Japanese, French and Russian are also taught. A student's general direction is set in Junior High School.

Back to the hotel for lunch and a rest, after which Joan bought a beautiful rubbing for ninety cents. It was just lovely walking along the streets, looking at the shops with the crowds, crowded buses, the absence of private cars. In the afternoon we visited the **Temple of Heaven,** the most perfectly round, beautiful and relatively small place with carved marble, painted wood with enormous wooden pillars recently replaced with British Columbia tree trunks, yet so light, like a lovely wedding cake in stone.

Of all the old buildings in Beijing, this is the one to which I most frequently returned. If you stamp your feet on the floor in the centre, you can hear a hollow echo, as you do when you whisper against the wall in the dome of St Paul's Cathedral in London. That dome and the temple seem to have roughly the same size. We had dinner with a bottle of wine, and packed, drinking vodka in our rooms and writing letters and post-cards.

In 1964 he felt that China's educational system was still *"fraught with problems, the most important of which is dogmatism . . . . The school years are too long, courses too many, and various methods of teaching unsatisfactory. The children learn textbooks and concepts which mainly remain textbooks and concepts: they know nothing else."* China was a poor country without even generalized decent primary education. The built-in advantages enjoyed by the children of well-educated parents were still very apparent. The school syllabus was simplified. In 1963, Chairman Mao persuaded the Chinese Communist Party that its members should take part in manual labour. Then came the *GPCR,* the end of which the extremist *Gang of Four,* lead by Mrs Mao, (*Jiang Qing*), thought was premature. They were all in prison during our stay awaiting trial. Thus, 1980 was a very crucial year to visit a high school.

On **Friday, September 12th,** we breakfasted on blintzes!

Then, off to a **Jade factory, the biggest in China with 1600 workers.** After a three year apprenticeship, they (men and women) are allowed to work alone. It takes ten years to become a master. Some of the works, so complex, become museum pieces. The work hours are from 8-12 and 1-5. There is a ten minute break for exercises in the morning and afternoon.

Workers whose families live away from the city can have three weeks off a year to visit them. There is a medical clinic in the factory and the local hospital is responsible for medical care.

We saw so many beautiful things being made of jade, coral, topaz, turquoise. Each worker starts with a piece of rock, visualizes in his/her mind the completed design. Some pieces may take months to complete, using small electric drills similar to those used by a dentist under a continuous water stream.

As always, our visits began with tea and introductions. The name of Bethune was the bond between us. We bought a lovely small jade plate which had taken one worker two weeks to make ($40), as well as some rings and loose stones, jade and amethysts. Irene was not feeling well, and stayed at the hotel that morning.

We had an early lunch in order to take the **12:20 train with Wan-ru and Cioma to Shijiazhuang,** four hours and two hundred miles away through flat-lands, a lovely trip south-west through miles and miles of corn-fields as far as the eye could see, with thousands of farm-workers gathering crops; everything so old, tidy and well-run, totally un-mechanized.

We would be away for three nights only, so we kept our rooms in Beijing, and only had to bring small bags with us, leaving the rest, well packed, behind.

I remember one stop in **Baoding,** the old capital of the Province of Hebei (60 million people). I got out off the train onto the platform of the old railway station full of flowers and had to run back, nearly missing it! Baoding is a very old city, with all the amenities of a Provincial Capital, political, educational, social, religious, military, and penal, just a day's carriage drive for the emperor when travelling south.

The prison has an enormous red-brick wall around it. It is one of the biggest and oldest in China. I never was able to find out how many inmates lived there. I guess in the tens of thousands. That prison seems be be the only institution left in this old city, most of the others transferred to Shijiazhuang.

Unfortunately for Baoding, it's very old military establishment was one of the two main military colleges in the whole country, the other in Guangzhu, both under the control of Generalissimo Chiang Kai-shek, thus its sad decapitation.

A small town at the onset of the 20th century, **Shijiazhuang** became an increasingly important railway junction when the Beijing to Guangzhou railway line was built. In 1980, the station was still very primitive, but one could catch a connecting train going east to Jinan, capital of Shandong province, or west to Taiyuan, capital of Shanxi province. To-day, twenty-five years later in 2006, it has become the starting station, the base, of the new line to Lhasa in Tibet on a Bombardier made TGV! This in a nut-shell demonstrates the fantastic development that occurred in China in general and in Shijiazhuang in particular just during the past quarter of a century. When we arrived there in September 1980, Shijiazhuang was on the threshold of its modern development. It was a young town, lacking the sophistication of Baoding, Guangzhu, or Beijing. Everybody seemed so young and comparatively immature. In 1995, my last visit there, its population numbered over six milion. The centre of the town was unrecognisable.

Shijiazhuang was the first sizeable town to be liberated by Mao's forces in October 1947. In **April 1948, the BIPH settled there,** one of the first if not the first new important institution. It was the site of the former Kuomintang Joint Hospital and before 1945, The North China Japanese Army Hospital, and before that just a small railway junction.

Thus it is a late twentieth century town, a new developing capital in the middle of an enormous and very old agricultural area totally lacking in modem technology, very poor by modern standards but with thousands centuries' old beautiful peasant villages.

We were met at the station by Mr Sun, Mr Lu, and Miss Chung, and were driven to the <u>Provincial Government Guest House</u> where we had another delicious banquet, with *very large prawns caught just off the coast of the province.* I still remember them. Prawns were not a usual dish in Canada at that time. Then, off to bed.

On **Saturday, September the 13th,** we went to the PLA's Bethune International Peace Hospital (BIPH) immediately after breakfast. The director, Dr Dung Guo Hua, and the senior members of the staff were waiting outside to welcome us at the main gate, with their white coats and white hats. They were all clapping and smiling, a happy occasion. We immediately felt at home. Immediately after entering the gates, Dr Bethune was staring at us from his statue, just as the new practically identical one in Montréal would be doing later that fall.

We then walked to the Bethune-Kotnis Memorial Hall, just around the corner within the compound. The reception room was quite charming, with comfortable armchairs, settees and low tables, the usual tea mugs, but in addition cigarettes, little dishes of locally-made candies and delicious apples grown in the hospital's orchard: on each wall, a large painting of four different places where Dr Bethune had worked, beautiful mountain scenes, some of them with him caring for soldiers, others of him galloping with adjoining clouds. There were also two smaller bronzes of him galloping. There was mysticism about the place reminiscent of my school-days. We were presented with Bethune ceramic pins and two booklets. But we wondered who this Kotnis person was. I gradually gathered appropriate information:

Late in the night of October 9th, 1910, in Sholapur, 200 kms east of Bombay, India, was born **Dwarkanath Shantaram Kotnis,** his father a supervisor in a local cotton mill. He graduated as a physician at *Grant Medical College* in Mumbai/Bombay in 1936 (3'). On graduating, he was asked to become an instructor in the Department of Physiology. He was twenty years younger than Dr Bethune.

The Chairman of the Indian National Congress at the time, **Pandit Nehru** (cfr Ch 40), was calling for the formation of a medical mission to support the Chinese People's anti-Japanese war. Young Dr Kotnis wanted a more active job, applied to be a member of the China Aid Committee and was accepted. There were five of them, Dr M Atal, head of mission, his deputy, Dr M Cholkar, and three other physicians, Drs D Mukerji, B K Basu, with the youngest, our friend.

On October 7, 1938, after seventeen days at sea, they were met in Guangzhou by Mme Soong Ching Ling, the widow of Dr Sun Yatsen. Dr Atal asked her whether they could meet Zhou Enlai in Wuhan, so that he could send them to join the Eigth Route Army. Zhou Enlai agreed with the proviso that they would first spend some time in Chongqing under Kuomintang control. They arrived in Yenan on February 12th 1939.

Dr Kotnis's Chinese name was Ke Di, but the five of them added 'hua' at the end of their Chinese name, meaning 'China', so Dr Kotnis's Chinese name became Ke Dihua. During the winter of 1939 he worked at the HQ of the Eighth Route Army north of Yenan and attended Dr Bethune's Memorial Service after he died on November 12th 1939.

By February 1940, three of the five Indian doctors had returned home because of ill health, and Drs Basu and Kotnis were assigned to the new Bethune Medical School, arriving there on August 17th 1940.

Jiang Yizhen was the President of the Bethune Medical School at that time; he would later become Minister of Health for the

---

3*   **Bombay** had been a British possession since 1662. The Grant Medical College was so named because it was founded by Sir Robert Grant, Governor of Bombay, who died suddenly just before it was opened in 1845. The program for medical students at that school would have been modeled on that of the Edinburgh School and very similar to the one to which I was exposed.

---

whole of China, solely responsible for the birth-control policies later implemented. Basu and Kotnis were both recalled home.

Kotnis refused to leave. By that time, he could speak Chinese quite fluently, helped in this task by a young nurse, Guo Quinglan. They soon married and had a baby boy. All his teaching from then on was in fluent Chinese. He became the first Director of the Norman Bethune International Peace Hospital during the summer of 1940.

Dr Kotnis soon passed a long pork tape—worm in his stools which he kept in a jar as a specimen for his students. Unfortunately, cysts sometimes settle in the brain causing epileptic fits, (cysticercosis), and from this Kotnis suffered and died at 0615h on December 12th 1942.

He had completed 177 pages of his book, 'a General Introduction to Surgery', He was then 32, and his baby 3 1/2 months' old; he was a worthy successor of Dr Bethune. He adopted all of Dr Bethune's ideas and added to them! What a marvelous combination those two made, two happy ingredients of a delicious cake! And what a sad and sudden ending they both had.

Dr Atal returned to China and also worked at the BIPH; he died in China in 1957. Half of his ashes were scattered there, and half back home in the river Ganges.

Thus, young Dr Kotnis had probably received one of the best possible training available on the Asian mainland at that time.

The only time in my life that I had been exposed to the problem of cysticercosis was at one of my examinations for obtaining my qualification for practicing medicine during the forties: I had to interview an old ex-Indian Army soldier with the same but milder problem, but luckily I had been forewarned that he might just be there as an examination participant!

The Bethune International Peace Hospital (BIPH) is situated in the south-west corner of a large walled rectangular compound, the wall it around one thousand by five hundred meters' long. It had eighteen departments and 800 beds.

The International Peace Hospital was founded in the fall of 1937, at first just as an improvised clinic in an old temple with a staff of twelve at the start of the Japanese invasion from Manchuria. Patients that needed a bed were accommodated in local homes. That was in a small mountain village, *Gengzhen/ Gengsuo*, just east the Provincial border with Hebei, in the mountainous Wutai County, Shanxi Province. Dr Bethune arrived in June 1938. He died on November 12th 1939. Dr Kotnis took over after a few months.

The International Peace Hospital, so named because it was funded by a gift of 24,000 GBPs from Britain, adopted Dr Bethune's name on January 5th 1940, one of only two hospital in the PLA named after a person, and in 1987 the only two hospitals in the PLA to have kept their **organizational system intact during their first fifty years**.

During the seventeen months that Dr Bethune spent there, he wrote two books, *Regulations for the Base Special Surgical Hospital,* and in July 1939, *Organization and Techniques of a Division Field Hospital in Guerilla War,* thus becoming the first person to apply western hospital management skills to the battlefield in China. Unfortunately none of these have survived; some were undoughtedly kept by old students.

During the second Chinese revolution, between 1946 and 1949, there were nine branches of the BIPH in the mountainous Wutai region, its staff participating in many battles. When it had finally settled in its present location, many patients stayed in the home of the peasants, most of the present buildings built after 1952. The original one, in the Wutai Montains, destroyed by the Japanese Air Force and rebuilt and also named after Dr Bethune. **Thus, there are two BIPHs, the original first one in the hills and the final one in Shijiazhuang.**

Until Chairman Mao's death, the hospital staff, including the doctors, were involved in physical labor in the afternoons, growing grain and herbs, raising cows, pigs, and chickens, helping to look after the orchard, the beautiful rock garden and its plants, and a large and lovely botanical garden, the many lovely trees lining the paths and roads, thus alleviating the burden of the peasants. More important, it tried to keep that special quality of the Army that retained its closeness to the people. Medical teams were frequently sent to the countryside to help the peasants.

The hospital, equipped with clean unbleached sheets on narrow metal-framed beds about three feet apart, its two floors linked by a ramp, is part of a compound where people work and live surrounded by walls with a large entrance with the statue, a second entrance for services, both with guards. There were also three other open side doors without guards at that time. Security became a problem after the first few years, and all side-doors were locked; only the main gate plus the service entrance with guards were left open.

Thus, the head of the institution is a director/mayor of a small hospital/town of over three thousand people, each family living in a small four room apartment with a small balcony in a six-floor red brick building with a central staircase and perhaps twenty-four apartments.

It took me twelve years to visit one of those apartments.

Each new brick would cost a cent at that time. The spouse who works nearby outside the compound cycles there and back. The best housing had been built by the Japanese, half a dozen separate small houses with a small garden of their own, reserved for the senior staff.

The head of Surgery had one of them, qualifying in 1948 from the prestigious No 1 Capital Medical School in Beijing. At the age of 22 he married his sweet-heart, an anesthetist, and they both immediately joined the PLA. She was also responsible for the blood-bank founded by Dr Bethune, the only one in town even when I last went there in 1995 when the population had grown to perhaps five million.

The *BIPH* also became involved in the Korean War. I later learnt that the head of Surgery spent some time on that front during the fifties doing emergency surgery, reminiscent of the Mash television series:

> He had to invent many different courses in treating wounds. One of them was a new successful way of stitching ruptured livers using thick catgut and a mattress type of sewing with a large and curved non-cutting needle; up to that time, rupture of the liver meant inevitable death from hemorrhage. He saved many lives, Chinese, Korean and Western injured military and civilian people including Afro-Americans. He had at least fifty framed and faded paper testimonials on the walls of his office, the only way one could be recognized in those difficult days.

The BIPH gradually became a comprehensive hospital involved in teaching, training and research. At present there were 1.4 workers in the hospital per patient. The ultimate aim was to build a new BIPH to meet international standards by the turn of the century.

After lunch at our Guest House, we visited the large **Cemetery of Martyrs where Bethune and Kotnis were eventually buried,** with beautiful trees, very well kept and peaceful. The two main monuments are to Bethune on one side and Kotnis on the other, each with its statue, the third we had seen of Dr Bethune, in front of their imposing burial site.

Irene laid a wreath brought from Canada, pine branches with sprays of wheat and maple leaves, quite an emotional moment, particularly for Irene. Other more simple tombs are for those who survived the Long March and for those who fought for Mao's China before the end of the Civil War. It was a large and historically very important military cemetery.

We then drove to *Tang Xian*, a small county town, about fifty miles away to the north. This part of the country was not open to tourists. It was a fascinating drive: a cortege of about six cars, led by an army Chinese jeep, with a red flag to warn the traffic we overtook to keep to the side until we had passed. Hebei Province is one of the poorest provinces of China.

We passed along roads flanked by rows of tall trees reminiscent of Holland and Belgium: carts and bicycles coming to & from market laden with dead pigs, crates of live chickens, vegetables, wood, drawn by oxen, horses, mules and even unexpectedly camels. There were no private cars, no foreigners and just a few tractors, cotton fields, sorghum, sugar cane, maize, vegetables. Much building with local red bricks (1 cent each) was going on. Naturally everyone stared, especially when we stopped for a short while because of an overheated tire. Corn was thrashed by scattering it on the road and allowing traffic to pass over it. We arrived in Tang Xian at about twenty passed six, to a fantastic welcome at the new small Guest House built just the year before for the fortieth anniversary of Dr Bethune's death. A large number of people were waiting outside to welcome us.

It was around this area that Kathleen Hall had established her Mission (ch 17), and that Lu Wanru had spent two years farming separated from her family during the *GPCR*. Drs Bethune and Kotnis, both foreign and long nosed, had become an important part of the cultural history of this intensely populated poor agricultural area of China.

We were received by the Vice-Chairman of the revolutionary committee for the county, Mr Chin Fu Da, and the Vice-Director of the office of the revolutionary committee, Mr Tien Ming Tien. We were shown to the main guest room with a large adjoining sitting room and separate bathroom, and an older gentleman with his Mao suit and cap actually proudly demonstrated how to turn the hot and cold taps on and off in the bathroom.

After a brief rest, there was a small reception with tea and persimmons; introductions were made, and a delicious banquet followed. Remembered are rare white fungus, turtle, and many little sweet cakes, including moon cakes: although it is no longer a religious observation, most people in northern China eat moon cakes during the evening of the first full moon of autumn and have a small party at home.

We were told about rural organization: twenty families make up a team, ten teams a brigade and ten brigades a commune.

We were then taken to the movies. It had started to rain a little and people were there to help with umbrellas. There was a large crowd outside the cinema. When we got inside, a jam-packed audience was patiently waiting for our arrival. Everybody stood up and applauded loudly as we went to our seats in the centre of the quite large cinema. A long table stood in front and above the seats just in front of us, and cups of tea were served during the performance, *"The Jade Hairpin"*, a traditional opera performed by the Shanghai Opera Company. On leaving, we received the same ovation, the whole evening a moving experience. What a day that was! That film was our introduction to Chinese opera.

There are at least two main schools of opera in China, in Shanghai and Beijing. Everyone talks during performances, quite disconcerting at first: comments, ah for approval, oh for disapproval, laughter, anger. The Yuan period (1279-1368) is considered the golden age of the classical opera; it had existed for many centuries before that. Everybody goes to the opera in China. It is literally as old as the hills. The design of the magnificent costumes and the different maquillages are centuries old.

We had breakfast in our Guest House on **Sunday, September 14th,** glasses of hot milk, herbal coffee, congee (rice with little pieces of meat in it—the rice is runny, not like the dry rice served with other meals). Also delicious were the hot doughnuts: we saw them being sold at stalls in the town.

We then drove through lovely hilly countryside to **_Huangshikou_** where Dr Bethune died. The narrow road had only recently been tarred for the first time. There was a large crowd waiting when we arrived at the simple peasant house where he died, now an important place for the Chinese to visit.

Tea had been set up in the court-yard, but, as it was raining slightly, we were taken inside the small house, to the small room, with just very simple little wooden stools with very low legs which were promptly put on the very kang on which Dr Bethune died, and we sat there drinking tea and eating persimmons as we listened to Ti Chun Sing, who was seventeen years old at the time, telling us simply and touchingly of his death. The Tang Xian town photographer had accompanied us and took black and white photographs in the courtyard and later during the day while we were in the area. The whole episode struck us as being very simple, civilized, touching and sincere. Persimmons are now presented to all visitors.

We then proceeded to **_Juncheng_**, where Dr Bethune was buried, just a few miles away. The site was so beautiful and bare: a small green field surrounded by quite tall mountains on three sides with this beautifully carved marble monument where Dr Bethune was buried until the end of the second civil war in 1950, plus just a few simple houses.

There was a three months' delay for the burial itself, because the Japanese were still quite close and the *PLA* had to bring in all the marble and other materials to build the Memorial. One enters the small cemetery through a lovely archway built out of two inscribed square white marble columns, about ten feet tall, linked at the top by wrought iron, beautifully built and maintained. Dr Kotnis was buried there, both considered martyrs to the cause. It was an emotional event, particularly for Irene. She had known Bethune before, had met Bethune in New York on his return from Spain in 1937; they returned to Montreal together.

We placed a large floral tribute made of vivid paper flowers, which our hosts had brought for us, and planted two commemorative trees, both pines. We walked to one of the houses, formerly one of the model hospitals, where we had lunch, the five of us at a long table in one room, the others in an adjoining kitchen-dining room. After lunch, sipping our tea, eating apples, dates and persimmons, a group of people who had known him were introduced:

> A short man, now 68 years old, sitting next to me and a veteran of the eighth Route Army, had a bullet in his leg that had been removed by Dr Bethune. He later became an assistant orderly. He remembered how good Dr Bethune was to the wounded, "working day and night" and very quick to attend them.

> A great big man, also a veteran, met Dr Bethune in the summer of 1938 at a recuperation centre. He stayed with him for more than an hour. Dr Bethune lived in their house for over forty days. He also cured his son's skin lesions, possibly impetigo treated with sulfur mixed in pork fat. He remembered his warm.—heartedness and his devotion to duty. He slept little, and used to rise early to sweep the courtyard, so his grandfather rose even earlier to do it himself! He insisted in sharing a little extra food he had with the old man. He had a very close relationship with the people. They all wept at his death, and to commemorate him the family often meet and talk of those times.

> The third speaker was an older lady of 64. The family heard of the kind foreign doctor who charged nothing and she became a patient in the hospital. "The other doctors talked of amputation, but Dr Bethune looked at my foot and told me not to worry. I felt such great relief. He said the patient's point of view must be considered. He cured me in two weeks. To show my gratitude I took him eggs and fruit, but he refused them saying 'the army and the people are one family'. This is how Bethune treated the people, so I can never forget him. Even after forty years I always remember him. Every year I and my family pay tribute to his tomb, and I tell my children to emulate him".

> The next speaker was a 64 year-old man. The Army HQ was in his village when his father fell and broke his arm on his way to work. "We took him home, but the wound became infected and painful. My father met Dr Bethune who operated and told him to come and have the dressing changed on the third day. When he didn't do so, Bethune went to see him, and not long after he was cured. He decided to take a basket of eggs in thanks, but Dr Bethune refused,

saying 'if you want to thank anyone, thank the 8th Route Army: I am a doctor of the 8th route Army'. My father lived to be 89, and always taught us not to forget. We have such a good life to-day, we must not forget Dr Bethune and give thanks to the Communist party".

The fifth speaker was a little man of 60 with no teeth, also a veteran of the 8th Route army. "In October 1939 Dr Bethune came to our village with an inspection team. I was a male nurse and heard his lectures on nursing care and observed him. The Japanese were isolating the liberated areas. We were very poor materially, cut off from the outside world, with medicine in short supply. We used many herbal products, dressings were used over and over again until they wore out. Dr Bethune initiated several methods of treatment: sun treatment, sterilization and physiotherapy. He lectured on theory and demonstrated operations. He taught sterilization of wounds by the sun, the sterilization of all equipment before touching wounds, and the use of heat therapy and cold therapy by means of compresses. He made up a sulfur powder mixed with pig fat for treating impetigo.

He was very concerned with the patient's well-being. The leaders would get special food for him, but he gave it to the patients, and he would give his own possessions, quilts etc . . . , to the soldiers. I remember very clearly a leg amputation Dr Bethune did: the staff laid bets on how many times he would visit the patient—he went eight times during the night. I knew him for two periods of ten days. The way to emulate him is to work hard for the party and the people".

The last speaker, now a High School teacher, a tall young man seated at the head of the table, told his story. "In the summer of 1939, when I was three, Dr Bethune came to my village. I had a cyst on my leg which older people said always led to death: it was very fast growing. My father was unwilling to bother Dr Bethune, who was very busy, but he operated on me and opened the abscess. He refused my father's gift, saying We are the 8th Reute Army, we serve the people'. My father always felt greatly indebted to him, and it is engraved on my heart. I will study hard Chairman Mao's essay and try to follow Dr Bethune's example. In my job I try to teach the young the same thing".

Then we said our goodbyes; the old lady kept filling Irene's pocket with dates, stuffing them in handfuls! When we left, the road outside was lined with people waiting to see our departure. Back to *Tang Xian*, another fascinating drive; we had a good rest writing letters, having a bath etc . . . . Our group had dinner alone and then went again to the cinema to see *"the 7th Grade Sesame Seed Official"*, a Ming period comedy opera: it was amusing and the scenery and costumes beautiful, but we kept falling asleep, tired and full of impressions after our early start and full day: we had been up since 6:00 am, awakened at 5:30 by the loudspeakers making announcements (telling people the news of the day, playing music, the same thing again at 6:30 and 7:30 if I remember rightly!). Not much chance to be lazy and sleep late there! We got to bed at 10:30 and slept as usual like logs.

After a good breakfast on **Monday, September the 15th,** we visited the **Tang Xian Museum,** We were met by the staff and saw mementoes of Dr Bethune, photographs of previous visits and, much to our surprise, **a large one of us taken yesterday!** The photographer had worked until 3am to get them ready and there it was framed on the wall. We each received a set of photographs as well, in an envelope with our names in Chinese script.

The average income in this area, as poor as any in China, is about $65 US per annum. In the countryside, people do not need as much money, having easy access to fresh produce more easily and cheaply than in the towns. We were also each given a bag of dates and another of persimmons, touching gifts.

We were driven to Baoding, had tea in the station, said farewell to our friends and caught the 10:45 train to Beijing. We shared a carriage with a German technician. Apart from the much loved Ambassador Arthur Menzies and his wife, no one from the Canadian Embassy had apparently been invited to visit the area (4*).

We had an excellent lunch on the train and arrived at around 2pm. How lovely these train rides in spotless compartments, the windows framed in lace and velvet curtains, hot tea constantly at hand, the fascination of the panorama passing the windows, the people, the good food in little bowls.

We were soon back in our hotel where our rooms awaited us, a good rest, then a return visit to the ***Summer Palace***: the weather was so beautiful but cooler. We wondered through the courts and pavilions of the Manchu period, admired the lakes sleeping under their thick carpet of lotus leaves, the intricately-carved marble everywhere, incredible in its variety and extent.

We were back in our hotel at 5:30 for a pleasant evening, vodka in Irene's room, a lovely dinner, Joan at the hair salon for a wash and massage, washing

---

4*   All Embassies, I soon realized, are liable to be exposed to a game of 'tit for tat'. Embassy staff may have to give notice in advance when traveling more than 'x' many miles outside the capital area. The country responsible for that embassy might do the same in retaliation.

and ironing a few clothes, the ironing board in the hall for the convenience of patrons, and to bed at 10pm.

> When one wants to visit China officially or not, one never ever obtains a visa until 36 hours before departure. In a country as large as Canada this is quite inconvenient. It is the same for the Chinese leaving their own country. A Chinese or a Canadian is promised a visa, but it is not officially confirmed until the last minute.
>
> It seems similar to the RCMP listening to telephone conversations or asking what you are doing going to the Chinese Embassy. It also means that the Embassy staff tend to <u>live together in the same block</u>. It simplifies life but is a problem if one wants to explore the country, leading to '<u>we or they' thinking</u>. That is why the Chinese visit to *l'HSC* just a year before was not confirmed until the last minute.

We were on our way to *Manchuria* on **Tuesday, September 16th,** getting up at 6:30 to pack our bags.

At 8:30 after breakfast, we visited *'The Museum of the Revolution'*, an enormous building. We were struck with the fact that, in the section devoted to foreigners who helped the Chinese Communist Party, the only ones mentioned were Dr Bethune, two German Journalists, and perhaps one or two other people—very few. There were very interesting maps and models.

Some of their means of defense were so primitive: bamboo spikes to stop the enemy, bandages of palm leaves, the same material used to make a vest for one of the commanding officers, even dummy wooden pistols.

Back to our wonderful Hotel to pickup our bags and off to the airport at 10:45. Madame Lu Cui was waiting at the hotel to say goodbye. She was a nice lady.

Mr Duan, acting like a Commissar, accompanied us to the airport and talked about the Bethune Foundation. He did not like the name, leading people to believe that it was a rich organization like the Ford or Rockefeller Foundations. The old name was preferred. He also would have liked the membership to be much enlarged.

He did not seem to understand much about the circumstances of its history, nor did it seem useful to discuss the situation. I did not feel he would understand any explanations about what was going on in Quebec at the time, linguistically, religiously or politically. He seemed to have a simplistic vision of democracy, which to a Communist must seem pretty chaotic and disorderly. He seemed peremptory. As Winston Churchill used to say, Democracy is not perfect but is the best form of government available. Neither did I feel at the time prepared for discussing the matter as I was not so well prepared myself, but I was learning fast.

I was appreciating Mme Lu Wanru's attitude more and more; she was like a breath of fresh air! We never talked about politics or party affiliation. She understood perfectly that some subjects are better ignored.

We all had lunch together at the airport, our plane's departure for Changchun, the capital of Jilin Province and of ex-Manchukuo (the new name of the Japanese Puppet State, 1932-45) delayed until 1:15pm, much to Wanru's disgust. The Chinese were not too happy about their airline nor about its services (5*).

> Chairmen Stalin and Mao never really trusted one another, their brand of communism being so totally different; the Russian Revolution starting in industrial cities, the Chinese Revolution in the countryside. But both leaders had to appear to get along. Chairman Mao talked about the particular Chinese brand of Communism.

In 1945, Stalin advised the Chinese to support the Generalissimo and, just two weeks before the end of WWII with Japan, invaded the whole of Manchuria which had been heavily industrialized by the Japanese during their occupation (1932-1945). All the contents of the large factories were shipped to Russia before their final departure in the mid-fifties. The Kremlin only gave up control of *Lushun* (Port Arthur) in 1954.

We flew in a Russian top-wing two engine turbo-prop, a small noisy plane. We felt cramped. We crossed the Great Wall and stopped for forty minutes in **Shenyang** (Mukden of old), the capital of Laoning Province and the old Manchu capital, then on to **Changchun,** the capital of Jilin province and the ex-Japanese capital of Manchukuo.

For a change, a minibus drove us to our government guest-house. a beautiful building containing just four suites. There is a small dining-room on the ground floor. We had the main suite, a big sitting room, a huge bedroom and an enormous bathroom. It was the one occupied by ***King Norodom Sihanouk of Cambodia,*** exiled to China while his country was under control of the Khmers Rouges (1975-79). It stands in extensive grounds, full of pine woods, and Joan felt it looked exactly as she imagined Russia would look.

After dinner, we went to the guesthouse cinema to see "Love at Noontime", a sentimental movie about a love affair between the daughter of a Kuomingtang officer and the son of a Communist officer, the two officers united in the end in friendship. The lady had a change of clothes in every

---

5*   Of The Han and Manchu Dynasties,—The Tartars.

shot! The cinema was extremely comfortable. We sat in armchairs flanked by tables with tea, the thirty or so soldiers that guarded the guesthouse sitting silently in the rear, so different than what we were exposed to in Shijiazhuang and Tang Xian.

"The Han Dynasty ruled China from 206 BC until AD 220, with only a brief interruption. During this period Chinese rule was extended over Mongolia, and the administration was in the hands of an organized civil service, Confucianism was recognized as the state philosophy, and detailed historical records were kept. The arts flourished, and technical advances included the invention of paper. It was to this era that later dynasties looked for their model.

Han is the term now also used to describe the dominant ethnic group in China, 80% of the population" (OERD) as distinct from the 55 minority groups.

A *Manchu* (meaning 'pure') is a member of a Tartar people who conquered China and founded *the Quing dynasty* (1644-1912).

At first, the Manchus only controlled Northern China. An energetic early Manchu ruler, Kangxi (1662-1722), with the help of loyalist Chinese commanders, gradually asserted his authority over South China, the last Ming resistance in Taiwan falling in 1683.

Louis XIV of France, the Sun King (1643-1715), might be his European twin, both enlightened rulers.

Adoption of the Chinese culture by the Manchu conquerors led in time to the loss of their own culture and customs. Their language is to-day only spoken in a small section of Northern Manchuria, and Manchu people to-day are just one of the minority groups.

A *Tartar* is a member of the combined forces of central Asian peoples, including Mongols and Turks, who under the leadership of Genghis Kan, overran and devastated much of Asia and eastern Europe in the early 13th century.

Tamerlane (14th century), established a large empire in central Asia with its capital Samarkand (one of the oldest cities of Asia destroyed by Alexander the Great in 329 BC) now in eastern Uzbekistan. Tamerlane was an ancestor of the *Mogul dynasty in India* who built the Taj Mahal, completed in 1649.

On **Wednesday September 17th,** after a good breakfast, we drove to the **Bethune Medical University,** a large compound based around well-built ex-Japanese multistoried Government buildings with wide impressive staircases dating from the 1930s. It had its own statue of Dr Norman Bethune in front of the Main building.

The University Hospital occupies a large ex-army barrack, the ground floor of which was originally a large garage-like area, with many strong concrete columns, to house the horses, now redesigned for administration and teaching; the new top floor is a recent addition for clinical obstetrics and pediatrics.

We were welcomed by the President, Dr Ho, and senior doctors: there was a large floral greeting painted by one of the nurses welcoming us. We had tea with some of the professors, then visited the Medical School, the department of anatomy etc . . . The staff was charming.

Amongst so many things to see, experiments were being carried out to investigate pain. We then returned to the guest-house with a walk in the park on the way. A magician was giving an open-air show, the audience sitting on benches. The weather was lovely, much like that in Canada in the autumn, warm sunny days and chilly nights.

After a forty minute siesta after lunch, we returned to the medical school and visited the museum. A round-table discussion had been arranged with the staff, at least thirty of them, with students sitting around the walls listening avidly. I talked about medical education in Canada, the number of medical schools, the curriculum etc . . . , with a map of Canada that I had brought along pinned on a board.

At that time, we had fifteen medical schools for twenty-two million people. I tried to give an idea of the extent of the country, bigger than China with so few people, with similar difficulties in communication. At the end, I gave the map to a student, and it was immediately confiscated by a staff-member for the museum.

After a question period, I went off on my own with about fifteen professors while the other four talked to students and let them practice their English. A number of them, perhaps a fifth of the class, learn the whole of their curriculum in English, taught by Chinese teachers in English with English textbooks. This was very impressive. They were great, intelligent, polite, so enthusiastic to find out about Canada, how we lived, what students studied, how they spent their spare time. Joan tried to get them all talking. One asked her if "everyone had a TV", "just about", "Even the peasants", "yes". She wondered what the peasants' would think. Another "we are sick of politics in China". Talking with them was a great experience.

We talked about medical education. They could not fathom why it took so long to train a specialist. This discussion centered principally about pediatrics: sixteen years in Canada after high school, four undergraduate, four graduate, and four postgraduate. Personally I agreed with them, but I tried nevertheless to explain the process.

I was struck by the physical appearance of some of my Chinese colleagues, and soon realized that when Japan was defeated in 1945, many Japanese professionals had been there for a number of years and had no desire to return home to their defeated country which was barely surviving those horrible attacks with atomic bombs.

There was a Japanese Medical School in Changchun in those days: some Japanese had Chinese spouses, some had taught there. They had lost some of their allegiance to their home country. Their departure from China would have created a serious void. So they stayed behind, changed their names and nationality. Wang was their most commonly accepted surname as far as I could tell. Changchun was their home.

I failed to appreciate at the time that the **Provinces of Jilin and Saskatchewan are of same size** (as big as France), with the same climate and similar soil. They were both settled during the nineteenth century, Jilin Province by people of Han descent following the Manchu take-over of the leadership of China, now numbering over twenty million, Saskatchewan by Europeans, now one million, most of them seeking to settle down in a hospitable environment and farm.

The Trans-Siberian and Trans-Canadian railways were twins in development during the end of the nineteenth century.

The farming in Jilin province is labor-intensive, its produce an essential component of the whole Chinese agricultural production. In Saskatchewan farming is highly mechanized, its products equally needed.

The first European settlements in Ontario occurred in 1673, Fort Frontenac in Kingston, and Fort Rupert on Hudson's Bay, while during that same period the Manchu emperor Kangxi was pacifying China.

Jilin is the smallest of the three provinces of Manchuria. Ontario is the same size as Spain and France put together,

That quite fantastic afternoon ended in a small room adjoining the large cafétaria. President Dr Ho Yun Qing, said that Dr Bethune would have approved of such a simple arrangement. We ate at two round tables and had a really wonderful meal cooked by the caferia staff, all sorts of delicious things, and many courses. The people were just charming. We got back at the guesthouse at 7 pm, went straight to bed and slept until 6.30 am!

We later learnt that Dr Ho was standing next to General Nieh, the young Commanding Officer of the Eighth Route Army, in a well-know photograph of Dr Bethune after he died. He was a survivor of the Long March.

After breakfast on **Thursday, September the 18th,** we went off to the Changchun Film Studios. A huge statue of Chairman Mao dominates the courtyard, perhaps the only one left in the whole country. Over tea with the director, Mr Gan, we learnt about the studios. They make twenty features a year, with an acting group of one hundred and fifty actors and actresses. They have all gone through an actor's school in Beijing for four years from where they are assigned to different studios.

Changchun is the third largest after Shanghai and Beijing. The technical crew is also trained there. Actors and actresses from anywhere in the country may be invited. There is a special group attached to the studio to write scripts, and they also absorb scripts from outside. Most films are made for the cinema and not for television. They also make scientific and educational films, the scientific ones to popularize science. Movies are very popular in China, most adults going once or twice a week for the cost of about ten cents. A popular movie might be seen by two hundred million people, including those that go to see it two or three times.

We saw the final sound recording of *"The Red Peony"*, a seemingly very good film on circus life before the revolution, the shooting of a rain scene from *"the Red Phoenix Turning towards the Sunrise"* directed by Lu Wen Yu, visited the enormous property room and saw a truly beautiful film on birds, *"Bird Island"*, shot in North West China on "Qing Hai Lake".

We were taken for a drive around the city and returned to the guesthouse for lunch. We gave our persimons, which were getting soft, to the staff, along with the dates, and left for the station where the President of the University and three or four senior professors had come to say goodbye, along with the Head of the Jilin Friendship Association, Wanru and Cioma thankfully with us as always.

We left for **Shenyang** on the old Trans-Siberian Railway line, on time at 1:23 pm, arriving at 5:30 pm. I would never have guessed that one day I would be travelling on that line. There were still concrete pillboxes built by the Americans and the Kuomintang at regular intervals along the line in an attempt to prevent Mao's guerilla forces from blowing them up.

We were met as usual by the Head of the local Friendship Association and drove to our hotel, The Laoning Mansions, an enormous brooding pile right in the middle of a large and severely polluted industrial town, seemingly built by the Russians, reminding Joan of some vast building in the Midlands in England. After dinner, we went for a short walk with Irene and to bed at about 7pm, sleeping like logs until 6am. Our beds had mosquito nets, a first for us in China.

We spent two days there. Liaoning Province (Liao, the river and Ning peaceful tranquility) founded sixteen centuries BC, now with a population of thirty-four million people, is an important industrial area (metallurgy, machine-building, electronics, coal, petroleum, power generation, petrochemical, textile and light industries), the second richest province in China. Shenyang (yang, bank of a river), over two thousand years old now has a population of three million people. It is is an important educational centre.

In contrast, Changchun was a much more recent poorer and backward consumer city of one and a half million. It did have a large new auto industry, making mostly large trucks, the third largest in the country.

On the morning of **Friday September 18th,** we visited The May 53 Commune adjoining Shenyang just to the south, growing mainly vegetables and grain and raising pigs and chickens.

In 1950, Mutual Aid Teams were set up.

In 1953, an initial Agricultural Cooperative Team for mutual aid and development was introduced.

The Commune was first set up in 1958, meeting quite a lot of opposition. Production increased and the standard of living gradually improved.

Between 1958 and 1979, the production of vegetables increased (×1.6), grain, mainly rice, (×1.2), the number of pigs (×6) and cows (×6).

Under the leadership of the commune (population 20,000 to start with and now 39,000, mostly a natural increase, 30% over the age of 56 years), there are now seventeen brigades with 86 production teams, 9,000 agricultural personnel, 17,000 laborers for 3100 hectares of land (a square, 31 Kms per side).

In 1979, 570 tons of meat was produced and 70 tons of eggs. Sixty trucks were purchased as well as 290 other vehicles, 360 electrically operated wells were dug, 90% of the land being arable and irrigated by this underground water.

There are 100,000 square meters of greenhouses, eighty beautiful storage rooms for vegetables, 100 hectares of cold frames for advancing spring planting by two month, also a medical clinic and a communal hospital in each production brigade.

There are three High Schools, seventeen Primary Schools and a retail centre with eight stores. We visited a medical clinic with a few beds, saw the medical record room, the dispensary and visited one of the small houses where **Korean** families had settled, beautifully kept with a goose and chickens running around in the small yard.

The average yearly per capita income is 240$. In 3 of the 17 brigades there is a voluntary retirement accommodation system for men, sixty years old and women, fifty-five. Further training is available for technicians of all kinds as well as for barefoot doctors.

The Commune's Revolutionary Committee was about to become the Commune's Managerial Committee (fifteen members with a director and a deputy-director, with sub-committees with specific tasks, educational, technical, etc . . .) with elections every two years.

If so desired, each worker had a personal plot of land (40×60m) for private use. I remember visiting some beautiful pigsties with happy clean pigs and beautifully built enormous thick-walled red-brick storage tunnels. Chemical fertilizers are used for grain, natural fertilizers for vegetables because the taste seems better!

After a visit to the Friendship store, we returned to the hotel for lunch and a siesta. The hotel was very busy; a thousand scientists from all over the province were attending a conference.

We visited <u>The Shenyang No1 Machine Tool Plant</u> that afternoon. As usual, we were received with tea. The managers seemed to know what they were talking about, an impressive bunch that would not stand for any nonsense. There are 6,800 workers of whom 20% are women, eighteen workshops and 24 laboratories, producing forty varieties of machine tools which may be divided into eight main groups.

The plant was built in 1935 as a maintenance repair plant for mining tools. It was stripped of all its equipment during the Russian period (1945-1953); it took its present shape between 1953 &1956. Since then, quotas have been overfilled. Much progress has been made in technology, and they now design their own machine tools, 5,000 of which are made per year. 10-15% of the production is exported to over 30 different countries.

Living conditions have improved, with 200,000 square meters of new housing for the workers, 75% of whom live in factory-provided housing. More buildings are planned. There are nurseries and kindergardens, special buses for transporting children, a public canteen. The workers are encouraged to attend skill-improvement classes; the factory runs a workers' University, with TV programs, technical programs and spare-time classes.

After this introduction, we were taken for a visit, and noticed especially women driving huge cranes etc . . . The whole place was very clean and uncluttered. Then back for more tea and talk.

There is an eight-grade wage system, ranging from 33 yuan (the yuan is pegged to the US $) to 108 yuans per month, the average being sixty. Each grade increases by about ten yuan, reaching the maximum in two years on average. Three conditions have to be met for passing from one grade to another merit (contribution), technical skill, and assessment by co-workers, the factory authorities making the final decision. Administrators are paid about the same wage.

A worker pays 5% of his wages for housing and receives a 20 yuan a year subsidy for heating. Housing is allocated according to the number of dependants and the length of service. Each worker has to reach a daily quota in his eight hour shift, six days a week. Workers rotate for shift work, some for two shifts, and others for three. A bonus of 20% for overproduction goes to the factory and is used for improvements. Individual workers receive 20 to 30 yuan a month for exceeding their quota, and there is a group bonus for those working as a team.

Workers share in management: representatives attend annual and/or quarterly conferences on major topics, such as production, welfare and housing; 30% of the workers participate, and in each shop, shift and group there are meetings for discussing management, In group meetings, 10% of the time is spent on pragmatic discussions.

One can start working there after a two year course in a Technical School. The children of former retired workers may enter as an apprentice in the same branch as the parent; 80% of the workers are middle-aged (over 35); 10% of the 6800 workers are technical personnel, 40% of which are university graduates, the rest technical school graduates. Some have just acquired the skills to function at the appropriate level.

After leaving the factory, we visited The North Tombs of the Ching (Manchu) Emperors (built between 1643 & 1651), encircled by a thick wall over 7 meters high. They have been gradually restored since 1945. An avenue of large stone elephants and other animals with lots of old trees led to the tombs with their beautiful red roofs and gilded and carved wood. These are really memorials, as the graves are actually somewhere within a huge burial mound, no one knows exactly where. There are no plans at present to excavate them. The emperors were probably buried this way to discourage grave robbers, just as where the pyramids in Egypt.

Then back to the hotel for dinner, vodka in Irene's room first, and wine in Hilary and Maryellen's room afterwards. We were to have gone to see the Ballet "The Silk Road", but we had already seen it in Beijing. We could quite happily have seen it a second time but felt tired. We had a chance for an early night and were in bed by 9:00. Cioma had'nt been feeling well and had stayed in bed that afternoon.

We were up at 5:40 on **Saturday September 20th,** an early breakfast (delicious French toast), to catch the 6:40 plane to **Shanghai.** Our local hosts were there to say goodbye. Leaving started to be sad events; we felt our trip was approaching its end! We crossed the Hei Shan plains and then the border to Hebei Province, with the Great Wall and its mountains, to land in Beijing, the only stop on the way, a forty minute stay during which Wanru and Cioma rushed to the telephones to say hello to their husbands.

Approaching Shanghai it started to rain, the palm trees writhing in the wind, the tail-end of a typhoon in Canton. Our plane almost touched down, when it suddenly rose again, why we didn't discover, and took off steeply. It landed a few minutes later at 1 pm. It was then that Hilary told us that the same plane, a Hawker-Siddeley (UK) Trident, had crashed near Heathrow in 1973 because it had not risen steeply enough at take-off! The engines had stalled and nobody survived. Hilary had been quite apprehensive!

We went to the **Ching Chiang Hotel,** most luxurious, with a really lovely room, beautiful wood paneling, a large walk-in fitted cupboard. We were there for four nights. It is where President Nixon had stayed on his first visit to China in 1973. We had an excellent lunch in the lovely dining room overlooking the city, and then a siesta.

Shanghai is a huge city with over ten million inhabitants. It has an ambiance we all warmed to, cosmopolitan, but very polluted. The weather was grey and overcast when it wasn't raining, and we failed to see the sun.

That afternoon, we visited the Shanghai Industrial Exhibition, a huge building with a permanent exhibit for buyers, everything under the sun, huge machinery or models of it, silks, all sorts of products. Originally a gift from Russia in 1954, it was called The Friendship Mansion of China and Russia. It has been in operation since 1969. We were served tea in the middle of one of the halls and talked about the exhibits. We bought Chinese records on Wanru's recommendations.

After dinner we went to the Opera, "The Disguised Demon" (17th century) performed by the *one thousand year old Kim Company,* with both men and women actors. In Beijing, all actors in opera are men, in other companies all are women. The scenery, costumes, acting, music (four musicians playing traditional instruments on the side of the stage), dancing, all were perfect. The use of the hands, and the way they let fall their long sleeves and then so easily shake them back in perfect folds was fascinating. The demon remained with his back to the audience, and when he did turn round kept his face covered with his arms and long sleeves until you could hardly bear to wait to see his face—and then what an effect it had when he suddenly revealed it in all its skull-like horror! The seats cost 80 cents, the seats were hard, the decor spartan but the performance wonderful and the audience spellbound.

What a day that was, each more exciting it seemed as the sojourn progressed.

On **Sunday September the 21st,** the end of our second week in China, we drove to the harbor for a trip down the Huangpu Jiang (River) after breakfast.

To go downtown, one passed through various concessions, German, American, British, French, and others, each with its typical architecture. The downtown area along the river has massive buildings of former colonial powers, banks, business headquarters etc . . . separated from the river itself by a lovely park, 'the Bund'.

Until 1949, there were notices "No Chinese or Dogs" pinned around the park. At the North end, the former British Consulate, in a strategic position by a small cantilevered bridge over a tributary river before it joined the Huangpu a few meters away, controlled the access to the Bund from that end. Walking over the bridge was free except for the Chinese who had to pay 10 cents per crossing.

We boarded our boat and went to our private cabin on the top deck furnished with comfortable chairs, little tables with tea, candies, moon cakes. Outside a wonderful view of the waterfront with myriad shipping, boats from all over the world, junks, barges, constant activity. There were many Chinese having their Sunday outing on this trip, and we looked on families seated around tables, talking, eating, drinking, chewing pumpkin seeds. We had a three hour trip to the delta of the famous Yellow River (Chang Jiang) in the middle of which you could not see mainland. On the return trip, we were offered beer and peanuts and treated with a show by a magician. Then, back for lunch and our siesta.

Then, off to The Children's Palace. We were greeted by the Directrice and five sweet children, each one taking us by the hand to act as our guide during our visit. We started in the usual fashion sitting round a table. Each of the children spoke, addressing us as 'Uncles and Aunts, Grannies and Grandpas'.

The Palace began in 1958 for after school education from 3 to 5pm. It takes 800 children from 7-12 years of age. There are technical and scientific groups, entertainment, art performing groups, many different activities, painting, folk music, recorder, dancing. The children chose according to their interest and the school recommendations. There are also group activities—reading, chess, table tennis etc . . . . The children come from their schools in turns: there are slogans 'we are happy, we will answer the party's calls' etc . . . .

There are ten districts in Shanghai, each has a Palace, plus one Municipal Palace, and there are also neighborhood communities including several 'homes for the young', a place to go after school, where they try to channel the children's energy properly and put the parents at ease.

Every week, this Palace will receive maybe 4000 children. Each Thursday they will have a special group: recently they have introduced a new program where the children make trips 'in their imagination'. They are contributing to the Tibetan Children's Palace. We were shown many of the activities and were much struck by the children's obvious enjoyment of all they were doing and the dedication of the staff.

Especially remembered, a very tall young man conducting very delicately and gently a choir group, a charming young woman teaching dance, absorbed youngsters making models, others queuing up for a turn at a type of push-button game.

Before we left we saw a little dance program done for us: the same lovely hand movements and graceful carriage that we had seen at the opera. Lovely! They all stood at the door having us goodbye.

We went to a <u>department store</u>. Joan bought some lovely cream silk at just over 3$ a yard, cheap even for Shanghai standards and I a Mao blue cap which I still have. We also had a look at a Friendship Store. Then, we had dinner at the hotel and to bed. Irene, Hilary and Maryellen visited the Peace Hotel. It was still raining. Joan wrote some letters and did some washing.

We visited <u>The Tianshan Residential Village</u> on **Monday** morning, a residential area built for workers on agricultural land in 1952: 500 buildings with 430,000 square meters of floor space for 11,000 families, a total population of 45,000. Most residents work in textiles, light or heavy industry, also, several processing factories (workshops). There are teachers and service personnel, such as shop assistants. There are four high schools, four primary schools, nine kindergartens, two hospitals, nine clinics, 40 department and grocery stores, a cinema and a swimming pool.

Four thousand four hundred retirees live there, men retiring at 60, women 50 or 55. Their pension is 70-80% of their wage. Medical care is covered by the state. Most live with their children on their retirement. Many do early morning exercises. They help to maintain the environment and educate the young. Study groups are organized for them two or three times a week.

The *Tianshan Neighbourhood Government* administers the Village with ten residents' committees, each with a full-time administrator, the cadres elected by the residents. Income has doubled during the past three years and the number of workers has increased by 4,000, requiring the living space to be increased by 50,000 square meters. Services for working parents with children are mostly organized by retirees. A *party committee* guides the neighborhood offices and a member is present on the committees. The neighborhood office is the executive.

We visited a kindergarten, sweet children singing, dancing, playing games, a garment factory making mainly embroided silk jackets and a private home.

There, we were received by a lady, 55-60 years old, a family of six, grandparents, son and daughter-in-law, grandson aged seven, and an older boy at High School. There were two large and airy rooms and they share the kitchen and bathroom with another family. The husband is a retired steel worker with a pension of 90 yuan/month, his wife a retired textile worker and a pension of 50 yuan/month. The son and daughter-in-law both work and earn less than the retirees. There are two TV sets and an electric fan. She was making lovely smelling soup for her grandson's lunch. She came from a peasant family in the country and was sent to an uncle in the city before the revolution to make some money: a textile factory, a twelve-hour day, looking after thirty looms, spending all day running from loom to loom without even time to go to the bathroom, earning a pittance barely enough to live on, always in poverty.

Lastly, we visited the neighborhood clinic, run by a very nice and competent 'public health' nurse with six months' training with three helpers working full-time, doing mostly prevention, visiting schools etc . . . There is a lot of propaganda for encouraging birth-control. A patient came in while we were talking, an older man; he was invited to stay and sat quite comfortably with us, very polite and sweet.

Then, back to our hotel, Joan went to the hairdresser for a shampoo and set. The hairdresser seemed quite tired, he and his lady assistant both snoozing while she was under the dryer. While we were having lunch, we talked to our American neighbors at the table next to ours, led by **Tim Gittins,** executive Vice-President of the Sister Cities International, Washington DC. He had never heard of Dr Norman Bethune and seemed quite interested. At the next meal he was much more interested, having realized that same afternoon the esteem the Chinese held for him.

At around the same time, walking around the busy streets in Shanghai, I was accosted by a nice thirty or so year old Chinese man talking excellent English: he felt I could not possibly be a teacher at the Norman Bethune Medical University in Changchun! I had a badge on my jacket to that effect, given to me when we were there the previous week. We explained what we were about much to his surprise and pleasure.

That afternoon we visited The Shanghai No 1 Silk Factory, built from 1956 on. It is based on the cotton textile mills, with 2,800 workers, 800 looms, producing forty-six varieties of materials, from raw silk, artificial silk and synthetics. There are mainly four workshops, a preparation shop, two weaving rooms and a finishing room. The yarn is sometimes died before weaving, sometimes after. The weaving machines are produced in Shanghai. Floor space is limited, so there are more machines for the space than elsewhere in the world. The facilities include a kindergarten, clinic, library, games room, dining-room, dormitory for single workers, 70% women. There are designers in the factory, and their designs both classical and modern can follow the buyers' requests.

As elsewhere, the management has three divisions, political, administrative and logistical; 40% of the administrators are women, and the workforce is very stable.

We were taken round the factory; it was indeed crowded, the noise deafening. Management was aware of the problem: it was caused by lack of space. It was only possible to hear by cupping one's hands round the other person's ear shouting at the top of your voice: even then it was difficult. Nobody seemed to wear any kind of protection over their ears that one could see, and surely the noise must lead to some hearing impairment.

We returned to our Hotel, which is really lovely, an aquarium, a comfortable lounge, covered portico, very nice park where, in the early morning, you may see everyone doing their exercises and Tai Chi. One morning early we went for a short walk before breakfast and saw groups of older people working under the guidance of another and many people exercising on their own. People often approached us wanting to improve their English. We went shopping in the hotel book-shop and the Friendship store close-by to buy presents for the family.

A movie *'Love and Legacy'*, quite corny and filled with propaganda, but something quite sweet about it too. Cioma thought it was wonderful and was sobbing; she had seen it before and thought it showed the correct attitude to love and marriage! Wanru did not say anything. Then back to dinner, packing and bed.

We always had our meals on our own, except when we attended banquets, on the train etc . . . , and Wanru and Cioma ate with other Friendship Association people, more simple fare. We always had a lavish meal with six or so dishes, with soup and beer.

On **Tuesday, September the 23rd,** we got up at 5:30 to catch the 9:30 plane to Guilin, We had so far visited three of the four autonomous cities in China, Guangzhou, Beijing and Shanghai. The fourth is Tianjin. We stopped for thirty minutes in Hangzhou, the capital of the Province of Zhejiang (44.5 million) just south of Shanghai, 30 minutes away, where the best scissors of all sizes in the country are made. Each one of us, including Wanru, bought some, a marvelous useful present.

Then, flying over Jiangxi province, (41.5 million) to land in Changsha, capital of Hunan province (over 64 million people), and Chairman Mao's home province.

??? in he sane basket one after the other!

We returned to the hotel for lunch and prepared regretfully to leave this lovely place—our trip was coming to an end and we were all beginning to feel sad at the thought of leaving. Hilary had discovered that she had left her passport and airplane tickets etc . . . in the bedside table of her room in Shanghai. Panic! But luckily they were still there and were to accompany Flora Macdonald's party to the guesthouse in Canton where we shall also be staying.

For lunch we had entire little birds but for the feathers: they were lotus pickers, eating the flowers, so are considered a pest. We had enjoyed various parts of the lotus at some of our meals. The night before we had delicious large frog's legs. Our plane left at 1:55 pm just ten minutes late, for the one hour flight to **Guangzou (Canton).**

We were met there by Mr Ma Fui and Mr Chou Jin Yi, an older man with short cropped grey hair, and the same two interpreters we had on arrival. We drove to the beautiful official Provincial *Kwantung Guest House,* a huge mansion previously owned by a 'capitalist', with a lovely garden, a lake, lotuses, a bridge, and stepping stones. Our magnificent room had a big bed and a single one, just the double bed prepared, with a lovely mosquito net in place. We had a short rest then went to the Friendship Store. Joan bought a lovely silk jacket and I a Mao's blue worker's jacket.

Back to the hotel to prepare ourselves for our farewell banquet at the Guest House, simply delicious—Cantonese cooking at its best! Beautifully hand written menus and name cards. Especially remembered, the 7-treasure soup that included lotus seeds served in a carved winter melon, the sweet and sour carp and delicious desserts. The room had stained glass panels, as in the old teahouse—such lovely colors, deep shades, dark blue etc .... Many toasts as usual, 'Gambay'. Then farewells and a last walk around, the shops putting up their shutters as it was around 9:o'clock. We could look into the tiny rooms, 8 feet long, often a ladder leading to a sleeping deck, I suppose, upstairs. People were sitting outside on the sidewalk playing games, talking and so on.

Back to our Guest House, we witnessed Flora Macdonald's arrival with Hilary's documents and to bed under the mosquito net, this one shaped like the stalactites in Guilin, gathered into a central sort of crown, unlike those at the Hotel there on a square frame. Joan did not feel too well that night.

Sadly the next morning the date of departure, **Friday September the 26th,** had arrived. We all had a farewell meander around the grounds, the nearby streets. Then a lovely breakfast and off to the railway station with our interpreters, Wan-ru, Cioma, and our local Friendship Association hosts. Mr Chou took Joan's hands in a warm grip and told her how delighted he was that she had bought such a beautiful jacket the day before. Finally the train was about to leave, we found our seats, and said good-bye, all in tears, Wan-ru and Cioma as well.

We all felt physically and psychologically drained, unable to absorb and comprehend all that we had seen. We felt really sad at leaving this wonderful country and its people, for who knows when we will see it again if ever. The train to Hong-kong was a direct and fast one; we kept thinking of our arrival just nineteen short days ago, but it seemed like another life. We felt that none of us will be quite the same again.

On the train, we sat next to Mr <u>Kivoshi Takai</u>, Foreign Correspondant of the Yomiuri Shinbun, 1-7-1, Otemachi Chiyodaku, Tokyo, tel. 242-1111. He was charming, interesting and interested. He had covered the People's Congress in Beijing. Joan felt really sick and we were both glad to get to our hotel, having a simple lunch in the Patio waiting for our room to be made up. We went to bed during that afternoon and stayed there, having supper sent up. Our exhaustion seemed more mental than physical.

To cut a long return story short, Joan had a suit made out of the silk in Hong-Kong. We left on **Tuesday September 30th** stopping in Honolulu for a night after a ten and a half hour flight. We arrived there at 7am Wednesday because of crossing the dateline, stayed at the Kahala Hilton, finally arriving in Montréal at 7am on **Friday October 3rd** after coping with several delays. What struck us most on our return was the reappearance of glary advertising, totally absent in China, the amount of money people were spending, particularly in Honolulu, and the increased girth of the people, obesity being completely absent in China at that time. We were actually missing the simplicity of life we had rediscovered in China. Irene stayed in Los Angeles with old friends, Richard Corcelli met us in Toronto with a red rose for each, Hilary went to Ottawa, and Joan and I to Montréal.

CHAPTER 46

Second Visit to the Far East, 1983.

Introduction.

Thanks to our old friend Lee St Lawrence (1923-2006), who retired from the American Foreign Service in the early seventies with Ambassadorial rank to live in Deal, Kent, UK, I was introduced to a publication of the DACOR-Beacon Press, Bethesda, Maryland (Diplomatic And Consular Officers, Retired).

Lee was an old Dacorian. He still had three whippets that he loved dearly. They are very active and love tearing paper-backs, so these have to be protected on suitably placed shelves. I rescued a book that had escaped just on time, one afternoon, the back cover ripped-off, the only damage. This dog-mangled one, published in 1994, was absolutely riveting. Lee gave it to me, and I repaired it with some tape and another book-cover.

All US Foreign Service officials are sworn to secrecy. However, after a suitable time, Dacor Press will publish US government sanctioned books, one of which was

'War and Peace with China'.

First-Hand Experiences in the Foreign Service of the United States. Published by DACOR Press in 1994.

John Herbert **Holdridge** (1924-2001), a Chinese language officer,

US Ambassador to

- = Singapore (75-78),
- = Indonesia (82-86),

accompanied Henry Kissinger on a secret trip to China in 1971 leading to President Nixon's visit there in 1972.

Marshall **Green** (1916-1998),

Consul General in Hong-Kong (61-63),
US Ambassador to

- = Indonesia (65-69)
- = Australia (73-75).

William N **Stokes**,

assigned to

- = Mukden (Shenyang), Liaoning Province, in 1946,
- = under house arrest in Mukden for a year in 1948, served in Tokyo during the Korean War, coordinator (deputy then principal) of US interagency advice to the Thai government in its struggle against Maoist insurgency and Vietnamese raids on US bases (67-73).

The three were all University Graduates, served in the Armed Forces during WWII, one in each of the three main branches. They married in wartime. They all had several children, entering the Foreign Service directly from the military.

There are just fourteen short chapters, 200 pages in all, a masterpiece for exact, factually correct, non-judgmental and comparatively unbiased information about the events that took place.

August 1945-October 1ˢᵗ 1949, the second Chinese Civil War:

From 1945 onwards, Civil War dominated the priorities of the official Kuomintang government, both parties attempting to control **Manchuria** vacated by the Japanese in the northeast.

In order to ensure Kuomintang sovereignty in the north-east, the US assisted the advance of the national army by guarding the railway lines, recalling some of those pillboxes we had witnessed there during our visit in 1980.

US misgivings were severe, having received realistic reports about Communist military and political potential during the anti-Japanese war: would the CCP

= become a tool of Soviet policy, or
= adopt a pragmatic middle path with reconstruction as a priority.

The Truman administration tended towards the latter view which was not popular in the US. In 1946, the Russians finally admitted military and political delegations of the Kuomintang in the principal cities under their control, of which Shenyang and Changchun that Joan and I had visited in 1980.

The US trained and equipped Kuomintang armies, made-up mostly of soldiers from the south, hating the climate in the North and the quality of the food there (rice, just one crop a year instead of three or more), drove the PLA armies (50% North-Koreans), towards the north-east in a series of sharp conventional battles.

Those fleeing Communist forces eventually crossed the Yalu river, just south of Hilin Peorvice, to the safe haven of North Korea where they were refitted, an important debt of the CCP to President Kim Il-sung.

It soon became clear in late 1949 that Chairman Mao would adopt a hard line, thus '**completing the Revolution**':

= Kim Il Sung made the long trip to Moscow four times during this period, present for the most active stage of the Stalin-Mao discussions in February 1950: the consensus there was that the Americans would not intervene. That was the only time Mao ever left China;
= Soviet aid experts soon arrived on the scene;
= in late 1949, two divisions of the new Chinese Fourth Army, mainly composed of ethnic Koreans, were sent to Korean border;
= in January 1950, all 30,000 remaining ethnic Koreans in the PLA were sent to Korea and organized into the seventh division of the 'Korean Peoples' Army', which spearheaded the original attack. The units committed by Mao were amongst the most effective in the Chinese Army (including the marvelous surgeon from the Bethune International Peace Hospital, Dr Zhao Po).

June 1950-1953: The Korean War.

South Korea was totally surprised and under-armed, US elements from Japan having to be thrown in piecemeal.

Two weeks after the initial attack, when it was still in full promise of total victory, Mao formed the <u>Northeast Border Defence Army</u> to prepare "an intervention in the Korean War if necessary".

On August the 5th, Mao told a Politburo meeting that China needed to help North Korea with military volunteers. <u>It is explicit in Mao's messages that he wanted total triumph over the Americans</u> **by military means.**

In late August, after the invaders had pushed the allies to the most southern point of Korea, MacArthur landed successfully at Inchon, leading to the complete reversal of the tripartite aggression when the original boundary at the 38th parallel was regained.

On September 14th Stalin asked Mao for help, and Mao gave orders for deployment of Chinese troops on October 2nd, disregarding the opposition of his own politburo, five days **before** the original 38th parallel boundary had been reached.

At the same time, Zhou Enlai was informed in Moscow by Stalin that <u>the earlier Soviet offer of air cover was withdrawn,</u> a lack that was to cost China the war.

Mao was the big loser in this whole episode, fatally ruining his reputation as "The Great Helmsman".

"Emperor MacArthur", who threatened to bomb mainland China, was <u>stripped from power</u> by President Truman.

"Emperor Mao" destroyed his critics compounding his error in Korea by <u>increasingly abortive attempts to prove himself</u>:

= the disaster of the Great Leap Forward, including megaprojects in industry and farming that we had witnessed during our visit to Shenyang,

= the horror of the Cultural Revolution (Xioma, Wanru and Dr Wang),

= his eventual obloquy among those who understood, <u>although his image remained as an icon of continuity for the regime.</u>

The Vietnam War (1964-1973):

is not mentioned at all in the book: it was not strictly a Chinese undertaking; 75,000 American troops were there in 1965, 530,000 in 1968. President Nixon's visit in 1972 to China took place **before** its official end.

The Aborted Indonesian Revolution (September 30th 1965):

The Indonesian Communist Party (PKI) had become the largest outside the USSR and China.

The PKI completely agreed with the CCP that revolutionary prospects were highly favorable in the old colonial world, Southeast Asia in particular.

The PKI favored President Sukarno (1901-1970), the first President (Dictator) of the Indonesian Republic (1948), and he favored them. He had become seriously ill that August. Should he die, the army would probably move in to crush the communists.

On the night of September 30th, the **PKI murdered six of the eight top Generals** and took control of Jakarta, the capital.

Within forty-eight hours, the Indonesian Army had moved quickly to suppress the Communist coup, leaving Sukarno weak and suspect. He was soon replaced by General Suharto (b1921), one of the two remaining generals. He abandoned power only in 1998.

The failure of the Communist coup in Indonesia shattered for ever the Indonesian relationship with China. The aborted coup was an entirely Indonesian effort. Tens of thousands suspected communists were assassinated mostly in the rural areas of Java and Bali. Many of these were of Chinese ethnic origin, perhaps because of their control of money lending and the retail trades.

These setbacks strengthened the hand of pragmatists in China, Zhou Enlai and his colleagues.

The US In Thailand from 1965-1972:

Forty thousand American airmen at six major bases in **Northeast Thailand** were conducting war over Vietnam and Laos. These bases were being threatened by Chairman Mao's efforts to try inexpensive and indirect guerilla type influences in the Northeastern Thailand countryside. There were similar to those used against the Kuomintang and the Japanese in mainland China a few decades before.

William N Stokes was loaned to Air Force GHQ to advise on the defense of the strategic air bases in Southeast Asia which were expanding because of the Vietnam War.

As in Mission Coordinator Bangkok, William Stokes advised the Thai Government on means of countering the insurgency, not by war but by **"nation building"**, which called for a balance of social and economic development, political reform and security measures, all more amenable to civilian leadership and much cheaper.

American advisors were strictly forbidden to participate or even advise in field operations while the operations were in progress. This was the first time that such a policy had been introduced by the American Military.

This policy resulted in the Thai government feeling responsible for dealing with the insurgency.

It was the first time a Foreign Service officer had become a leader of a national interagency program to counter insurgency: with timely advance warning from Thai villagers through Thai civil channels, cross-border attacks were thwarted without American casualties or serious damage.

There were parallel gains, such as increased Thai investment in rural infrastructure and a more responsible rural administration with increased sensitivity to the needs of the rural population.

Maoist support eroded and the Chinese inspired insurgency collapsed. <u>By 1972, Chinese leaders recognized that the Maoist insurgency in Thailand had no future, all this just in time for President Nixon's visit.</u>

What happened in Thailand at that time was of particular interest to Joan and I for two reasons:

= **Lee St Lawrence** was much involved in the Peace Corps in Bangkok during those years. As a true Dacorian, he never talks about his experiences there. Occasionally, a story emerges such as flying illegally at low altitude for hours to some remote place in China to collect somebody.

He and Anne were very happy in Bangkok. It was an exciting and productive period of Lee's professional life. In his early fifties, he retired to Deal with a very good pension because he had been given the status of an Ambassador, and, just for a few weeks, early retirement had been promoted.

Deal is a Cinque Port in Kent north of Dover. Although he never talks about it, I strongly suspect Lee had misgivings at the ambiguous position in which he must have been, sandwiched between the Central Intelligence Agency (CIA) with its horrible boss and the true original objectives of the Peace Corps.

We had lost touch when we emigrated in 1958. In **Cleveland (1961-63),** we had been told of his address in Alexandria, Virginia, and had telephoned. It was so nice talking together. Lee lost my address/phone number, and we discovered years later that he had put an advertisement in the Cleveland Plain Dealer asking us to get in touch, but by then we had returned to Canada.

We knew they were living in Deal, but did not have their address. We visited the town in the early eighties, and knowing that Anne loved antiques, we stopped at the first antique shop we saw: *'oh yes, there is this somewhat eccentric American with an English wife living on the London Road in the oldest three storey house in town'*, late 17th century, with an important water well, Jenkins' Well.

Searching for Anne and Lee took exactly five minutes. We had a lovely leg of lamb for supper that evening with a nice bottle of wine. Fresh lamb from Kent is as good as any in the world. We stayed there for a couple of days and talked. The beautiful old three storey house had many Thai antiques and beautiful photographs. It was as if we had last met just two weeks ago! It had been forty years.

= **our youngest son Paul** had met Malee Leeaphon at CEGEP in Montréal during the eighties. Malee was the youngest of two children of a Thai family that had emigrated to Canada exactly ten years after us in 1968. There is much more about P&M later in this book, quite a fascinating story.

Malee, trained as a Research Inorganic Chemist at Purdue University, Indiana, obtaining her PhD. She then worked for 'Air Chemicals' in Allentown, Pennsylvania. We have a grand-son, Remy, born on September 24th 1998. Before we went to Asia that second time in 1983, I was still very ignorant about political matters in Asia. We were hoping to better understand what was going on.

The Trip, May 5h 1983-July 3rd.

I had met *Dr Donald Rice, Executive Director of the Canadian College of Family Practice (CCFP)* at his request at Dorval airport a few months before:

= he wanted information about the BIPH in Shijiazhuang and my help in organizing a doctors meeting lasting 36 hours;
= the College was planning to visit Beijing, Shijiazhuang, Shanghai, and Canton after the 10th WONCA (World Organization of National Colleges and Academies of Family Medicine) Conference in Singapore in May. Up to one hundred and fifty Canadian Physicians would participate.

Joan and I felt it would be an opportunity to go to Japan on the way, briefly visit Bangkok and attend the conference in Singapore before proceeding to China, mostly Shijiazhuang and Changchun.

We took with us ten copies of the latest edition of the Merck Manual, a welcome gift from Jack Frost of *Montréal*. He had sold his drug business to Merck Sharp & Dome and worked there in a senior position. I agreed with Dr Norman Bethune that this Manual is an excellent textbook, beautifully produced, reasonably priced, the best gift you can give a young impecunious physician with little access to English-speaking book stores and libraries.

It was a fascinating eight weeks. We received two pewter seals and two certificates to prove that we *'flew on SQ 11, May 5th 1983, the Inaugural Flight of Singapour Airlines' BIG TOP, the biggest 747 of all'* from Los Angeles to Tokyo!

> We stayed in Japan until May 13th (6 days),
> Bangkok until May 18th (5 days),
> Singapore until the 24th (6 days),
> China (5 weeks),
> returning via Hong-Kong, San Francisco and Chicago with a stop
> in Honolulu on July 2nd.

We knew little about **Japan**.

We travelled around by ourselves by metro and railway, first to ***Kamakura*** to see the largest bronze Buddha anywhere, built in the thirteenth century, once enclosed in a spacious temple destroyed by a tidal wave in 1495, since then exposed to the elements. It is 42 feet high and weighs around a hundred tons, a merciful Buddha in perfect repose. Admission tickets were themselves works of art, a beautifully printed card of the Buddha on one side and an explanation on the back, all with a nice tidy ribbon, a perfect book-mark.

A Buddhist undertakes to abstain from taking life, not to take what was not given, to abstain from sexual misconduct, not to tell lies and to abstain from intoxicating beverages, such simple precepts without dogma.

We spent a few hours in ***Nikko,*** a small town ninety-one miles north-east of Tokyo and a main religious centre. A **Shinto** temple seems to have existed there from time immemorial, revering ancestors and nature-spirits and emphasizing ritual and standards of behavior rather than doctrine. Shintoism is strictly Japanese.

In 767 AD its first Buddhist temple was founded. Some of the first shoguns, commanders-in-chief in feudal Japan, were buried there in the seventeenth century. The 'abbots' of Nikko were princes of imperial blood, all this making Nikko a mysterious and mystical place. Nature there is fantastic, several shrines and temples, one of them with sixty-two wooden pillars each eight feet in circumference, supporting an enormous superstructure, in the middle of beautiful old trees, some on hill-tops, the whole area between the two branches of a river that join just beyond a beautiful old bridge leading to the many monuments.

We wish we could have stayed for a week, as did Ulysses Grant (1822-85) two years after he had retired from the US Presidency in 1879.

We returned to Tokyo via Utsunomiya, another route to catch a faster train to Omiya where we joined the Underground railway back to town. We had supper there, asked for chop-sticks, and saw one of the waiters run out to borrow some from a neighboring restaurant: they were no longer using them!

We took the _Shinkansen_ to **Kyoto,** our first experience with a high-speed train, so smooth, comfortable, safe and fast. We had Sake with our lunch, a first experience.

Dr Hideo Matsumoto, an old co-student and friend in Cleveland (1961-62), was professor of Legal Medicine at the Medical School of the University of Osaka, just down the road from Kyoto, one of the most reputed in the country.

Hideo had become a well-known authority on East-Asian blood groups, and was applying this knowledge to the study of the evolution of different races. He believed that the Inuit and North-American Indians, as well as the Japanese and most of the Chinese, originally descended from the Mongolian race. He was gradually accumulating data to prove this theory, but was lacking two-hundred samples of Han blood. I had written asking to meet him.

He had invited us to stay at his club for three nights, the **Diamond Kyoto Society,** by the narrow Kamo river, a most beautiful and peaceful place, a somewhat austere modern building with a few beautiful objects placed in the best locations, our delicious meals on partitioned lacquered plates, beautifully served, perfect service. We seemed to be the only foreign guests!

Kyoto was founded in the 8th century. It was the capital of Japan for over a thousand years (794-1868).

**Wooden Nijyo Castle** was the domain of the last shogun. Its enormous reception room had a creaky floor, the visitors a hundred feet away, so that there was no way to creep up silently to attack the master.

There are many beautiful temples with dry stone gardens that are raked daily with beautifully scattered rocks and perhaps a small fountain, a small continuous stream of water to a small pond and the delicate sound it made: the

Golden Temple with its lovely garden, the _Daito kuji Zen Buddhist Temple_ still in use with a priest addressing some children seemingly an accomplished actor and teacher, attached, a famous dry garden. The city is a Buddhist stronghold.

Kyoto is still considered as the western capital, Tokyo the eastern one.

We were escorted by three charming and able junior colleagues, Drs Kawai, Suzuki and Hara, one day each, _two of them with cars!_

We boarded this quaint and old fashioned but beautifully appointed train for _25 miles to_ the old town of **_Nara_**, a beautiful trip. We bought packed lunches at the station and ate on the train. Nara was the metropolis for seven consecutive reigns (709-784).

Its favored existence during those few years was enough to build and furnish some imposing temples and shrines, the casting of an enormous Buddha, and the laying out a lovely park, now with tame deer. The weather was perfect and some trees were still flowering. We just walked around the beautiful gardens. We had tea in an original old tea-house, the hostess dressed in traditional clothes serving the tea in the traditional way, sitting on cushions on the floor, not an easy task for me. Thus, old traditions are kept alive, some of the costumes, gestures and dances similar to those twelve centuries ago. The east seemed to have been far in advance of the west during that early period.

Professionally, at Hideo's request, I spent a few hours to improve an English text to be published in the American Journal of Microbiology and Immunology the following October. Before leaving, Hideo and his wife, a pediatrician, invited us to a magnificent dinner at a French restaurant in neighboring **Osaka**: we had foie gras, lobsters and lobster bisque, Kobe beef (massaged cattle) and a delicious dessert, with French wine! We exchanged gifts, Hideo gave me beautiful Nikon bird watching binoculars, and we gave our hosts a North American Indian Print and each of our tour guides, a Merck Manual, a last minute gift for them. They were delighted. We saw **Mount Fuji** clearly twice from the Shinkansen, such a beautiful and rare occurrence as it is usually hidden by mist!

We flew straight to _Bangkok,_ **Thailand,** with one stop in _Taipei,_ **Taiwan,** on the way: I bought some current stamps at the airport post-office.

The Thai people immigrated from South China and Yunnan Province to south-east Asia during the 13th century, the first of a small group to do so, later with Laotians and Ammanese. They speak a tonal language distantly related to Chinese, with several dialects and their own script. They came down the _Menan river_ to the fertile plains where they grew the best rice in the world, becoming the only part of mainland Asia to have escaped European domination. It was the only Asian country that was never colonized.

P'ya Taksin, a royal Prince, founded his own dynasty in 1767 in _Thon Buri,_ a small village on the west side of the river just before it becomes the Gulf of

Siam. In 1782, P'ra P'utt'a Yot Fa Chulalok became Rama I. Bangkok became the capital, on the opposite eastern bank, and Thon Buri is now just a suburb. Thus Bangkok is a comparatively new City, just 60 or so years' older than Ottawa.

By Royal decree in 1895 a Legislative Council was established. In 1932, a coup forced the King to adopt a Constitution with a Parliament and a Prime Minister. In 1939, the Prime Minister declared that Thailand would replace Siam as the new name of the Country

Thailand was peacefully but unwillingly occupied by the unpopular Japanese after Pearl Harbor(1941-44).

The present King, Rama IX, Bhumidol Adulyadej, has been on the throne since 1946, the longest reigning monarch in the world to-day. The original Rama was the hero of one of the two great Sanskrit scripts of the Hindus, the Ramayana (c300 BC), a Hindu model of the ideal man, widely venerated by some sects as the supreme God (OERD). Thus, there is a mystical nature about Thailand, the Land of the Free, and its ruler, Rama IX.

He and his generals have little hesitation in calling states of emergency whenever doubtful behavior by politicians occurs: those events, although disconcerting, were usually benevolent and relatively free of violence. These have occurred many times during the reign of Rama IX. He works very closely with his Armed Forces' Generals, some of whom are provincial-lieutenant governors. Elections are free, voluntary and taken very seriously.

Joan and I walked a lot in Bangkok, took motorized tricycles, some drivers sniffing drugs, and clean buses with beautiful teak floors. We saw many golden Buddhas and a solid gold one (5 1/2 tons), many temples and palaces, all relatively new. I saw an efficient optician with the most modern equipment and bought a pair of reading glasses. I had lost my own somewhere on the way.

We went to the **Oriental Hotel,** the equivalent of the Mandarin in Hong-Kong but so much more crowded and noisy. We had a glass of fresh orange juice ($ 4,00 each). We had a delicious Thai meal with gracious Thai dancing. We stayed at a moderately priced German owned hotel with good honest food. One could buy beautiful jewelry, and cheap mock beautiful-looking Rolex watches as well as the expensive Swiss variety. We just bought small items of Jim Thompson silk, the best in the world!

> At the turn of the 19th century, a bright young man from Guangdong Province in China, **Mr Lee,** about 22 years old emigrated, taking a boat from Shantou to Bangkok. He founded a successful business, mainly growing and exporting Thai rice. He married a young Thai. As was custom and to abide by the Law,

his Chinese name became Leeaphon, so that all over the world he would be easily identified as a genuine Thai.

He sent his oldest son to China for schooling, and later to Duke University, Chapel Hill, North Carolina.

In turn, this eldest son, born during the first decade of the century, also married a Thai, and sent his own eldest son, now called Don, born in 1930, to school in Hong-Kong and then to Duke for three years. Don married a Japanese young lady in Bangkok, Etsuko Ohara, not a popular event in Thailand; they had two children, Dan and Malee. However, Don much preferred the North American way of life.

The family emigrated, first to Japan for twelve months then to Canada in 1968, ten years after the Delva family, first in Vancouver then Montréal (1975), and the parents later to Burlington in the State of Vermont in the USA. Paul and Malee met when they were at CEGEP in Montréal, fell in love, and married in Montréal in July 1988. Both Malee and her brother Dan had truly become bonded to Canada. The senior Leeaphons and the Malee and Paul live close to one another in Cape Elizabeth, Portland, Maine, close to the Atlantic Ocean.

Whereas Bangkok is modern, **Singapore** is an ultramodern City State with lots of skyscrapers and straight and wide streets. It consists of the island of Singapore and about 54 smaller islands with four and a quarter million people (2005). It lies off the southern tip of the Malay Peninsula to which it is linked by a causeway carrying a road and a railway. Sir Stamford Raffles established a trading post there under the East India Company in 1819.

Singapore was incorporated with Penang and Malacca to form the Straits Settlements in 1826, was under British colonial rule in 1867, falling to the Japanese in 1942, becoming a British Crown Colony in 1946, a self-governing state within the Commonwealth in 1959, federating with Malaysia in 1963.

Two years later it declared **full independence.** It is now an important world trade and financial centre (OERD). It has, in a very short time, become a sort of a new modern Venice.

Singapore is extremely well organized, but somewhat strict: one is not allowed to cross roads except at pedestrian crossings and chewing gum is banned without a doctor's prescription. There were 369 executions between 1991 and 2005, a world record according to Amnesty International. It is very stable, with an emeritus prime minister, Lee Kuan Yew, from the beginning in 1959 to 1990, 31 years. Thus, the administration has been trusted and continues to be since the beginning. A third prime minister has only just been appointed.

The Tenth WONCA World Conference on Family Medicine was an extremely well-organized grass-roots kind of meeting with well over one thousand attendees. Twenty-nine countries from the five continents were represented. The Proceedings were rapidly sent to all participants, a cheap but well-produced and attractive paperback (7"×10"); each page had two columns of print. The key-note address and plenary cessions are covered in the first 185 pages, the remaining 350 pages devoted to free papers. I thought it was an excellent well-organized meeting, my first and only experience at an International Medical Meeting.

Our own Dr Donald Rice gave the Keynote address: **"a survey of the Challenge faced by Family Medicine around the World in the 1980s"**. <u>The first WONCA meeting had been held in Montréal in 1964</u>. Dr Rice then reviewed what had happened since, presented the results of a survey regarding the present stage of development of Family Medicine throughout the world, and proceeded to identify some of the challenges facing it in the future, 12 interesting pages.

Dr M K Rajakumar of Malaysia, the new President Elect:

> *"the spectrum of Health Care, from urban sophistication to city slums and rural isolation, exists in all countries . . . . Health expenditure in the developing countries has tended to remain in the groove of the colonial pattern. It consists of heavy investments in building hospitals and the training of specialists for these hospitals, responding annually to population growth by mechanical increments in hospital investments.*
>
> *As a result, the health budget hemorrhages into hospital building. The result is that a great many capital cities in the developing world may not have a safe water supply, have poor standards in primary care, but nevertheless will have more than one CAT scan, cobalt bombs, coronary care units and so on. The hospitals are rest and recuperative centers for the trivially ill amongst the rich, and the hospital specialists are their primary care doctors".*

WONCA finally decided to join the WHO and has applied for membership with the status of a 'non-governmental organization' (NGO). Dr Rajakumar: "At present, WHO gets advice on primary care from everyone but family physicians. We must attempt to change that".

Dr Marian Bishop, Professor and Chairman, the Department of Community Medicine, University of Alabama in Huntsville, has a PhD and a Master's degree in Social and Preventive Health. She mentioned <u>the rigidity,</u>

separateness, and unaccountability of the climate in medical schools in the US. Incidentally, there was many more Canadian than US representatives present:

> *"The process of gaining and holding medical school curriculum time and the process of defining boundaries between medical specialties has less to do with a rational division of labor than with power and politics. Dividing curriculum time is not an educational process but a political process which is ultimately an accommodation to forces which have little to do with teaching goals and objectives".*

Socially, we met old acquaintances in Singapore:

Liliane Laporte, a pediatrician with experience in school health in Montréal, was more oriented towards Community Medicine than most pediatricians; her husband Pierre was a sociologist. They were both on the staff of the Faculty of Medicine in Sherbrook, having started at the same time as I in the fall, 1969.

They had both left Sherbrook soon after us, settling in Outremont three streets from where we lived

= Pierre had become *Directeur de la Régie de la Langue Française,* a difficult and important job;
= Liliane worked in a senior position in the Department of Family Medicine at McGill.

They both had a lot of charm. Liliane had known Pierre Trudeau since their student days. It took me a while to realize that she would welcome a transfer to *l'UdeM,* her Alma Mater.

Liliane had become a member of the Board of Governors of the **Canadian Research and Development Council.** The CRDC, based in Ottawa, was created in May 1970, its philosophy being to help countries to help themselves. Its East-Asian headquarters were in Singapore, and that is what brought Liliane there. The CRDC complemented the Canadian International Development Agency (CIDA), created two years before in 1968 in the aftermath of the successful International EXPO 67. This event really put Canada on the Map and was also a follow-up to Lester Pearson receiving the Nobel Peace Prize in 1957 for his help in resolving the Suez crisis. He later became Prime Minister. Lester Pearson, after he retired, became the first Chairman of CRDC until he died in 1972.

Personally, I did not at first have too much confidence in these new institutions with such a sudden large amount of responsibility, but one has to start somewhere, and eventually, perhaps after twenty five years, they might become mature and efficient. Such is the development of a new country like Canada and the United States. It took me a long time to realize this. In the Europe, governmental institutions and NGOs <u>seemed</u> all so ancient and immutable.

That year the *National President of the Canadian College of Family Medicine* was **Dr Robert Bourret,** a colleague from *l'UdeM* who had started a Teaching Family Practice Unit in his multi-doctored office in a street of Verdun, a sincere, honest and hard-working Family Physician. He introduced several measures at the College that supported bilingualism.

I was so new in the Federal Political Field that I had never heard of the CRDC at that time.

Liliane, representing the CRDC, invited <u>six people for dinner</u> after the conference, all six from the University of Montréal: Robert Bourret and his wife, Ronaldo Battista and Sylvie Stachtcenko, basically epidemiologists and researchers in Health Care working in the field of Community Medicine, plus Joan and I. It was a lovely evening for me particularly. As the new Head of Family Medicine at *l'UdeM* with such a wide-spread department in a large cosmopolitan City, it was an occasion to become more closely acquainted with some of my own colleagues! The people I knew best at that meeting were Liliane and Pierre. That had to happen in Singapore!

Joan and I explored the City. We travelled north to the border, visiting the beautiful Orchid Gardens. We sent some to my mother, delivered within twenty-four hours; the only thing she could say about them was that they were very beautiful but on sale in Marx & Spencer's in London at half the price!

<u>Sandy and Don Smith</u> from St Andrews, our neighbors, were also there; we had meals together on several occasions, once at Raffles, with its famous long bar where gin-based Singapore slings had originated and where Somerset Maugham had spent many weeks. The decor there seemed totally unchanged, lovely, perhaps all that was left of those old Colonial days. The old city houses had mostly been destroyed.

China

We spent one night in Hong Kong on our way to **Beijing** arriving there on May 26th. Caroline and Xioma were there to meet us. Caroline had been invited to teach English at the College of Foreign Affairs in Beijing for a whole year (1983). We spent six days there. It was nice being back. We felt we knew the town a little. With Caroline and Xioma we saw a Peking Opera, an Art exhibit and visited the Ming Tombs.

I was invited to give a talk at the prestigious *College of Foreign Affairs*: the one hundred years before Dr Norman Bethune died in November 1939 could be divided into four quarters, each of which covered a totally different period in the history of Medicine. That is what I talked about: during the

= first quarter, physicians such as Addison, Graves and Bright in England described diseases for the first time, such as pernicious anemia, hyperthyroidism and nephritis.

= second quarter, scientists became interested in the physiological aspects of these conditions, what actually happened to the body of those affected. Hughlings Jackson, neurologist, was a prime example.

= third quarter, people became interested in the dissemination of all this newly-acquired information to physicians and in teaching medical students. William Osler, Canadian-born, was one of the most effective medical scientist/teachers during this period.

= last quarter of that century, people became interested in applying all this information to caring for people. Health care became a priority, for soldiers and civilians, during and between wars, civil and national. Politics became fundamentally and irretrievably involved mostly for the first time. Dr Bethune, also Canadian-born, was a front-runner on both national and international global health care issues.

He had a scientific approach to his own career as a surgeon and to the problems of Health Care. Politically, he could not stand Facism, Franco, Hitler, Mussolini, Chiang K'ai-shek. **He was a humanist and became a social activist, only joining the Communist Party three years before he died.**

Since then, organizations such as *'Médecins sans Frontières'* have become involved, and there is no longer a need for an individual physician to work himself to death for a cause. Both Osler and more so Bethune, became world renowned, both starting their active careers in Montréal, Canada.

I tried to present Bethune as a well-rounded scientist rather than just a political activist. The audience was interested and delighted with our gift, the Foundation's book about Norman Bethune which they had received in advance. They requested a second copy.

Oslerians get very upset that anyone could be compared with Dr Osler. My point is that the joint achievements of those two Canadian Physicians complement each other perfectly during a fifty year period full of horrible world events (1890-1940). What an impact they had.

By that time, I had received a nice letter of appreciation of our book from Mr Wang Ping-nan, Head of the Friendship Association, and the senior experienced retired Chinese Ambassador to Poland, the link of China with the whole world after 1949 when Mao had come to power.

We had written to the *BIPH* in Shijiazhuang offering to stay there for ten days and teach. A delegation of four arrived in Beijing to talk about the teaching program: Dr Li Xifa, the director of the Department of Pediatrics, Dr Chu, general surgeon, Dr Lin, internist and Dr Zhang Ching Xi, Associate Professor from the Academy of Military Medical Sciences, **Xian.** I had offered a choice of one of three main topics: general pediatrics, community medicine or clinical genetics. Genetics was chosen.

> Dr Zhang was great: he was a brilliant person, unpretentious, with a great sense of humor, his English impeccable and instantaneous. He suggested and I thought it would be great, that I would write headlines of what I would talk about on plastic sheets for an overhead projector, and, before the morning's meeting, we would meet for an hour and he would translate what was on my plastic sheets to a Chinese set for a second projector: a first class way of doing things.

I had never heard of doing something like that before! I gave him a copy of the Merck Manual, so that we both had the same 'reference' book. There was also a long-term unexpected benefit of a different nature: when I claimed expenses for the trip from my income-tax, I was asked to prove that I had actually taught, so all I had to do was send my Chinese-written overheads to Revenue Canada/Quebec.

Dr Wu Chieh-ping with a few colleagues met with the 150 or so Canadian Family Physicians at *the Chinese Academy of Medical Sciences,* on Monday September 30th. **A senior urologist,** he was the most powerful physician in China, responsible for caring for the prostate problems invariably associated with ageing, the geriatric nature of senior government officials in China a source of much permanent revenue and power, just as cardiologists in the Western World in earlier times. He was pompous, sanctimonious and condescending. He could not have been much impressed by 150 Canadian Family docs!

He did give some interesting statistics: out of 116 Institutes of higher learning in China, 63 are devoted to western-type medicine, 22 to Chinese medicine, 2 to Pharmacology, and 25 were called junior medical colleges. The medical curriculum lasts from five to eight years.

Thirteen of those institutes are under the responsibility of the Ministry of Public Health in Beijing, the remaining 99 under provincial authority. Amongst the thirteen, the Capital Medical University in Beijing, subsidized with Rockefeller money since its inception, one of the best, admitted 30 students per year.

The Bethune Medical University in Changchun that we had visited in 1980 admits **500** students a year. The small Hunan Medical College in Changsha has long been associated with Yale. None of the colleges are presently closely associated with a University. Finally, Dr Wu barely mentioned the 1.4 million barefoot doctors who receive a very elementary few weeks training (full-time/part-time) before returning to their commune to give essential first-aid and help with preventive procedures. They continue to earn their living farming without any remuneration from the government. Plans were afoot to pay them a part-time salary; the commune itself might partly finance the operation.

I also learnt later that the three branches of the Armed Forces, the Post Office, Underground Mines, had their own medical schools, not mentioned in any publication that I have read or by Dr Wu.

Joan and I caught the train to **Shijiazhuang** at 3:30pm. We were served excellent food.

Dr Wang soon introduced himself, travelling alone, a Hong-Kong graduate who became a cardiologist, speaking perfect English, married to an artist who talked Russian. Perhaps she was Russian. During the Cultural Revolution he spent two years working in one of the coal-mines in Hebei Province; his hands were certainly permanently stained, and his blue fingers so thin.

After 1976, he had visited Frankfurt, Italy, and Queen Square (neurology) in London. He was quite fascinating and knew all about American movies. It seemed his youth had been spent at the Hong-Kong movies. When he realized Joan's name, he immediately mentioned a pile of film stars whose first name was Joan! He helped us off the train in Shijiazhuang and disappeared. He was a good conversationalist.

We often wondered whether this meeting had been planned in advance, who knows by whom. Such meetings happen in China seemingly more often than elsewhere.

Shijiazhuang is the thirty-year old capital of the **Province of Hebei,** one third as large as France and one of the oldest, with, in 1979, 51 million inhabitants, just 11% in the towns. Some areas in the west, within fifty miles of Shijiazhuang, are just as poor as any in the world with a yearly income of US$65.

It has a long history of farming, wheat, corn, sorghum, millet and potatoes, very little rice. The frost-free period varies from 220 to 110 days, the period shorter from south to north. It is also rich in mineral resources, coal, iron, petroleum, lead, zinc, copper, gold, asbestos and refractory clay. The beautiful red building bricks cost one US cent each, one hundred dollars buying 10,000 of them.

We stayed at the government guest house, down town. It was quite comfortable but the service more erratic than in sophisticated Beijing, the staff having a more *laissé faire* attitude, and this at all levels. There was a noticeable lack of interest in the job, cleaning china milk-jugs for instance, so unlike the other places we had stayed in China, perhaps the reality of the new China, the bread-basket effect.

> *"To be Chinese according to Confucius, one had to obey the sovereign, the father, the elder brother and the husband. For Mao, one had to obey the orders of the Party. In both cases, one owes total submission to someone during one's entire life and each individual is treated like a child all through his life (Jorge Svartzman, Spanish Journalist, in 'l'État de la Chine' 1989)".*

The College of Family Physicians of Canada study tour of the PRC officially devoted four days to professional encounters, the first one in Beijing mentioned above, on Monday May 30th, in Shijiazhuang on the Wednesday and Shanghai on the Friday and Canton on Saturday. I was co-chair of the afternoon meeting in Shijiazhuang. I remember very vividly some of the events that occurred:

= a presentation of Dr Zhang, quite brilliant, contrasting **Ying,** the passive principle of the universe characterized as female, sustaining and associated with the earth, dark and cold, and **Yang,** the active principle, male and creative, associated with heaven, heat and light. Then about **Zen** enlightenment, such as meditation or maintenance of a seated posture.

= a second Chinese presentation on medicinal herbs for treating peptic ulcers, and a third on acupuncture.

= the Canadians, so much less philosophical, talked about family planning, the treatment of hypertension and arthritis.

= ??? hypertension and arthritis.

The contrast was there between the west and the east for all to notice, but this seemed no basis for a discussion between the benefits of both the Eastern and Western approach, our mostly Canadian audience seemingly with deaf ears. I knew and respected a few of the Canadian visitors and was disappointed by the dismal impressions they had of what they saw and heard of the Chinese medical situation after just five days in the country. People just listened; there was little interchange. The mere thirty years since the chaos that had lasted over a hundred years had seen immense progress in the health status of the people:

= 10.3% annual growth rate higher than any other in the world except Botswana (1980-88).

= the annual growth rate for farm output was 2.1% in the 70sand 6.2% in the 80s.

= life expectancy was 63.2 years in 1970, 66 in 1980, 71 in 2003, in spite of the Great Leap Forward and the Cultural Revolution.

= a health system had gradually been installed right from scratch, priority from the beginning on improving sanitation, the quality and quantity of the water supplies, then the fantastic work of the barefoot doctors, with primary care as the main objective, the retirement system.

= there was electricity practically in every farm in the country.

= two hospital beds per thousand had been made available for over a billion people,

= the UN Human Development **1991** Report places China among the medium human development countries, due to its real (not exchange rate) per capita GDP in 1988 ($2,470, US) and other human development indicators such as life expectancy, health care, education, child care, the elimination of poverty, and little unemployment.

We visited a couple of wards at the BIPH and I was quite horrified by at least a half-dozen Canadian physicians with camcorders, then a relatively new pastime, taking pictures of patients in bed and even close ups, seemingly enchanted with their 'take', showing complete lack of respect, a behavior that would never have been attempted nor even thought of at home. The Chinese were noticeably shocked and I felt so ashamed. Camcord permission had been given, but no-one expected such an onslaught. Mum was the word. As my mother used to say, *l'homme est un loup pour l'homme*.

There were three Canadian nurses in our group: I organized an **informal nurses meeting,** totally unplanned, for the nurses of the BIPH: 30-40 of them participated, and it was the liveliest I could ever had imagined:

> **Mrs Jennie Wong MacLean** from Antigonish, Nova Scotia, was a probationer at St Martha's Hospital when I was there as a pediatrician, working in the obstetric department (1963-65). She was a daughter of Mr Wong, the founder/owner of the one excellent Chinese restaurant in town. She told me a tale that I had never heard before. One of her patients on the ward had just given birth to a child with a heart murmur, and Jenny had suggested to the mother, her patient, that I might be asked for a consultation. That patient might well have been an old friend. People knew one another there. The doctor involved complained to the nursing office that Jennie had trespassed her duties, and poor Jennie had to go and see the matron to receive a reprimand.
>
> She had seen a notice about the Asian meeting with my name on the program, and, as a result, joined the group. She was also so happy to be able to visit the country from where her parents came.

A second nurse was retired and came from Vancouver, she had had a mastectomy and worked as a volunteer with cancer patients.

The third nurse from Ontario and Jennie both worked full-time, one in an obstetric unit and the other as a public health nurse:

> **what** do you do in Canada if you want to change your job within the institution because you cannot stand the doctor in charge?
> "   do you do when you retire?—
> "   about continuing education, particularly if you are working in the premature unit, in the coronary care unit?
> "   are salaries like in Canada?
> "   about holidays and sick leave?

The meeting could have gone on for hours. There was an obvious companionship there that was lacking in the medical meetings. Everyone enjoyed themselves and there was lots of laughter, and it went on and on. Whereas the docs seemed miles apart, fundamental problems nurses had were identical on the two sides of the pond, and they had the opportunity, perhaps for the first time, to talk about them with people from the Western World.

Everyone visited Bethune Memorial Hall within the hospital compound; many photographs were taken; many visited his beautiful tomb close-by.

By Friday morning Joan and I were thankfully on our own. Those three days were illuminating if somewhat disturbing. Joan and I had by that time acquired a considerable knowledge of Dr Bethune, knowledge which was not shared by most Canadians. Still, such a meeting in China had been important, probably the first time a large group of Canadian physicians had visited China for a professional meeting.

For this Dr Rice deserves a lot of credit. The official celebration dinner in Shijiazhuang on Thursday evening had been cheerful with lots of toasts of goodwill. The small but numerous toasts, with thimble-full doses of strong Sorghum based 75% liquor similar but cheaper than genuine Mao-tai, proved to be a new experience. The Chinese are fantastic hosts. After a while I realized that one can keep the thimble-full of liquid in one's mouth and transfer it immediately to the invariably present glass of water nearby! I cannot take more than seven thimble-full of those drinks, but twenty-five is not an unusual number! Even teetotalers have a way out. That is what many of the Chinese ladies do, I later learnt!

The Provincial **Hebei Medical School** (HMS) was founded in 1913, thus one of the first in the country, first located in Baoding and now in Shijiazhuang, the old and the new provincial capitals. It was just two or three miles away on the same straight road as the BIPH.

Its president was an esophageal surgeon. Cancer of the esophagus is common in that area of the world. Dr Yang Tianzhu spent two years at the Montréal Neurological Institute, and we knew him well, sometimes inviting him at home for a meal. He ha become director of the Institute of the Basic Sciences, one of the four in the School, the others in Cardiovascular Surgery, Orthopedics and Tumors.

He showed us around his own Institute. It was becoming well equipped with Western research tools and a new Japanese electronic microscope. Its first CAT scan was on order. Their language laboratory was the most advanced we had seen, accommodating fifty students at a time.

Dr Yang loved ball-room dancing and was very good at it: that was how he and Mrs Yang kept fit! He was himself very fit and elegant, as was his wife. He could be quite funny. We spent half a day there and were guests at a dinner given by the president.

The priority in health care to date had been to give essential primary care to the whole population, and now they had to raise the technical standards and needed help, avoiding an over-emphasis on ultra-specialized care. This message was emphasized everywhere we went.

The School had a **large unit that produced many audiovisual tapes** in different subjects pertaining to teaching medicine that were highly respected and available though-out the whole of China. I had never heard of anything like that before, a library stacked with tapes.

There seemed to be little communication between the BIPH and the HMS. The two medical schools, so close, competed with one another, just as had occurred in my old medical school in London. Just as in England, the civilian hospital medical staff (HMS) was somewhat scornful of the military, although the BIPH was older and better funded being a federal and military organization.

The Military were paid 25% more than their civilian counterparts, a large differential in a poor part of the country.

We then spent ten days teaching at the BIPH, Joan conversational English and the use of English in the basic Medical Sciences to a group of twelve Chinese men and women, physicians, surgeons and at least one pharmacist and an English teacher: this was enthusiastically received and successful. Joan, as for everything she does, was extremely well-prepared. She had studied the problem, and arrived with small specialized books on the matter, mostly from the Oxford University Press that she had read and re-read.

She subsequently obtained a Certificate as a Teacher of English as a Second Language (TESL) from Concordia University (a two year part-time course). Caroline was a beacon for her. It is in China that Joan realized the importance of TESL by a native English-speaking person. The Chinese teacher of English had not previously been exposed to Joan's methodology and told Joan that his own methods of teaching English would be greatly enhanced. At the end of the course, the 'students' had tears in their eyes.

My contribution was split between lectures and participation at grand rounds.

Six of the formal two hour teaching cessions with Dr Zhang as interpreter were devoted to clinical genetics following the plan in the Merck manual.

Three cessions were devoted to pediatrics,

One cession, on my insistence, to the problem-oriented medical record and medical research (experimental trials, observational cohort studies, case controlled studies and associated trend studies). I knew my audience would find this boring, but I felt it was necessary to do so.

This was totally new to most of my audience, yet fundamentally important in the study of the epidemiology of diseases and the basis for any planning for health care and for teaching.

In grand rounds, patients would be presented in the wards, and a quite noisy discussion would follow in the classroom. In the interval I could look things up in the Merck and provide page references that could be consulted in the hospital library where two other copies had been left permanently.

Dr Zhang, Chinese-written plastic overheads and the Merk manual were my salvation! I tried to avoid dogmatic teaching and encourage discussion, no question deemed inappropriate.

We had a two-hour long <u>administrative meeting</u> with the director (surgeon), the associate director (ex-primary care physician/administrator) and the political officer.

The hospital's top priority was to develop cardiovascular surgery, then abdominal surgery (liver, pancreas), cardiology, immunology and microbiology, and the third line, ophthalmology, pediatric surgery and neurosurgery.

I tried to explain something about primary secondary and tertiary continuing care, Much had to be accomplished. I had visited the operating rooms, water on the floor, electric wires with connections practically floating on parts of it, and I could not envisage any University employed Canadian surgeon working in such an environment.

I was privately unhappy at the extent and lack of sophistication of the priorities.

We agreed that life was more pleasant when a couple was invited, the Chinese looking after all expenses and arrangements after landing in Beijing.

I realized how misnamed was the Norman Bethune Foundation. It was poor, taking three years or so to settle debts after the Bethune Conference; yet the name created expectations that could never be satisfied.

All this I attempted to transmit, emphasizing that Canada was a new, developing, huge but under-populated country, with a smaller population than Hebei Province yet larger than China itself, with comparatively small financial resources. It takes time to get things going.

We were driven around to visit three impressive old sites:

=   the <u>Zhaozhou Great Stone Bridge</u> built in 605AD during the Sui Dynasty just a few miles north west of the city, more impressive than a European Roman bridge, one beautiful wide long arch with iron crampons to consolidate the beautifully positioned hand-carved blocks of granite;

= the <u>Longxing Buddhist Temple</u> built in 586AD, "a tower temple with nine high buildings and four towers", a large complex with many old buildings, plus one of the oldest beautifully carved steles in the country and a enormous revolving wooden scripture cabinet one thousand years old;

> Some of the old isolated buildings worth preserving are dismantled and rebuilt here, or just transported.

= on a Sunday we travelled south-west in Jeep-type army vehicles for seventy kms to visit the solitary <u>Qialoudian Palace in the Cangyan Mountains</u>, deep ridges between large vertical rocky escarpments linked by a beautiful stone bridge half-way up with an inaccessible road on each side, small beautiful temples and palaces on both sides of the road which can only be reached by climbing 300 or so steps.

> Princess Nanyang had founded a monastery and lived in it a thousand or so years ago. It was not yet on the tourist run, so there were few visitors. It was an agreable surprise to see this site at the end of that famous Chinese film, **"Crouching Tiger, Hidden Dragon"**.
> Before coming back we had a picnic: Chinese Army tinned spam, sitting in the grass by the roadside, with delicious home-made bread and a glass of cold beer, quite delicious.

On Friday May 17th **we left Shijiazhuang** for Beijing by train, spent the night at the new wing of the Friendship Association Guest House in Beijing before **flying to Changchun,** capital of Jilin province, 23 million inhabitants. There, we stayed at the same small, luxurious, comfortable and welcoming Government Guest House for two weeks as we did nearly three years before.

The contrast between the two medical schools was even more remarkable: I was never told how many students per year entered each medical school in Shijiazhuang, whereas the big boss himself, Dr Wu in Beijing three weeks previously, had informed us of the intake at the Bethune Medical University in Changchun, five hundred annually (a figure never mentioned in Changchun itself) from all over the country, the largest in China if not the largest in the whole world and controlled by the Ministry of Health in Beijing. The intake is now 600.

There are three other large teaching hospitals in town, each with over five hundred beds. The main campus was enormous and much building was going on. Manchuria is a new rich place, whereas Hebei is poor, but so much older and richer culturally and historically.

We were escorted from Beijing by a very bright young urologist, Dr Zhao from Changchun. His English was perfect. I asked him once what he would like best in the world, and he answered immediately 'a Benz'.

A couple of years later, I received a telephone call from an old colleague from Sherbrooke who had become head of the Department of Urology at Mc Gill. He asked me what I thought of Dr Zhao, who had become one of two applicants for a basic research job in his department. I was very supportive of Dr Zhao, and he got the job.

We never heard from him in Montréal! But he proved to be a great asset, able to micro-dissect the kidneys of rats better than anyone else in the whole world. He immigrated to Canada and probably bought a Mercedes. He exchanged his clinical skills for a basic research position in a permanently-paid top-notch surgical department in the Western World.

The First Teaching Hospital in Changchun, an old Japanese Army building with 650 beds, is one of four equally large teaching hospitals. A group of students were taught entirely in English.

There was a department dealing with **Chinese medicine** with 30 beds, specializing in the treatment of enuresis with acupuncture and moxibustion (heating the needle). It was staffed with young medical graduates who had received an extra two years training in traditional medicine. Bed-wetting boys, 6 years olds, were flown in from all over China for one month, returning home cured. I had a long talk with the young lady, head of the section: I was not impressed, because it is a well-known fact that enuresis at that age will usually improve without specific treatment, and this was a perfect place for having a control group who would not receive real acupuncture. She was quite offended: **'we know this works, and that is all there is to it'**! Mothers have to stay in the same adult-sized bed with their child up to the age of seven to look after them.

Joan and I repeated the same kind of program in Changchun that we had offered in Shijiazhuang but with larger classes and much younger students than in Shijiazhuang:

> Joan was totally submerged, teaching conversational English, in the morning to forty students, in the afternoon to well-over one hundred at a time! It ended up by the students asking questions in English about 'life in Canada', and Joan answering: where does one shop for groceries, about holidays, sports, Christmas and New Year celebrations, about spare-time, about medical schools, about life in general. On several occasions they mentioned how fed-up they

were with politics. They seemed so keen, so intelligent, laughing and enjoying the cessions. It was probably the first time for many of them to listen to a University educated native English speaker. They appeared to understand English very well. They were good totally unplanned cessions.

I presented the same medical material in the same way as I had done at the BIPH with the same Chinese plastic overheads and a couple of remaining Merck Manuals, the whole experience quite exhilarating but exhausting for both of us, Monday 20th to Saturday 26th (9:30-11.30 & 14:30-16:30).

Professor Chen Yuan Yao was Director of the Basic Sciences Department, and had spent two years in Quebec, the first at *l'UdeM*, the second at *l'Université Laval* in Quebec City. We had met several times in Montréal, and he was occasionally our guest. He was a very sociable person, very kind and considerate. I liked him very much. He had arrived in Canada at the same time as Professor Yang Tiangzhu, now at Hebei College, and they both knew one another. They were both good dancers, and that was how they kept fit.

I have since met some of Dr Chen's four 'bosses' from two Francophone Quebec Universities, all four respected scientists, Drs Jean Dussault, Jean Joly, Georges Pelletier and Gilles Richer.

They all thought Dr Chen was a wonderful person, always helpful and cheerful, but they had little good to say about his scientific abilities. They were absolutely astounded that he was now occupying such a senior position so soon after his return.

He was soon to become Dean of the whole school, perhaps the largest in the whole world. How could that have possibly occurred? Those four Quebec Medical Scientists, highly intelligent and motivated, had failed to fully understand the difficulties a young Chinese physician, totally untrained by Western standards, would have during a two year stint in Canada. Dr Chen was obviously not too interested in what they were doing.

Unless a young graduate is interested in a particular narrow technique such as to how to investigate a particular group of diseases or to learn about newer diagnostic techniques, or some other specific and concise field of endeavor, he had no hope to reach equivalence with a Western-trained person.

The reality is that, during those two years in Quebec, Dr Chen had the opportunity to reflect, read about and observe what was going on during a two year period in two old established North American University affiliated Medical Schools, thus preparing him for a leadership role in his own country.

It reminded me of the old monastics spending a couple of years in the wilderness, in a desert or up a tree, returning finally to do great things. But in Canada, Dr Chen had it easier, having access to libraries and living in a Centre of Learning. He had the opportunity to reflect on his own problems at home and how these might eventually be tackled. Insufficient value is given to reflection to-day.

Professor Gou, Head of the Department of Pediatrics, a suave and efficient older lady, was very frank. Her husband was a top, probably atomic physicist who apparently spent half his time in Beijing attending political meetings.

I tried to explain that scholarships to study outside China should be conditional on return to the homeland where the need was greater; she implied unexpectedly *'for me that this is somewhat undemocratic'*:**the greatest achievement for an educated Chinese family is for their children to enter a university in California subsequently emigrating there, nowhere else!**

Canada was not in the picture, neither was the rest of the US. I understood for the first time that the ultimate success for a Chinese intellectual family is for their children to settle permanently in California in an academic position. The success of the family is paramount. San Francisco is the port of call. There seemed to be a lot of support from within the faculty for Professor Gou's attitude. Thus, they would encourage our young urologist Dr Zhao to leave his home town for good. They had no wish for him to stay there.

The difference between Shijiazhuang, an Army-based affiliated Medical College in one of the poorest areas, and Changchun, a Federal Government Medical College in a wealthy area, was remarkable.

Dr Gou remembered with pleasure **Dr Gloria Jeliu,** a senior member of *l'Hopital Ste Justine pour Enfants, affilié à l'Université de Montréal.* She had spent four weeks in Shijiazhuang and in Changchun teaching paediatrics in 1981: Dean Bois saught my help in organizing the exchange. Each night, she would spend hours preparing for her teaching the next day; she had worked so hard. I did not know Dr Jeliu personally, but I knew she was well-liked and admired in Montréal; I never was able to find out what she felt about her experiences in China, and I regret this deeply. She retired around that time.

I was much impressed by the President of the Medical University, a senior physician, **Dr He.** He had participated in the Long March, had met Dr Bethune, had attended his funeral. He had been present at several small banquets given for Joan and I, always in the corner of the staff cafeteria. The food had always been quite delicious, with dishes following dishes interminably.

Likewise, there was **a senior ophthalmologist** on the staff, who must have been 75 years old: he had also known Bethune. It was he that I saw one morning surreptitiously cleaning with his handkerchief the bird droppings off the hand-painted notice by the front door of the Institution that had been hand-painted by General Nieh himself, black on cream, 'Bethune Medical University'. It was a custom for senior leaders to personally write such inscriptions.

I met **Mme Kotnis,** the Chinese nurse who had married Dr Kotnis, the Indian physician who had succeeded Dr Bethune and who had died two years later of an epileptic fit caused by cysticercosis. She had become a pediatrician and still worked there. Her son and only child had died violently during the Cultural Revolution. So in Changchun there were interesting links with the past.

We visited a beautiful deer farm close-by, a lovely large water reservoir where we had a delicious picnic with Dr Chen and his family, including his mother and a lovely grandchild.

We visited an old Palace close-by where lived the last Emperor under the Japanese occupation in the thirties, Pu Yi. It had become a museum, many cupboards with drawers full of old small unclassified valuable beautiful objects that could be so easily stolen!

We left Changchun Wednesday June 29th at 1:30 pm by train. The weather was unpredictable so flying seemed uncertain. We arrived at 7:30pm on Thursday. Caroline was there to meet us. We spent two nights at the Friendship Hotel, had a lazy day on Friday, meeting Wanru, doing some shopping, being interviewed by Radio-China.

We got up early the next morning to catch the 8:45am plane back home. **What a fantastic eight weeks had flown past!**

CHAPTER 47

Lee 5 Lowrence

CHAPTER 48

Living and working in Montréal, 1975-1990; of Paul, our youngest child.

Montréal is one of only six old large cities north of the State of Mexico which have retained much of their own original individuality:

= four are of <u>Roman Catholic</u> origin, three French and one Spanish:

- **Montréal** (1642) is on the south shore of *l'isle de Montréal*, 50 kms long, in the St Lawrence river at its confluence with *la Rivière des Outaouais*, its largest tributary;
- **New Orleans** (1718) is on the Bay of Mexico in the Mississipi delta;
- **Saint Louis** (1764) is at the confluence of the Mississippi and Missouri rivers;
- **San Francisco** (1776) is on the Pacific Ocean.

= **Boston** (1630) is on the Atlantic Ocean, of <u>British Puritan</u> origin and the capital of Massachusetts, the only one of the six cities to become a State Capital.

= **Neuwe Amsterdam** (1626) was taken over by the British in 1664 and renamed **New York,** in honor of the Duke of York, later King James II. The Dutch were Calvinists*.

Most of the other large cities are newer and oh, so similar. There must be some exceptions.

The big difference between Montréal and the other five cities is that it has kept its original French language. It is to-day one of the largest French speaking Cities in the world after Paris, its *Université de Montréal* the largest French speaking University outside Paris.

I qualified in Medicine at what has now become the Royal London Hospital (1948) at the age of 24. I then

= inherited my Belgian father's general practice in the East Ham, four miles from the City of London, after he died in March 1949.

= married Joan Campbell in 1950 and had three children before immigrating to Canada as a general practitioner in 1958. During that time, the family spent a year in Germany and a second in Belgium when I became medical officer in the British Army of Occupation of the Rhine (1951-53) Our fourth child, Paul, was born in Cleveland in December 1962.

= passed the Royal College of Physicians and Surgeons of Canada Certification examination in Pediatrics (1964), after four years of work at Dalhousie University, Halifax, Nova Scotia, (1959-61), Western Reserve University in Cleveland, Ohio (1961-63) and after two years (1963-65) during which I became the first qualified Pediatrician outside the capital area in Antigonish, Nova Scotia, the home of the cooperative movement in English Canada, of St Francis Xavier University and its Coady Institute: my four-year slavery period, **plus** a two-year thinking period in Cleveland, Ohio.

= entered 'academia' as a member of brand new Departments of Social and Preventive Medicine at old Queen's University in Kingston, Ontario, (assistant professor, 1965), then, by invitation, at the 'new' *'Université de Sherbrooke' in Quebec* in 1969, later becoming *professeur agrégé.*

= was invited in 1975 to join the faculty at *l'université de Montréal,* becoming *professeur titulaire plein temps géographique, département*

---

* John Calvin (*Jean Cauvin*, 1509-1566) was the founder. The French Catholics call their French Calvinist colleagues Hughenots. The only Calvinist/Huguenot church in the North America is in Charleston, North Carolina.

de médecine sociale et préventive on June 1st 1978, later becoming a founding member and the first *professeur titulaire* in the new *département de médecine familiale.* My retirement rank was *professeur titulaire de clinique* (1990).

It was nice to finally settle down in Montreal! We would stay there for 22 years, for the longest period of our married life in the same location. I retired on December 31ˢᵗ 1989. I was sixty-five and a half.

How lucky we all are in Canada to have such a cosmopolitan city within half a day's drive by car for many Canadians. **Montréal is a University town;** two of its four downtown Universities are francophone (*l'Université de Montréal et l'Université du Québec à Montréal*) and two anglophone (McGill and Concordia* Universities). Mc Gill is the oldest and truly international; all four have many non-Canadian born students.

- Sir George William (1821-1905) founded the YMCA in 1844 in London. Its Canadian branch named after its founder had started a college in Montreal eventually becoming a University.
- Loyola College, the English component of *le Collège Jésus-Marie,* founded nearby by Jesuits in 1848,from which it grew.

During the academic year 1982-83, there were in Montréal a total of **121,458 University students:**

- *l'Université de Montréal,* 48,858, founded in 1920.
- *l'Université du Québec à Montréal,* 26,545. *L'U du Q* system was created in 1968 to increase access to post-secondary education, now with eleven diverse campuses from Rimouski to downtown Montréal to the Saguenay, with 80,000 students. Modeled on the University of California system, it remains to-day the only province—wide university system in Canada.
- Concordia University has 24,564 students.
- McGill University had 21,491 full-time and part-time, undergraduate and post graduate students.

James McGill (1744-1813) was born in Glascow, Scotland, immigrated to Canada in the 1770s, made a fortune in the NW fur trade and in Montréal; he bequeathed 18 acres of farmland

---

* Two Colleges had amalgamated in 1974 to create Concordia:

and money to found McGill College in 1812; it became McGill University in 1821.

Montréal is a **Music town:** the four Universities have excellent faculties of Music, each producing excellent concerts of all kinds continuously it seems. The city has at least **seventy churches** of all denominations, mostly Roman Catholic, **each with a beautiful organ.**

The largest of them weighs 40 tons, a <u>Rudolph von Beckerath</u> monster, 32 feet high with 78 stops, one of the largest mechanical action organs in the world, in *l'Oratoire St Joseph,* with the largest dome in the world after St Peter's in Rome. Its corner stone was laid in 1924; it was inaugurated in 1955, with 3,500 seats plus room for an extra thousand standing.

The new organ was similar to another made after WWI by von Beckerath for *la Cathédrale Notre-Dame de Rheims,* where most of *les Rois de France* were crowned. Most Sunday afternoons at 3pm one can listen to a free organ concert. The new organ was inaugurated on November 13th 1960 by *André Marshall, organiste à St Eustache* in Paris.

Frère André, functionally illiterate, unimposing in speech and stature, was the spark behind this whole project, working mostly by himself; certainly he had vision and guts! At the start, he had little support from religious and civilian authorities. Both jumped on the band-wagon when they realized the potential of the project. He died on January 6th 1927 at the age of 82. His Oratory is still Montréal's most imposing landmark, the only major urban shrine in Canada with half a million visitors a year from all over North America.

There are now **nine organ manufacturers** *au Québec,* the largest and best-known of which was founded by *Joseph Casavant* (1807-1874), a blacksmith who discovered organ manufacturing in Ste Hyacinthe, just a few miles north of Montréal. Between 1840 and 1866 he produced 17 instruments. His two sons, *Samuel* (1850-1929) and *Claver* (1855-1933) founded *Casavant Frères* in 1879; at the beginning of this new millenium, it had produced its four thousandth organ with the help Swiss and German experts working for them, over forty of those organs in Montréal. So there are literally hundreds of organ concerts a year in Montréal, without doubt the <u>Organ Capital of the world</u>.

L'Orchestre Symphonique de Montréal became world famous during our stay. *L'OSM* gradually became a good orchestra after its start in 1935; many well-known guest conductors came to Montréal, Leopold Stokovski, Charles Munch, Bruno Walter, Igor Stravinski, Georges Szell, sir Ernest MacMillan, amongst many others. A young Zubin Mehta (b1936) guided l'OSM between 1961 & 1967, during which it became the first Canadian orchestra to tour Europe. **Claude Dutoit** took over in 1977; he was born in Lauzanne, also in

1936. Under his leadership, *l'OSM* visited many European, North and South American as well as Asian cities to much acclaim.

In 1980, *l'OSM* signed an exclusive contract with London's Decca. This led to an impressive series of digital recordings, all made in *l'Église de St Eustache* just north of *Montréal* which has the most perfect acoustics, and the producer for Decca was none other than Ray Minshull, Decca's world-known acoustic and electronic recording expert. By December 1984, Decca had sold over 1 million copies of Ravel's Bolero, earning Platinum status. Many other *OSM* recordings earned international acclaim. *L'OSM* had become internationally well-known.

What is even more interesting is a recording *(Les Productions Richelieu, RIC2-1809)*, discovered recently following **a violin/organ recital** in Kingston just round the corner from where we now live: *Anne Robert,* ex-first violin for twelve years of *l'OSM* (her violin made by Vincenzo Panormo in 1790), and *Jacques Boucher,* since 1986 *titulaire du grand orgue Casavant opus 615 de l'église Saint-Jean-Baptiste de Montréal.* He gave a recital in *la Cathédrale Notre-Dame de Chartres* in August 1996, following which he joined the jury in the Chartres International Organ Competition.

I would never have imagined a recital with such a small instrument and a church organ, yet it seemed so perfect: this event to me symbolizes the inventiveness and perfection of the Montréal musical scene. The recording was made in *l'Église Sainte-Famille de Boucherville,* just east off the Island on *le Fleuve* on an *Orgue Casavant opus 3749.*

Public transportation in Montréal is excellent. There are frequent buses everywhere, and a brand new metro with rubber tires was being expanded, similar to that in Paris, and much less noisy than that in London. Montréal was also preparing for the 1976 **Olympic Games,** the first in Canada. This would actually put Canada on the world map.

The expensive stadium was being feverishly being built, and visiting the site regularly was soon to be an obsession for so many Montréalers, including yours truly with his wife and children. Its mortgage has only recently been paid off (2007)! The big question was whether the Olympic facilities could be finished on time. We bought quite a lot of tickets for attending the opening and closing ceremonies and for a few of the hundreds of activities; we shared them with the children.

At the opening ceremonies, Nicholas was walking around peering over a large site, and he thought his elegant neighbor looked familiar: he realized suddenly he was *monsieur Roger Taillibert* himself, the French architect of the stadium. Nicholas introduced himself, and *monsieur Taillibert* drew on an old envelope with his ball-point a sketch of his stadium, addressed it to Mr Nicholas Delva and signed it! I am staring at it as I write. The leaning tower that he designed is still to-day the tallest and largest leaning tower in the world. *Roger Taillibert* is to-day the architect-in-chief of *'les batiments publics pour le Gouvernement Français'*.

There is no question in my mind that the **1967** Centennial World Exhibition and the **1976** Olympics, both held in Montréal when *monsieur Jean Drapeau* was mayor of the town, plus the repatriation of the constitution in **1982,** were three fantastic events that confirmed the maturity of Canada as a nation, the first two an introduction of our country to the world. The Canadian Charter of Rights and Freedoms soon followed that same year.

Where will we live in Montréal? That was a problem. While in Sherbrooke, a friend, Dr Rodrigue Johnson, a sociologist at the *CHUS,* was always talking about Outremont, a small sophisticated town of 23.000 people just on the other side of *la Montagne de Montréal* and about *la rue Querbes* in particular: the favorite location for a place to live in the whole of Quebec and the whole world according to Rodrigue!

Many Quebec leaders lived in Outremont, Prime Ministers Robert Bourassa and Lucien Bouchard for instance, as well as many of the senior staff of *l'Université de Montréal* which is just round the corner adjoining *Outremont.* Montréal is made up of many small towns like it, each with their own Churches and organs, Town Hall, shopping streets and restaurants: many *Montréalais* chose to live in their own relatively small town, rarely leaving it except for going to work.

But for many French Canadians, Outremont is no 1.

Outremont thus became the choice for our new home, an easy decision. The town is divided into three, separated by two main roads going from east to west, *le Chemin de la Côte Ste Catherine,* on the northern edge of the hill dating back to the 18th century, and *l'Avenue Van Home,* a little further north and more recent. On the south, adjoining the famous beautiful old cemetery on *la Montagne,* live the wealthy in large houses and beautiful large gardens; in between the two, many professionals in individual houses with small gardens, and the northern third with many blocks of apartments, some with outdoor staircases, all three districts quite distinct but all three just gorgeous in their own way.

There are many small parks, beautifully kept, with nice lawns, trees, ponds and small water-falls, flower beds, some with tennis courts, two lovely municipal swimming pools. There are three shorter shopping streets with many nice small restaurants, the ones in the south quite expensive, those in the north very reasonable. There are two beautiful and large Catholic churches with beautiful organs and large wide stone steps to get there, and it seems that most people from miles around get married and attend funeral services there. A large community of Hasidic[*] Jews live in Outremont.

There is a narrow paved alley between the backs of houses for car access to back-gardens and parking. We bought a lovely quite large red-bricked frame house between the two horizontal roads on *la rue Davaar*, no 554, built before WWI just behind *l'Hotel de Ville*, itself in the middle of the town on *le Chemin de la Côte Ste Catherine*.

It had an imposing wide wooden staircase leading to the front door, a large basement with a small bedroom/bathroom and a large comfortable room for watching TV, cool throughout the summer. The ground floor had a large living room/kitchen at the back with an open fire-place lined with beautiful tiles, a large dining room and a large sitting room. There were four bedrooms and two bath-rooms on the first floor, one bedroom with had a large balcony over the back living-room. A small fenced-in garden with a picnic-table and two benches on the grass included a parking lot for two cars.

Three or four houses up the road is the Town Hall and the town Library. My University office was just a ten minute walk westward on *la Cote Ste Catherine*; *l'Hopital du Sacré-Coeur* in *Cartierville* on the north shore of the island was just twenty minutes away by car, driving north out of town in the morning thus avoiding traffic. I soon bought a second-hand bicycle and would use it when the weather and my desire and need for exercise cooperated!

It took us a while to realize that our Town Hall, one of the oldest houses in town dating back to the 1850s, had started as a place for the fur trade, manned by Scots, and that *la rue Davaar*, leading to it, was named after a very small rocky uninhabited island called Davaar Island off the west coast of Scotland. Nicholas had driven past it during his Sabbatical year in Oxford in 1993 and had sent us a post-card of the wee site. It took us a while also to realize all of the above, perhaps twenty or more years. Such 'history' is what life is all about, and, as one gets older, one's activities become restricted and one is readier to think about the past and try to reconstruct what went on. *La rue Davaar* ends at the Outremont town-hall, the old fur-exchange.

Of mainly **PAUL**, our youngest, born in Cleveland in December **1962**:

He was always such an easy child, breast-fed for over six months like the others: a first experience for our pleasant black cleaning lady, for she had never

---

[*]   Hasidism is a mystical Jewish movement founded in Poland in the 18th century to counter the rigid academism of rabbinical Judaism. It emphasizes religious enthusiasm rather than learning, and is still a force in Jerusalem, New York (OED) and Outremont.

seen a white lady breast-feed her baby. Joan was in hospital for just forty-eight hours, the cost of her care thankfully only around $300! We had no health-care insurance during our two years in the US. Paul grew up with five relaxed doting parents (two sisters and a brother included), an excellent experience for all concerned, most of all for Paul.

Apart from adjusting to a cooperative nursery school in Kingston just before his third birthday, when dear mum had to go to school with him for a while, sitting quietly nearly out of sight, waving a little when he looked around to make sure she was still there, he sailed through school, ending a second grade VI in French immersion at the end of the **1975** school year in Lennoxville. For that year, he had an excellent much-loved young teacher, *Mile Luce Turgeon.* He was very happy at his primary school.

By that time Paul loved the water, rowing a little boat in the summer at *Lac des Isles* in the Laurentians, or by the sea in Maine. He loved accompanying us for weeks-ends to Concord (MA) for instance, visiting Louise May Alcott's house where she wrote Little Women, and Fort Knox not far from Ellsworth (ME) built in 1844 when the borders between Maine and Canada were being finally being discussed. Sherbrook was near the border with the US, so it was so easy to travel south. Littleton (northern NH), was just ninety minutes away, very near the headquarters of the Appalachian Mountain Club (*vide infra*).

Paul also loved assembling and painting plastic aeroplanes, and he pushed small toy cars on the tracks, a design at the periphery of a large old red carpet in the basement, making a gentle motor noise brbrbr . . . that one could hear from upstairs. He basically did not think he should be doing this anymore, so he would stop and ask us what we wanted in a stern voice if we opened the door.

With his friend Steve Thompson next door, he spent many hours building a lovely fort in a old tree. He loved constructing 'museums' in the basement, charging one cent for admission via a ticket that he had made and that had to be officially stamped on entry at the door. His pet objects would be lined up on a table, all properly labeled. One of them would be our much loved black and white cat in a paper bag until he jumped out unexpectedly when he got fed-up with the game, much to Paul's frustration. That final year in Lennoxville, he made us a lovely Valentine card, *et une carte de Pâques.* Nicholas graduated that spring as a physician (1974).

Paul's only year at middle school in *Outremont,* grade VII **(75/76),** at the Strathcona Academy, just around the corner from our new home in Montréal, five minutes away, was a delight.

Paul then started high school for four years, at Outremont High, just six minutes away in another direction, where most other students were Greek, some of them quite rough and tough, noisy and unsophisticated. Many thought

Paul might attend a private school, such as St Georges, where he would have to go by bus. We thought it more satisfactory to meet more new Canadians and be able to come home for lunch. He made few Greek friends who all seemed to know one another and had little interest in meeting people from elsewhere. Keon, a nice Chinese boy, would frequently come home for a sandwich lunch, frequently making one himself. Paul rarely visited Keon's home. One day Keon broke his arm at school and I drove him to hospital (*Ste Justine,* just down the road) and then home. Paul and Keon totally lost touch after high school.

The fall and winter months during that first year were an exciting time. The new *Concorde* flew from Paris to the new *Mirabel* airport, 30 kms away, and it appeared most Montréalers, including us, were on site: Paul fell in love with them both. Mirabel was from then on a favorite destination. We celebrated our 25th wedding anniversary, Nicholas supplying delicious wine, a *Château-Neuf du Pape,* and Paul writing a superb menu including the various wines to be served! Ken Read, whom we had known ten years before in Kingston, won the down-hill at Val d'Isère with three other Canadians in the top ten. They became known as the mad Canucks.

Philip Delva, son of my cousin Luc, a pediatrician in Ostend, spending a high-school year in Buffalo, visited us for a week-end in **January 1976.** We did our best to give him a good time. He was a pleasant guest. We tried to instill in him that life in Canada could be quite civilized! One of my Belgian cousins had asked me quite seriously if we ever heard music by Mozart in Canada! Europeans can be so condescending about Canada, just snow, snow-shoes and *quelques arpents de neige* as Voltaire once said.

Bibi, my mother, had a hip replacement in February 1977; just before her discharge from rehabilitation, Joan flew to London at the beginning of March so that she could help care for her. While my mother was in hospital, my step-father, **Sir Alun Rowlands,** was being looked after by Wenna, a cousin of his from Wales. Sir Alun died suddenly in London on **March 1st 1977** at the age of 91; he was cremated on March 7th at the Golders Green Cemetery.

It was quite a sad affair: he had a cancer of the stomach that he kept secret; suddenly and characteristically he started vomiting blood. Wenna immediately sent for the ambulance to take him to his cherished London Hospital, but the ambulance staff felt it was too far away and drove him to the Westminster Hospital close-by; he died shortly after his arrival on a stretcher all by himself in a corridor.

So when Joan arrived two or three days later, the situation had completely changed. Wenna was a wonderful lady, but an atrocious cook, so Joan took over the cooking much to my mother's relief. Joan was very busy, seeing the family lawyer, giving six months notice to end the lease of the apartment, literally sorting things out An old friend/patient of Sir Alun, Mrs Eileen Howarth who lived in Highgate, helped find a first-class home for Bibi nearby, an old well-endowed institution, **The Working Ladies Guild,** that had started as a retirement home for working women, mostly nurses.

I met an old senior nursing sister from the London there; we talked quite a bit, and she gave me an old book about the Hospital. But there was a waiting list of ten to twelve months. So my mother, in September, rented a room at Mme Zavalani's, an Albanian royalist lady who had known King Zog (1895-1961); he had resigned when the Italians had invaded the country in 1939. My mother seemed to have been quite happy at Mme Zavalani's.

Joan, Paul and I were back for 10 days towards the end of the lease, and Joan stayed for a further two weeks that **September.** She tried to get a global price for the contents of the apartment, but the amount offered was ludicrously low, so we advertised several times in the Times and the Daily Telegraph and sold the whole lot ourselves, quite an exciting process. We raised several thousand pounds, much to our surprise. Paul spent a lot of time on that occasion exploring the London Underground Railway and the Tube, the most extensive in the world. He was absolutely fascinated by London's public transportation.

A quite extraordinary event occurred in **July 77:** the opening at McGill of the new Ernest Rutherford Physics Building in honor of Lord Rutherford of Nelson, OM, FRS, (1871-1937), Macdonald Professor of Physics, McGill University (1898-1907), by none other than Professor Norman Feather, an old student of his from 1926 onwards.

I had lived with the Feather family for two months in Barrow Road, Cambridge, in the spring, 1940; the French Lycée, had been evacuated there. I returned for the academic year 1942-43 when I was studying the basic sciences for my first MB at King's College: Queen Mary College in East London had been evacuated to King's College just round the corner from there.

> After WWII, Professor Feather, FRS and FRSE, became Professor of Natural Philosophy at Edinburgh University for the next thirty years (1945-75). He demonstrated that nuclear transmutations were produced by neutrons very shortly after Chadwick's discovery of the neutron. He then led the Cavendish group working on neutron multiplication before nuclear weapons became a reality.
>
> We met at the Four Seasons and he came home for dinner one evening, for us a memorable occasion. Professor Feather died shortly afterwards in August 1978.
>
> What I remember of him was his excellent photography with a large old-fashioned box camera on a stand with a hood with which he made wonderful pictures that each took 30 minutes to take!

Everything had to be perfect, the exposure, the pose, the light. There was nothing instantaneous about it. He also made Welch Rarebit every Sunday evening, which took hours to prepare; it was delicious but left a mound of washing-up for the rest of the family to do.

Grace Feather, his wife, was so understanding and patient. She was a RC, and saw to it that John, my brother who lived there in 1940, and I would not miss church on Sundays. She liked the fact that I practiced my violin, a good example for the twin girls, who in fact took up music later professionally in Sheffield. The older boy, Michael, about 7 or 8, could be quite naughty and would get into trouble, one morning emptying a box of thumb-tacks at the entrance of Barrow Road, thus preventing many professors arriving on time at work that morning on their bicycles.

Mrs Feather came back home very happy because her grocer had given her an extra quarter of pound of butter that her husband asked her to return immediately. I also remember the secret meetings that went on in the sitting room, with the likes of Chadwick, Oliphant and other professors that no one was allowed to mention.

He came to East Ham on one occasion for lunch, and my mother was most upset because Professor Feather went to the lavatory with his briefcase. My father and he corresponded benevolently after the war on the subject of the bomb. I developed mumps during the winter in 1943, and went home for a couple of weeks. On my return, Dr Feather had taken up smoking, much to my surprise. He had developed trouble sleeping. His doctor had advised him to sit down for fifteen minutes after each meal and smoke a maximum of five cigarettes a day.

So he had this lovely old small cigarette case in which he would religiously place his five Sobranie cigarettes every morning. To my amazement, the habit had remained identical when we met over four decades later in Montréal, using the same cigarettes in the same old solid silver case.

Old *Tante Maria*, aged 90 from Ghent, my father's sister, the eldest of eight children and last of that generation of Delvas, died on October 20th 1975. She never had children of her of her own but always treated her nine nephews and nieces with absolute fairness.

Her recently received inheritance ($23,000) paid for most of the cottage that we purchased in **1978** in St Andrews-by-the-sea at Passamaquoddy Bay just off the Bay of Fundy, three miles by water from Maine, such a beautiful small official Heritage House (the first so-named in the whole of New

Brunswick) built around 1830. The St Croix River joins the sea there. Whales arrive for their yearly holiday at the end of the summer when whale food, sprats, was plentiful and cheap.

The Bay of Fundy, with the highest tides in the whole world, 28 feet at St Andrews, was full of delicious fish, particularly haddock, lobsters and scallops, some of it caught by the local fishermen. Wee **St Croix Island** is round the corner, where Samuel de Champlain established the first year-long settlement in North America north of Florida in **1604**. The whole area is now a World Heritage Sight.

We had no intention of buying such a house. On that first visit, we were on our way to Charlottetown for a medical meeting. We arrived in St Andrews on Wednesday, saw the house on Thursday and bought it on Saturday, arriving in Charlottetown on Sunday. The children were all quite flummoxed.

The house had been restored by the St Andrews Civic Trust, their first such endeavor. Plastic siding had all been replaced. In fact, our purchase helped put the St Andrews Civic Trust on the map. The house had belonged to the same family for over a century. The Trust had purchased it and its restoration was a voluntary contribution from the citizens of St Andrews.

We soon discovered that we could spend just a couple of days in St Andrews, leaving Montréal at 5pm, arriving at 1am, a lovely drive, sometimes a last-minute decision. We crossed the Appalachian Mountain Club trail every time, whichever way we took to get there. It was a beautiful trip. You can walk along the AMC trail from Quebec to Georgia. There was comparatively little traffic on the roads in those days. There was never any waiting at the customs.

Paul would usually accompany us. He loved it. We most often crossed the whole of south-eastern Quebec, beautiful and isolated villages, *La Patrie, Notre-Dame des Bois,* entering Northern Maine at Coburn Gore. Kingfield, surrounded by woods, was the half-way mark. We soon had our favorite stops on the way, pic-nic tables, spectacular views, lakes of various sizes, crossing or driving along beautiful streams, water-falls and rivers with lovely smells, fish jumping around. On our way, we got to know all the gas pumps, small cafés, some useful shops where reasonably-priced clothing could be found. We loved the trip.

Our three eldest rarely needed help in their school-work, and Paul was no exception. We always took it for granted the four of them would well cope by themselves. We always supplied them with their own desks and chairs, and there were always lots of books around, dictionaries of all sorts. Joan and I were always looking things up in dictionaries, a habit that was transmitted automatically. Joan would read to each one of them in turn an appropriate story before bedtime, 15-20 minutes each. They looked forward to it and Joan read beautifully. At 8:30pm, everything was quiet and one could hear a pin drop. I never remember any of them crying. They always seemed to sleep like logs.

Mont St Hilaire, 414 metres high, 40 kms from Montréal, is one of the eight Monteregian Hills, including Mont Royal, that rise prominently from the floor of the St. Lawrence River Valley. It is the least disturbed by human activity and the richest in natural history, with Lac Hertel (32 hectares) at its summit surrounded be the only remaining primeval undefiled forest in the region, exceptional for its 600 or more plant species, some 400 year old trees, over 800 species of butterflies and moths, 372 types of minerals 50 of which are new to science. In 1978 it was designated as the first Canadian site in the <u>UNESCO Biosphere Reserve</u> program. **Gault's Natural Reserve,** 1000 hectares, is a park, part of the mountain, with trails, owned by McGill and open to the public, a truly exceptional place to explore. We went there several times and Paul in particular loved it.

In 1972, our book club sent us **'The Complete Walker'** by Colin Fletcher, published by Random House. I was quite taken by it, and gave it to Paul when he was about 13 or 14. He just loved it. He seemed particularly fascinated by the equipment used for long treks, what food to take that was easy to carry, how to prepare it, what mini-stove to buy, how to carry it around, which back-pack to buy, what bedding to use, clothes to wear, particularly the boots, etc . . . . With his allowance, he started to buy stuff, usually seemingly carefully planned purchases. The book was also an introduction to the **Appalachian Mountain Club (AMC)** and its trails, its headquarters near Gorham, NH, on old US route 2.

My mother **Bibi** came to stay six weeks for Christmas and the whole family flew on Quebecair from Mirabel to the Grand Bahama Hotel and Country Club, a Jack Tar resort, landing on an airstrip in the grounds of the hotel, such an easy access **(Jan 22-29, 1978)**. It was just a three-hour trip. We enjoyed the sunshine, the swimming and the sea, just lounging around. My mother, 81 years old at the time, thought the sea there was so dull: no boats or sirens, compared to the beeches in Ostend with so many ships in the Channel. But we nevertheless had a lovely time, the whole experience so new. We rented a car for one day, motoring to Freeport, the capital.

What follows is a 'sample' list of events attended during an **eight week winter period, Feb 15th to April 15th 1978.** Paul often accompanied us:

=   a talk by Conor Cruise O'Brien, Irish author and diplomat, a severe critic of the dangers of extreme nationalism.
=   *l'OSM* with James Conlon, and the mezzo-soprano Gabrielle Lavigne.

= 'Giselle', *les Grands Ballets Canadiens*, with Anton Dolin and Ludmilla Chiriaeff.

= at *'le musée des Beaux-Arts'*, an exhibition of paintings by the Belgian painter, Alfred Stevens (1823-1906).

= Royal Winnipeg Ballet, three shorter works.

= a new film with Simone Signoret *'la vie devant soi'*. She had received an Oscar for her role in 'Room at the Top'.

= Guarneri String Quartet playing Schubert, Lutoslavski and Brahms.

= *musée d'art contemporain*, a Dennis Oppenheim Exhibit, the pioneer conceptualist of land art, body art, video and sculpture art forms.

= Dietrich Fischer-Diskau with Jorg Demus at the piano, Schubert's *'Winterreise'*.

= the last concert of the year of radio-Canada at *la salle Claude Champagne (l'UdeM)* 'Lakmé', with *Louise Lebrun*.

= Debussy's *Pelleas et Mélisande à l'UdeM*.

= *au centre d'essai de l'UdeM*, a medical student production *'une fantaise hellénique' de marc-gilbert sauvageau*.

= I received a nice letter from dean Bois advising me *'de ma titularisation'*, as of June 1st 1978.

The three of us **flew into La Guardia** for a week, from **Friday March 2nd 1979 to the 9th.** We stayed in the Holiday Inn, 440 West 57th Street. We had a whale of a time:

On that **Friday afternoon,** we walked around and visited the World Trade Centre's observation deck. It's twin towers, 110 stories high, a symbol of the economic power of New York itself and of the United States, had been completed just seven years before. It was a beautiful afternoon, and one could see for miles around. How could one ever expect at the time that its life-span would be such a short thirty years, its end such a horrible tragedy.

We took the subway to Greenwich Village and had dinner at the 'Vineyard' with Susan, Caroline's best friend, and her husband Dan Leigh.

We spent most of **Saturday** at the Metropolitan Museum of Arts (MMA), principally at the Temple of Dendur, built during the 1st century BC on the banks of the Nile 600 miles south of Cairo. To avoid it being submerged permanently after the completion of the Aswan High Dam in 1960, the Temple and its gateway were dismantled and carefully rebuilt inside the Sackler Wing of the Metropolitan Museum, where the controlled environment would be beneficial for its preservation.

It was truly magnificent, and one could sit down and contemplate it, thinking of its history, for as long as one wanted.

We saw <u>Peter Ustinov</u> signing copies of his recent book at Scribners.

We viewed an exhibit at the <u>Rizzoli Gallery</u> by an extrordinary artist from Sri Lanka called <u>Tilak</u> Samarawickrema, beautiful black-ink/white paper drawings, simple curved lines, imaginary people and objects, a first in North America. We also saw a quite striking film there, <u>Andere of Sri Lanka</u>.

We went to the Kennedy Centre that evening, <u>WINGS</u> by Arthur Kopit with Constance Cummings, a wonderful play directed by John Madden.

That **Sunday,** we saw the <u>Frick Collection</u>, East 70th Street. Particularly remembered are Gainsborough's (1727-1788) 'The Hon. Frances Duncombe' and 'Mistress and Maid' by Johannes Vermeer (1632-1675). In the afternoon, at the <u>Carnegie Recital Hall</u>, chamber music, *Leopold Teraspulsky* at the cello with *Marion Gaffney,* piano, playing Schumann, Hindeminth, Brahms, plus two First New York performances of music by James Yannatos and Charles Fussell.

Paul then went to the 'Museum of Holography' while we had tea at Rumpelmyers.

On **Monday** we walked around the <u>Rockefeller Centre</u> and took a guided tour of the <u>Headquarters of the United Nations</u>. After lunch, we visited <u>The Museum of Modern Art</u>, remembering in particular Paul Cézanne's 'Still Life with Apples' and Joseph Pickett's 'Manchester Valley'. That evening, at <u>Carnegie Hall</u>, we heard an excellent recital by soprano *Grace Bumbry* accompanied by Geoffrey Parsons.

She sang one of our old favourites, Berlioz's *'Nuits d'Ete'*. After, we went to <u>The Russian Tea Room</u> (RTR) next door, an exciting place as our neighbor was none other than Grace Bumbry* herself! That is where we discovered that Peter the Great was the first monarch to invite ladies to dine at his diner table. He insisted on fashionable hair-styles, décolleté gowns, discarding veils, discouraging the 'painting' of teeth black. He loved Dutch cheeses and meats served with fruit preserves.

On **Tuesday,** we returned to the MMA and spent a lot of time admiring the <u>Treasures of Tutankhamun</u> (1334-1325 BC): amongst so many

---

*   Grace Bumbry, born in St Louis, Missouri in 1937, trained as a mezzo-soprano, made her début in Paris in 1960, then appeared in Basle, Bayreuth, Covent Garden, Salzbug, Milan, finally at the NY Met since 1966. In 1970, she also sang soprano roles. She has a beautiful and vibrant voice and a powerful dynamic personality (Concise OUP Dictionary of Opera, 1979).

objects a stopper in the form of a human head from a canopic urn used to contain different organs of an embalmed body in an ancient Egyptian burial, the Deity Netjerankh in the form of a gold snake, a beautiful wooden folding stool, a child's chair, gold jewelry—a wide hinged bracelet with a scarab (beetle). In the evening, we went to the Martin Beck Theatre, **Dracula** with Raul Julia, most enjoyable.

We might stop for meals in local brasseries, such as O'Neals' at 57st street, and Wolfe's, 57th × 6th, or the restaurant in the museums.

Wednesday was devoted mostly to visiting 'The Cloisters', a branch of the MMA devoted to the art and architecture of medieval Europe, four acres overlooking the Hudson River in northern Manhattan's Fort Tryon Park. The sophisticated building incorporates principally elements from five medieval French cloisters: gardens, medieval works of art (tapestries, stained-glass windows, column capitals), to-day 5,000 works of art from AD 800 but particularly from the 12th-15th centuries. According to a former director of *le Musée du Louvre*, The Cloisters is "the crowning achievement of American museology".

It is quite an incredible place where one could spend a few days. What we remember in particular is the *Cuxa Cloister* in the center, incorporating within its design features suggested by a small chapel in the Church of St Nazaire at Carcassonne, the tapestries, and a limestone statue of the Virgin and Child, from l'*Ile-de-France*, XIV century, of which we bought postcards.

We stopped in Lower Manhattan on our way, seeing five of the fifteen sites on the Heritage Trail: City Hall, the Woolworth building, St Paul's Chapel, Trinity Church, and Wall Street's stock exchange.

That evening, we saw the new musical, 'Annie' at the Alvin Theatre; it had won seven Tony awards. We had a drink with Susan and Dan (friends of Caroline's) at Ziegfeld's. What a day that was!

On our last full day, **Thursday,** we went window-gazing plus shopping around 5th Avenue. Paul went up the Empire State Building and further explored the railway!

In the evening, we saw the premiere of a new production by the Metropolitan Opera Company, Kennedy Centre, of Richard Wagner's *'Der Fliegender Hollander'*, a one act opera, three scenes without an intermission. It lasted two hours and twenty minutes.

James Levine was the conductor, and Jean-Pierre Ponnelle the Producer and Set Designer.

James Levine was born in 1943, becoming music director at the Met in 1975; he was considered the most gifted young American conductor at the time.

Jean-Pierre Ponnelle was born in Paris in 1932, He was "a highly gifted painter and producer whose work exhibits great originality, charm and style, though occasionally he has been tempted to overload the stage and action with too much detail" (OUP concise dictionary of opera, 1979).

This exactly describes what we saw, quite literally a wonderful performance with fantastic sets that were interestingly greatly booed and applauded at the same time, much standing, a first such experience for us! The production was created by the San Francisco Opera Association and designed to be shared with the MET.

On **Friday,** we shopped; Paul went to a rubber stamp store while Joan and I went to the Park Plaza Hotel for tea. We suddenly came across the official 'Office of Tourism' of *'le Gouvernement du Québec'*. We took the 7.20 pm plane to Montréal and were home by 9:30. New York is such an exciting, vibrant and stimulating city, just one hour by plane from Montréal!

Paul obtained *The Certificate of Graduation* from **"The Protestant School Board of Greater Montreal"** in June 1980, just a week after completing his last biology examination on the Friday the 20th; he was 17 and a half years old, one of 168 new graduates. He excelled in Arts and Crafts for which he got the annual prize.

We left at 5pm for St Andrews, and felt quite guilty dropping Paul with his back-pack off just after crossing a bridge over a small tributary of the Androscoggin River on the eastern side of Gorham. There was **this sign for the Appalachian Trail.** It was raining and dusk was fast approaching. It was Paul's first experience of that kind. But he was all gung-ho! We were sad and a little anxious leaving him. It seemed the first real separation. Joan and I had supper a few miles later by ourselves at Tatone's in Mexico, Maine. We arrived in St Andrews at 4:30am on Saturday.

We spent most of our time there steaming wallpaper off the walls, sometimes six layers of it. We still have samples of this beautiful old stuff, some of it mid-Victorian. We returned on Tuesday, July 1st, Dominion Day, to find Caroline, Nick and Di there. Paul arrived soon after. He had had a minor fall, spraining an ankle, cutting his trip short, but this did not discourage him one bit, just slowing him up a little for a short while!

Within two years, Paul became the only Canadian (with an American passport however) to be employed by the **Appalachian Montain Club** (AMC) every summer for next few years. Many Quebecers visited the area and Paul spoke French, a real asset. Paul soon really felt he belonged there, still remaining a member to this day. The AMC, the eldest nonprofit conservation and recreational organization in the US, was founded in 1876; the first trail opened in 1879. Huts were built at regular intervals where one can spend the night. **This summer, 2007,** Paul spent a night with his son Remy, nearly nine, and a twelve year old Japanese cousin, at the trail's hut closest to Mount Washington, the highest AMC hut on the highest peak (1918m) of the eastern United States.

Joan and I spent a couple of nights at the AMC headquarters in Gorham: permanent staff of Paul's age had to cook for 20-30 people every night for a couple of months, and the food was very good! If you worked at a Hut higher up in the mountains, every morning, you had to trek down the mountain with all the garbage and return with all the supplies, an 80 pound load in a back-pack each way, over steep and slippery paths. On one occasion only did Paul fall on the way up, breaking three dozen eggs. But there were fewer customers in those more distant smaller Huts with just a staff of two.

Every year, people would fall and perhaps break bones, or have hypoglycemic attacks, diabetics who had failed to judge properly the climatic conditions that prevailed, and they had to be rescued, sometimes by helicopter. Several deaths occur every year. It certainly was a life-forming experience for Paul. Much later we learnt that much pot had been smoked! He ended by driving the shuttle bus around, and distinguished himself by, for the first time, always being on time. Joan and I couldn't get over how excellent Paul's cooking had become!

Much to our surprise, **Paul decided to become an engineer,** and the two years that followed were spent in a relatively new anglophone *Collège d'Éducation Générale et Professionelle* (**CEGEP**), **Vanier College,** founded in 1970, not too far away on Decarie Boulevard near Queen Mary road. A young lady student of his own age, Malee Leeaphon, born in Thailand, in Canada since 1968, asked him whether he would be her partner in the chemistry laboratory as they had to work in pairs.

He accepted. They rapidly became good friends. After two years in CEGEP they both transferred to University, Malee to McGill in inorganic chemistry, Paul in engineering to Concordia, from September 1982 onwards.

An engineering degree is a demanding proposition, so much rote and detailed information to remember. Paul always got through exams, but usually with medium results. At Concordia, he quickly found himself a niche in the editing and publishing of the Concordia Student Journal. He just loved working at it. At the end of his first year there, he decided to switch to Journalism, with quite a strong new academic department, founded in 1975. He obtained credits from his first year in engineering, so no time had been lost.

This change, from science to journalism, was unusual, but it proved beneficial in the long run, giving Paul a definite advantage that was unexpected when the decision was made. Few journalists have an engineering background. Joan and I felt journalism was more in character with his personality and capacity.

Joan and I felt somewhat cheated for a short while: shortly after Paul was born, we had purchased an 'educational insurance' that would pay for undergraduate education. We had paid over $2,000 for it by installments over the years, and this insurance had paid for Paul's first year at Concordia. But there was a clause in the agreement precluding transfer to another field, so the insurance was cancelled. What a stupid insurance we thought: how can one guarantee what one really wants to study after high school for one's future career. However, we received what we had paid, and that was that.

> We first met Malee Leeaphon accidentally on <u>March 27th 1983, Jane's 28th birthday</u>: we were having lunch together at home with Jane and Ray Philip and the four of us decided to go and have coffee and a pastry at Stachey's, a pleasant small tea/coffee/ pastry shop: in walked Paul and Malee!

We went to Kingston, 183 miles in 2-1/2 hours that same evening with Jane; Nick and Di had invited us for a steak dinner and the annual birthday cake, probably a Victoria sponge, by then the family favorite. We were back home by 10:30pm.

> The first time Malee visited us at home was on March 31st 1983, just four days later; the first photographs we have of Malee date from May and July that same year, taken in our house in

Outremont. Malee, a lovely young lady, lived with her brother Dan, her only sib, in a small student semi-basement apartment near the western campus of Concordia (old *Loyola*), not too far from her family home in Montréal-West, a small town beyond Westmount and Côte-des-Neiges. Bibi, my mother, visited us that summer from July 15th to September 7th. She met and thought Malee was great.

Dan was finishing his studies in computer science and had recently married, his new wife the daughter of German immigrants. Thus, Malee was living alone. Paul came home one evening, asked us to sit down because he had something important to tell us: we couldn't imagine what it was: 'I want to go and live with Malee'—'is that all' we replied. So we adjusted his allowance to compensate him for his not having meals at home. Also, as he had a permanent summer job, his yearly allowance was paid in eight monthly amounts, September to April. Bibi typically failed to emit any opinion whatsoever regarding her approval or disapproval of the two of them living under one roof!

On September 16th, the six of us, three Leeaphons and three Delvas, had dinner together at home, a successful evening. It was the start of a positive relationship.

We had a lot in common. Both families were new Canadians, one from Europe in 1958 and the other from Asia in 1968, both middle class for at least a century. It was a typical and exciting Canadian situation, east and west meeting in the 'new' continent.

Both mothers had different backgrounds than the fathers, Don Leeaphon of Thai (Chinese) and Etsuko of Japanese origin, my Dad, Joseph, of Flemish (Spanish) and my mother, Lucienne (Bibi), of Walloon (French) backgrounds.

I had married Joan, from Northern Ireland. Her Dad was a Scot, and her mother from Northern Ireland since 1604, of Scottish descent before.

Don had spent two years at Duke University in North Carolina during the fifties; Canada for him was just a transition area until he could go and live there permanently. The Leeaphon seniors were soon to move to Burlington, Vermont.

We had also lived in the US for two years in Cleveland, but had returned to Canada to which we had become bonded. The two Leeaphon children remained staunch Canadians. Our oldest son, Nicholas, had married (1979) an Ontario lass, Dianne, whose middle-class family had lived there for over a century.

What a soup of genes all those relationships produced, but how typical of the times in North America.

Paul received his BA diploma on Monday. June 16th, 1986. The convocation address was given by Lise Bissonnette, a lawyer and a writer in *"Le Devoir"*, the only truly national independent daily in Canada. Paul received the Journalism Book Prize. Malee also received her BSc certificate from McGill around that time. She sent applications for a post-doctoral scholarship to twenty institutions and was accepted in nineteen of them, much to her family's surprise!

> *"Free and Independant, Le Devoir is not influenced by ideology or political party. It defends values, liberty, equality, solidarity and integrity. It has the freedom to defend ideas and causes that promote the advancement of Quebec society, politically, economically, culturally and socially"* (web-site).

Of mainly Paul and Malee, 1986-1990:

Life is so unpredictable: what would those two young twenty-three year olds do during the next five years, Malee with six years of chemistry, and Paul, with his newly acquired love for the AMC plus three years of engineering and three in journalism?

Paul was immediately offered a job as a reporter at the Montréal Gazette, with a salary of around $40,000 a year. The wonderful thing about journalism is that one can just observe what is going on in society, describe it and be paid for doing so! Many of us are doing some of that all the time without pay!

Malee wanted to be independent and to continue her studies. Her parents and male friends had suggested nursing or school-teaching, She applied for post-graduate positions to enable her to pursue a career in inorganic chemistry and obtain a PhD. Malee completed and dispatched admission formulas to twenty institutions to be accepted by nineteen of them. The University of Toronto was one, but the grant offered there was insufficient. However, much to her parents' surprise, **she was accepted with a generous grant at Purdue University, Lafayette, Indiana,** so off she went, quite independently. But she remains a Canadian citizen to this day. None of us relatively recent immigrants had ever heard of Purdue University.

---

*   *"Le Devoir"* was founded by Henri Bourassa in 1908. It's proprietor is *'L'imprimerie populaire Ltée';* the editors in turn are responsible for the control of the investment. Lise Bissonnette became editor (1990-1998). Thus, for one hundred years,

So Paul and Malee decided to live apart. But it was only for twelve months. Paul lived at home during that time. After an interesting year as a journalist at The Gazette, based in its Pointe-Claire office from where he had to cover the activities of the Council of *la Ville de St Laurent*. Bombardier's aeronautic works were based there, and the population, particularly the immigrant population, was rapidly expanding. It was just around the corner from Cartierville where I worked at *l'Hopital du Sacré-coeur*. Paul has since believed that municipal politics are ethically the worst of the three levels of government.

So, on Wednesday the 27th of July 1987, his last day at the The Gazette, Paul left for Burlington, Vermont, at 7pm. Malee was staying with her parents who had recently moved there. Both of them returned to Montréal on July 31st, and we had lunch together at the Katsura, the best Japanese restaurant in Montréal at the time, a favourite of Pierre Trudeau. On Saturday August 1st 1987 Malee and Paul drove off to Lafayette, each in their own car with all their stuff. What would Paul do there? But first, an introduction to The State of Indiana and to Purdue University:

Indiana was colonized by the French in the 18th century, ceded to Britain in 1763, passed to the US in 1783 to become the 19th state in 1816 with its capital Indianapolis. The Indy 500 miles long motor-race takes place there every year. Its most important river, the beautiful **Wabash**, 765 km long, starting in western Ohio, flows west across the State, turning south to form the border between Indiana and Illinois; it then joins the Ohio river, where the States of Indiana, Illinois and Kentucky meet.

On Christmas Eve, **1824,** 22 year-old **William Digby** purchased land on the Wabash River on the banks of which lived a loose confederacy of nomadic Wabash Indians, linguistically Algonquins. At that point, 100 Kms or so north-west of the capital, the river banks were low so that supplies could be easily loaded and unloaded. He platted a town on the grid system with a public square and resold it within the next six months making an $8 profit. The new town, built on the east bank, was named **Lafayette** in **1826.**

Marie Joseph Paul Yves Roch Gilbert du Motier, Marquis de La Fayette was born on **Sept 6th 1757,** orphaned at the age of 13 and left a princely fortune. At 16 he married Marie Adrienne Françoise de Noailles, of the highest nobility. He then joined the Cavalry, becoming a Captain of the Dragoons.

He remained a royalist all his life, but promoted the idea of a King and Queen with less centralized power. He was never thrilled by the Revolution or by Napoleon. He was enthralled by the American War of Independence, and promised his help, landing near Georgetown on his way to Philadelphia. He could not speak a word of English. On July 31st 1777, at the age of nineteen he became a major-general in the US Army. On August 1st he met George Washington who became a life-long friend. He returned home on Jan 11th 1779 for a short period; he was promoted Colonel. Back in the US he continued to participate in battles, terminating his military career in the US after the battle of Yorktown on **October 19th 1781;** he was then 24.

Le Marquis de La Fayette returned to the US forty three years later, from **July 1824 to September 1825** and was overwhelmed with popular applause. He was offered $200,000 and a township of land. He died in 1834.

Lafayette, Indiana, was so named within one year of *le Marquis de La Fayette* returning to France.

In **1860, <u>Abe Lincoln</u>** was elected President and the **South seceded:** the Northern States started to pass laws previously spurned by the South to encourage economic growth and expansion towards the west, such as the railroads. In **1862,** Congress passed two fundamental measures:

<u>**The Homestead Act**</u> allowing any citizen to receive 160 acres of public land and purchase it later at a nominal fee after living there for five years.

<u>**The Morrill Act**</u> making it possible for new western states to establish Colleges for Teaching agriculture and mechanics: over **70 "land grant"** colleges were established. But only in 1890 were the land grant provisions extended to the sixteen southern states. Justin Morrill was a Congressman from Vermont.

In **1865,** the **Indiana State Assembly** started to make plans to establish such an Institution. It received gifts in support of the project, $150,000 from **<u>John Purdue</u>,** a local Lafayette business leader, $50,000 from Tippecanoe county and 150 acres of land from Lafayette residents.

On <u>May 6th 1869</u> it was decided the college would be built near Lafayette; it would be called **Purdue University**. It opened on <u>September 16th 1874</u> on the west bank of the Wabash, in West Lafayette. The first degree, a BSc in chemistry, was issued in 1875, and the first female students were admitted that fall.

Historically, its main strengths are the two original colleges of agriculture (twelve departments) and engineering (nine schools and three departments); more recently, it has expanded in many other areas, the whole university now organized in eight colleges and fourteen schools, with over 39,000 undergraduate and 8,000 postgraduate students.

Its **aviation school,** ranked <u>first in the nation</u>, was the first of its kind in the country: twenty two American astronauts are graduates, including Neil Armstrong, the first person to walk on the moon.

> **Amelia Earhart,** (b 1898) served as 'Advisor on Careers for Women' from 1935 until she disappeared in 1937.

Purdue now enrolls the <u>largest international student population</u> of any US public university. **The College of Science** has seven departments, Biological Sciences, Chemistry, Computer Science, Earth and Atmospheric Sciences, Mathematics, Physics and Statistics. Malee's Chemistry department now ranks 22nd in the US.

Professor Henri T Yang, Dean of the **College of Engineering at Purdue** from 1984-1894, is a very impressive person. He obtained a BS degree in Civil Engineering at the National Taiwan University in **1962.** He then attended **Cornell University,** Ithaca, NY, the youngest of the eight Ivy League[*] Universities founded in 1865. He was granted a doctorate degree in Structural Engineering, as well as honorary doctorates from Purdue University, Hong-Kong University of Science and Technology and National Taiwan University.

He might have arrived at Purdue in **1973 or 1974,** because, in **1975,** he received his first 'academic' award there that I can ascertain, as an "Outstanding Teacher of the Purdue University School of Aeronautics and Astronautics". He soon held a professorship in the Department of Mechanical Engineering and subsequently the Neil A. Armstrong Distinguished Professorship of Aeronautical and Astronautical Engineering. Many awards followed.

In **1994,** Professor Yang became the fifth chancellor of the **University of California, Santa Barbara** (USCB). He is still there to-day (2007). Five recent Nobel Prize Winners are amongst the teaching staff. Professor Yang still teaches undergraduates and guides PhD students. With his wife Dilling,

---

[*] 'Ivy League' a term that applies to eight old universities with common interests in scholarship and athletics: Brown, Columbia, Cornell, Dartmouth College, Harvard, Pennsylvania, Princeton and Yale. The three 'seniors' are Harvard, Princeton and Yale.

he spends a lot of spare time on voluntary activities. They were both named honorary alumni of UCSB in 2001.

An unforseenable serendipitous occurrence: guess who gets an interesting job!

Professor Yang at that very moment wanted someone who could help him with editing the revamped engineering journal of the College, and at the same time help him improve his own working knowledge of the spoken and written English language. So he searched for a person who, in addition to editing the journal, would understand the difficulties an East-Asian-born person might have with the written and spoken English language.

Paul was good at that, with Malee's help, her parents, immigrants from East Asia (Thailand), who had had identical problems. His sister Caroline was an experienced TESL teacher with whom he had always been very close. He had his own experiences as a qualified experienced journalist in Montréal with three years' study in engineering at the CEGEP and University levels. Joan, his Mum, was also interested in TESL, later getting a university certificate in the subject from Concordia. Paul was offered the position within a few weeks of his arrival although he was the last of over twenty applicants for the job. By chance, he had landed on his feet at Purdue.

Paul edited the spring magazine of the Purdue University Schools of Engineering, **'EXTRAPOLATIONS'** (Vol 15, no 2, Spring 1988, twelve pages). It combined two pre-existing magazines, 'Extrapo' (six pages) & 'Extrapo Extra'. It was well produced, attractive to look at, beautifully illustrated and easy to understand. In that first number, Dean Yang wrote:

Building on Strength.

"This is an exciting time for the Schools of Engineering. Our Mechanical, Aeronautical and Astronautical, Chemical and Civil Engineering schools have in recent years celebrated their 100th, 40th, 75th, and 100th anniversaries (in 1982, 1985, 1986, and 1987, respectively). Electric Engineering marks its centennial this year . . .".

The names of the editor, Paul Delva, and of the designer, Dallas Pasco, are inscribed in a box on the back page, as well as its publisher, the Office of the Dean of the College of Engineering.

Paul was able to study for two years on a part-time basis enabling him to obtain an MSc from the Department of Communication, the College of Liberal Arts, Purdue University. This was his first US University degree. He got a lot of support from his new boss. Although Paul never talks about it, they developed a good relationship.

Malee obtained her PhD in the spring, 1990. They both moved to Allentown, Pennsylvania, where Malee had been offered a research position at 'Air Products & Chemicals, Inc', an international corporation whose principal business is selling gases and chemicals for industrial use. It provides amongst so many other things liquid hydrogen and liquid oxygen for the Space Shuttle External Tank.

Its revenue in 2006 was nearly 10 billion, and its net income over 800 million. It has 20,000 employees world-wide. Malee, a highly principled lady, worked very hard, earning for the firm several important copyrights.

More recently,

Paul subsequently worked for a while for **Crayola** in Easton, not too far away. He then became a **law student at Temple University** in Philadelphia, travelling every day from Allentown by car. We all went to his graduation on May 16th 1993.

Paul then trained as a **corporate lawyer for Dechert LLP in Philadelphia.**

Remy was born on September 24th 1998, shortly before Paul had joined **Fairchild Semiconductor in Portland, Maine,** as their first lawyer in 2000. He is now Senior Vice-President General Counsel and Corporate Secretary. Malee is a full-time housewife. They live in Cape Elizabeth, as do her parents.

Chapter 49

1: Of mainly the Children's Birth and of Jane, our Youngest Daughter.

Of Delivering Babies:

Delivering babies, particularly in the patient's home, and having one's own children are quite different experiences:

I had the best experiences possible in <u>learning</u> about it all. Miss Dear was my heroine teacher, the senior midwife at The London Hospital, with a special medal given to her for delivering over 4,000 babies, a record, during WW1.

She was my mentor in 1947 for my first month when I was attached to **the 'District',** and I would accompany her towards the end of her career, carrying her bag, walking to the patient's home, day or night, usually within a half mile of the hospital. Some of those streets were not safe for new-comers. She wore her dark-green uniform that the people in the street would recognize, much affectionate smiling on both sides, quite an experience and by far the most memorable of my student career.

Allan Brews (Bonzo) was head of department, a well-known and experienced senior person, whose father had been a colleague general practitioner of my Dad: Dad had insisted in attending his funeral in East Ham three months or so before he himself died. Bonzo's textbook on Obstetrics was the classic of his time.

When he was confronted with a problem in the delivery room, he would turn around and ask for Miss Dear's advice before proceeding: 'where is Miss

Dear?' She was often there and would invariably follow-up on the request, 'thank you Miss Dear, I thought so, thank you'.

Bonzo had one big fault, that of calling all his pregnant patients 'mother'. He never bothered remembering names. He looked after Joan when Caroline was on her way and Joan felt this was dreadful but she never felt any discomfort when she was examined: this was unusual.

How lucky I was to have been exposed to home deliveries by midwives: they were all qualified nurses (3 years) plus another three to become midwives, infinitely better trained than general practitioners who had just to complete 12 or so deliveries 'under supervision' during a regular two months' obstetric rotation. Miss Dear was *la crème de la crème* who loved teaching, mostly by example.

Miss Dear died shortly after of a cancer.

On arrival in the patient's house, we would be welcomed simply and lovingly. Miss Dear and her patient were well acquainted and would soon have a cup of boiling hot tea. Only the second, third and fourth pregnancies were allowed to be born at home, the whole experience a well-tuned operation. Miss Dear, calm and serene, was never in a rush. We would stay until everything was over, cleaned-up and tidy, seven or eight hours sometimes more. Time was never a consideration. Calm and patience was of the essence. Midwives might deliver on average fifty babies at home a year. It was not a high volume operation.

The homes themselves varied. It could be in Jubilee Buildings, a beautiful enormous red-brick complex of small apartments with enormous open but covered corridors and wide staircases built to commemorate Queen Victoria's Jubilee in 1897 by some millionaire American/Scot, or a small old store with a small apartment on the first floor, or a new prefabricated small cheap temporary house dumped on a bomb site after the war without any sound-proofing.

An example of what actually happened of the second kind was the young Jewish baker with small living quarters over the small shop, who celebrated by opening a small cupboard and offering, as we were leaving, a choice of delicious French *digestifs/liqueurs* to all participants; of the third, a husband who played the trombone in a well-known West-End band and practiced his profession during the whole time we were there, thus insulating himself from the proceedings. I was shocked but dear Miss Dear never batted an eye-lid. The noise was quite deafening. He played beautifully. That was my only ever exposure to a two-hour solo trombone concert, let alone while assisting at his baby's birth.

My second month followed immediately. **The Forest Gate Maternity Hospital,** a West Ham municipal hospital, was a couple of miles away from our house in East Ham, a short bus drive. This was a pleasant break in the routine. Four thousand babies were born there every year, an average of eleven every day. Bertie England was in charge, a devoted middle aged obstetrician who lived on the premises with his family. He was assisted by a wonderful younger lady, a physician, who also lived in, and four or five experienced midwives who lived out and worked on shifts. The medical personnel acted as consultants for the midwives. The midwives did all the routine deliveries. It was a very efficient operation with a relatively small staff. That was where Jane, our second daughter, was born in 1954.

Unfortunately, one never seemed to have eleven babies born each day: sometimes, on an eight-hour shift, one might have ten deliveries, and the midwife on duty and I would have to cope, trying to avoid if possible calling for help from the next midwife on call. I remember one such night, one rushed from one bed to another, to delivering a baby immediately followed by a placenta (after-birth) being delivered by another lady, not having quite enough cribs immediately available, putting two babies in one crib temporarily, all at 3am. I well understood the ease of making name-labeling mistakes. I delivered sixty babies that month single-handedly and felt pretty good about the whole affair.

I was very happy there, so much more informal than at the London itself.

My dear father, during his 'best' years during the mid-thirties, delivered over three hundred babies (charging 5 GBPs each) a year. Dad's secret was that, on that day, he would do house-calls in the immediate vicinity, thus returning quite frequently to keep an eye on the progress of the confinement. He had the help of retired midwives.

His large six-cylinder Renault car, black with large racing-green mud-guards cost 450 GBPs, the nicest I can remember as a child. A small two-door car (Austin/Ford) would cost 100 GBPs, a small row-house maybe 350 GBPs. I had a patient, a middle-aged humpbacked Welchman (from tuberculosis) with 2,000 GPBs in his savings account: I liked him very much; he was a small builder and bought about eighty bombed-out houses in East Ham during the war, 25 GBPs each. They were all rebuilt by the State after WWII, and then all he had to do for a living was to collect rents. He helped me such a lot on many occasions.

I did just a few deliveries myself **after I succeeded him in 1949;** I would answer calls from midwives, should some procedure be needed, mostly for stitching small tears of the perineum.

I remember vividly being asked by a midwife to help look after unexpected twins born at home whose birth weight was just below three pounds each; she was keen on looking after them at home; I was quite apprehensive, but the midwife thought nothing of it. I learnt a lot from her: to keep the place damp, two clothes-horses borrowed from neighbors with continuously damp cloth diapers hanging round the two cribs. It was winter and the coal fire in the grate had to be kept alight day and night. My hands had never been so clean! It worked like a charm much to my relief! The neighbors were so helpful.

On a second such occasion, the unexpected second twin was housed in a chest drawer on the floor: he had the sniffles and I examined him in his drawer on the floor. As I stood up, I developed this acute pain in my back, for which I treated myself with large doses of aspirin. Within forty-eight hours, I developed an acute intestinal hemorrhage and was admitted to the London for 8 days. I received six units of blood. The Queen's physician, Sir Horace, later Lord Evans, was on duty, and, believe it or not, felt my tummy with his Royal Hands! I felt quite honored! That painful episode in 1956 was a leading and final prod for the Delva family to permanently leave East Ham.

On another occasion, a senior neighboring physician who did quite a lot of home deliveries had a problem with a patient about to deliver and needed to use instruments (forceps) to help deliver the baby; he asked for my help in giving an anesthetic. I was quite horrified by the open coal-fire in the grate, and very carefully gave some ether. It worked like a charm but I had been quite apprehensive.

In **Glen Margaret, Nova Scotia,** I had a painful experience, my only delivery in North America. A very fit and intelligent older newly-wed pregnant teenager, a Christian Scientist, wanted my help. This was early on in her first pregnancy. She refused medical 'interventions' of any kind, drugs and instruments. I thought her risks of developing complications were quite minimal, so we planned together the birth at the Grace Maternity Hospital, Dalhousie University, in Halifax. She came to see me regularly at my office/ surgery in Glen Margaret for instruction and prenatal examinations.

I gave her simple pamphlets/books to read about natural childbirth (Grantley Dick Read, the authority at the time) and she devoured them. I instructed her on the course we would follow during the pregnancy itself, push and pant/relax when told and we practiced it. She was the best patient I had ever had, and the one I prepared the most thoroughly for the experience.

What happened at the Grace Maternity Hospital was a disaster in medical ethics and public relations. There were two English-trained midwives on the scene, plus the senior male resident in Obstetrics, the first two whispering in my ears reassuring comments, and the resident issuing threats in a loud whisper about the need for an episiotomy (cutting of the perineum) with scissors, ('my God, she is going to tear'), which, much to my horror, was done routinely in the whole province.

The British midwives at Dalhousie were only allowed to deal with deliveries when there was no MD present, the doctor otherwise occupied to attend on time. I felt so sorry for those fully trained midwives who were unable to follow their careers in their new country. Some of them, usually single, did excellent work in the Canadian Far North where no doctors were available.

The local textbook on obstetrics, written by Dr Attlee, ex-Head of Department, read throughout the Maritimes, strongly recommended routine episiotomy.

A beautiful baby was born without problems of any kind. The new Mum had a tiny tear that needed just one little stitch. But I was shattered, and unwilling to go through such an experience again. Had I stayed, I would have concentrated on doing home deliveries for the second, third and fourth pregnancies. I went to see one of the senior obstetricians shortly afterwards to talk about the plan, but Joan and I soon decided to improve our education and would be leaving the practice, so my plan was never put into effect.

As to my own four children, their birth was not so simple!

Nicholas was born in the British Military Hospital (BMH), Wuppertal, Germany, on December 13th 1951. He had arrived in Germany just three weeks before in Joan's tummy, an exception having been made to the rule that pregnant ladies were not allowed to travel by air during their last month of pregnancy. She was not exactly welcomed on board that plane, a British Airways Dakota III that had to circulate around Dusseldorf for an hour before landing because the sky had too many planes expecting to land.

Joan had a large private room in the BMH with a lovely view. The Royal Army Medical Corps obstetrician, a Regular Army Major in Wuppertal, felt Joan was getting tired and applied forceps under anesthesia at the last minute to help deliver Nicholas's large head. Otherwise, things proceeded like clock-work. Joan was home after a couple of weeks, the normal schedule at the time. I could drink my usual stout during my visits, as was usual throughout Britain for encouraging breast feeding, a much loved routine especially for fathers throughout the UK.

Miss Domagk was the technician at the BMH Wuppertal who took samples of Joan's blood for the usual tests. Her brother Gerhard had discovered sulphonamides in 1935 in that same hospital, a discovery that my Father praised so much: as far as he was concerned, there were two fourteen year periods during his medical life in the UK, pre-and post-Domagk. Gerhard Domagk (1895-1964) had been offered the **Nobel Prize in Physiology and Medicine in 1939,** had refused it at Hitler's request, finally accepting it after WWII.

Wuppertal was a wonderful industrial city of half a million people with a suspended tram going through it. People were at first unwilling to use such seemingly dangerous locomotion, so to show how strong it was, the authorities placed an elephant in the cabin and the elephant got scared creating havoc, breaking up the floor! It reminded me of Prince Edward, the son of Queen Victoria who succeeded her as King Edward VII, having a dinner party in the first tunnel under the Thames to encourage people to trust its construction and travel through it. That same tunnel was used by the new underground railway many years later.

Caroline was born at the London Hospital, Joan arriving there in the early hours of the morning of January the 3rd 1954. After a thorough examination, it was decided that the cervix of the uterus was not yet dilating, the second stage of labor having not yet started. So Joan went to sleep, waking up suddenly two hours later with Caroline nearly born. She had had a silent second stage. A short harmless chaos followed while the staff including midwives in training and medical students all rapidly appeared on the scene. Miss Dear would not have approved!

The SRA (senior resident *accoucheur*) on duty that night was John Bury, an old friend who had started medicine at the same time as I did in Cambridge in September 1942. John subsequently immigrated to Saskatoon and we still correspond and have met a few times in Canada, the last time in August 2009 just six weeks ago. He became a staunch member of the NDP.

On hearing of Caroline's death in 2004, John claimed she was the first of his deliveries whom he had been told had died. His father was a chemist who taught us all inorganic chemistry that first year in Cambridge (1942-43). He had a strong Scottish accent that took me three months to understand. Thus, I failed my first Christmas exam (3%!) and I went to a cram school during the Xmas vacation: got 73% the second time. Major Bury had become an army officer during WWI. His comment after that first exam was that such students should be in the army!

Joan unfortunately developed a breast abscess and was re-admitted for a few days. It was quite a troublesome period for she continued to breast-feed dear Caroline, weighing her before and after breast-feeds giving supplementary bottled milk as needed.

So Caroline was a Cockney, born within the sound of Bow Bells. She entered our world precipitously; her life was full of unforeseeable events; she died suddenly of Acute Progressive Multiple Sclerosis within a year at the age of 52. Her epitaph, 'Live, Laugh, Love', describes her well.

Jane, was the only one born with the help of a midwife on March 23rd 1955: there were no problems whatsoever at the Forest Gate Maternity Hospital, the West Ham Municipal Hospital, with our old friend Bertie England and his efficient team. She was such a contented child, playing for hours with her hands and fingers, never crying. There is much more about her below.

Paul was born in Cleveland, Ohio, on December 3rd 1962, at Western Reserve University's Maternity Hospital, built during the nineteen-twenties. It was an entirely new experience for Joan and me on a new continent. Choosing a physician is not so easy a task when you are yourself an uninsured student/physician on a limited budget, and I felt deprived by the total absence of Stout given routinely to new Mums in the UK for decades to supposedly encourage lactation.

We asked a well-known and well-liked obstetrician for help, but as soon as he realized we lived on a scholarship he referred us to a University paid physician, EJ Quilligan, an excellent and approachable full-time associate professor, who was later appointed Head of Department in an important University of California Teaching Hospital.

Then there was the transportation question. My landlord, who lived in the duplex next-door, insisted I drive Joan to hospital, a mere mile away, in his own large bath-tub car as he felt our little two-door Morris Minor, the only one in Cleveland, was too small and dangerous for the task, particularly in December.

Then there was the problem of timing: one had to pay the hospital by the number of 24 hour periods starting at midnight. So, we arrived at the hospital at five minutes past midnight Joan having started having pains around 10pm.

Dr Quilligan couldn't have been more efficient: he stayed at Joan's bedside all night with his hand on her tummy: Paul's head had not engaged in the pelvis as it normally should have, suggesting the possibility of a low placenta that might cause a severe hemorrhage as the cervix dilated; I remembered Miss Dear and her patience. Dr Quilligan reminded me of her. But everything turned out to be perfectly normal. Finally, Dr Quilligan allowed Joan to leave the hospital within three calendar days, so the total hospital cost was only $179.85. I still have the receipt. This had to be paid on discharge. We were very lucky: a physician friend had a child born prematurely, and his debt on returning to Canada was over $10,000.

Dr Quilligan did not charge us a penny. Joan and I gave him a lovely mantle-clock, which was the nicest object in the whole house according to Dr Quilligan's daughter who was in the same class at school as Jane. We had bought it at Higbee's, a beautiful prominent large Cleveland store down-town.

A very nice black lady helped us a lot during the next two weeks; she was quite amazed that Joan breast-fed Paul: she had never seen a white mum breast-feeding her child. The nurses at the hospital were of little help in this field. Our four children had all been breast-fed for at least six months.

More of Jane, our third child and our youngest daughter:

Jane weighed 8 lbs. at birth on **March 22ⁿᵈ, 1955** and doubled it at five months (six months is the norm). She smiled at 5 weeks, was on three feeds a day at 15 weeks being breast fed for six months. She never ever cried and loved playing with her fingers. Joan kept such marvelous notes. Jane was christened on Sunday, September 11th 1955. Pop and Granny were there, and Joan looked positively gorgeous.

My old school friend, Andre Roberti, made his final vows as a Jesuit Priest that same day in Leuven (Louvain) in Belgium. Erika Kloock, our maid when Nicholas was born in Germany had her first child called Petra that month, and Patricia Clayton had her third child, Julian.

Patricia's husband Trevor (Gus) had introduced us to each other on April Fools 'day, Saturday April 1st 1950, the evening of the Oxford/Cambridge boat race ball at the Dorchester Hotel.

Patricia and Trevor had met in Oxford during the post-war period: they both rowed, Patricia, short and light, a coxswain. Trevor had a fantastic collection of Newfoundland stamps (amongst the most expensive in the world). He hated his job in London and finally decided to join the Colonial Service as a District Officer in what is now Malawi, a very damp place where the lovely stamps promptly congealed to the paper to which they were lightly attached with light hinges, a disastrous occurrence. That was a tough period. Patricia had a tough time there.

Jane's First Lovely Interlude, Devonshire, June 1956, One year old:

Our only month-long family holiday ever in Britain was in Exmouth, 12,000 people, in June 1956, 120 miles away. It is an old holiday town on the river Exe twelve miles south of the county town, Exeter. We spent the whole month there. Joan and I had reconnoitered the place nine months before; "Maer Cross", an old Victorian house with quite a large garden close to a long and wide sandy beach was booked on the spot; Mrs Lanyon promised to help us out with house-keeping. She was an older efficient lady with an admitted 'passion for sherry'.

It was Jane's first holiday and our last long one for thirteen years. There were pony rides, lovely walks, small fairs with roundabouts, a children's railway, a Punch and Judy show, plus lots of rides in our car: we visited the small seaside towns around, Topsham, half-way to Exeter, Budleigh Salterton on Lyme Bay at the mouth of the River Otter, a beautiful spot between two hills, and Sidmouth a few miles further east, also between two hills. It rained a lot during that month.

One afternoon, we visited the headquarters of the National Health Service in the Shire Town, Exeter, to find out whether it would be possible to move there to work as a general practitioner: there were no vacancies at all anywhere in Devonshire! And none seemed likely in the near future.

> Exeter is such a beautiful City with its Norman Cathedral (1107-1136, completed in 1206). The town dates back to Athelstan (c895-939), grandson of Alfred the Great (849-899) and son of Edward the Elder (c870-924) whom he succeeded as King of Wessex and Murcia. We drove around, staying just a couple of hours.

Jane, eternally happy, seemed to take a lot in during her first real holiday. It really was a lovely family affair. Little did we realize that two years later we would just be arriving at the seaside in St Margaret's Bay, Nova Scotia, where we lived for exactly two years.

Jane's Second Lovely Interlude, Tunbridge Wells, Kent, 2-3 years old:

From January 1st 1957 until the spring 1958 when we emigrated, we lived in Royal Tunbridge Wells, a beautiful old spa town founded in the 1630s after the discovery of iron-rich springs; it was patronized by royalty; it had many beautiful green spaces. During the later period there, Caroline and Jane both attended a nursery school in a beautiful house a stone's throw from our house, a happy experience for both. Joan and I had decided to leave East Ham first, subsequently deciding where we would go from there.

Tunbridge Wells was a happy interim period: we had rented a ground floor of a Victorian corner house, the top floor rented by a 40 year old or so post-office worker and his little dog, and the first floor by a Russian émigré, a classical pianist, over 70 years old with bad cataracts: he played his beautifully tuned Bechstein Grand Piano (1916, the vintage year apparently) so perfectly, perhaps 2-3 hours a day! It really was lovely, and the music was always welcomed. His first wife was related to Prince Ioussoupov who had assassinated Rasputin on December 1st 1916. Our land-lord was a famous Kent cricketer, Frank Woolley (1887-1978).

Widowed, he had recently remarried a delightful young very fair lady, a student; Vladimir, also fair-haired, was about eight months old, sitting happily in his pram in the garden: such an incongruous and happy three-storey household of nine people was a joy to behold. Vladimir was loved by everybody. We all got on like a house on fire. The plaster ceiling below the piano actually fell down within a year of our departure. The pianist's sister owned the ballet-school on the other side of the road; Dr de Briger worked there as the pianist in residence.

We visited them one evening and were introduced to vodka, consuming a half-bottle in about 30minutes. Dr de Briger had trained as a physician in Tsarist Russia and had been examined by Dr Pavlov for his finals: Pavlov (1849-1936) was always very polite, and told his failing candidates that he would happily see them again in six months' time. He had become director of the Institute of Experimental Medicine in St Petersburg in 1913 after being awarded the Nobel Prize for Physiology or Medicine on 1904. Unfortunately Dr de Briger's medical degree was not valid elsewhere in Europe, and that is why he changed professions. His ancestors were engineers who came from Germany to build the new fleet of Peter the Great in St Petersburg.

Pop and Granny, Joan's parents, had moved to Tunbridge Wells a year or so before; we lived half a mile away, the only time of our lives that this was so. They were both so good to us. Pop drove Nicholas to school and back without ever missing a day for the whole time we were there. We shared many short trips and meals.

During that Tunbridge Wells period we would frequently drive to the coast for a few hours, Eastbourne usually, most often with one or two of the children living close-by: just on hearing we were going for such a drive, little Richard Mc Neff would immediately say 'I am going to ask me mum'!

Jane's Third Lovely Interlude, Nova Scotia, June 1958-June 1960, 3-5 Years old:

That was our first two years in Glen Margaret, St Margaret's Bay, Nova Scotia, Canada, a small village with a post office. We had just one of a few telephones with a single line: French Village 8 was its number. The local counselor, an arch conservative who distributed real Scotch at election time two months after we got there, owned the telephone exchange and his two daughters ran it! In addition to knowing where I was at all times, he knew exactly what was happening in his constituency.

For the many preschool children around it was paradise: little traffic on the only newly-paved road just outside our Cape Cod cottage on half an acre by the sea, no fences between houses, small swings just about everywhere, all bought from Sears, the most beautiful bays and gentle hills just beyond the road with spectacular views. Jane was then three years old.

There were no constraints of any kind for the children in one of the most perfect places in the world at that particular time of their lives.

Jane at School: 1960-61, Kindergarten at the Convent of the Sacred Heart, Halifax, Nova Scotia, 5 years old:

We had a problem that year because Joan and I were both working full-time, Joan as a teacher and myself as a pediatric resident. Caroline was of school age but Jane needed kindergarten for just a few hours a day. We both left home in Halifax at 8am and Joan returned at five. So we asked the nuns whether it would be possible for the girls to arrive at 8.30am and stay until Joan could collect them after Joan had finished teaching. They immediately accepted. Jane and Caroline would stay for *gouter* as they really called it.

The Nuns at the Convent soon realized our Belgian connection, immediately mentioning that their Order in Canada had been directed for many years by a Belgian nun who had eventually become Head, Reverend Mother Minette de Tillesse. She was a tremendous administrator.

My grand-mother on my mother's side, Gabrielle Cambier, (1873-1951), was the eldest of three sisters. The second sister, Lawrence, had married Alphonse de Hauleville. They had six children, the eldest of which, Melusine, had married Charles Minette de Tillesse, one of the Reverend Mother's nephews. As they put it, the Halifax Nuns were pleased to accept two young students who were members of <u>their</u> family.

At that time in Belgium many middle class families had several children; one of them, boy &/or girl, so often joined a religious order, a boy the armed forces, law school or joined the family business. Medicine was not an acceptable profession, my father becoming the first doctor in his family much to everybody's surprise and disappointment. He had questionable family support. They never understood what medicine was really all about: the first thing they thought of was venereal diseases and prostitutes.

Jane was happy at the convent. She loved wearing her blue uniform and was forced to look up to see the faces of so many of the students; she loved the ribbons and the colored sashes some of them wore: this is was what she remembers most of her first year at nursery-school.

Jane at School: grades 1&2, 1961-63, Cleveland Heights Elementary School, Cleveland Heights, Ohio, USA.

During that summer I had accepted to be medical officer for a Jewish Holiday Camp on Lake Pembina in the Laurentians, two-thirds of the way to Cleveland. The children would participate in all the activities of the camp;

Joan and I kept away from them as much as possible so that the campers would not feel our children were favored. I was paid $1,000 a month for board and lodgings for the whole family, plus free camping for the three children.

It was our introduction to the Jewish way of life; some of the senior staff there had gone through horrible experiences during WWII. We were asked to return the next summer; we accepted but just for one month. It was a good deal for both parties. The three children did not particularly enjoy the experience: a holiday is a holiday without constraints, and they found the experience too constraining, particularly their lack of contact with their parents who they saw so often but with whom they could not talk.

Joan and I decided that Joan should take the bus and go to Cleveland; she would meet with Dr Steinberg's office for help to find a house for rent near the best school in Cleveland Heights, as close as possible to the University. She would spend the first and last night with her old University friend and brides'maid, Joyce Atkins-Manners, who had married in Toronto and moved to Syracuse with her two children: her husband, an engineer, was working there for General Motors. In Cleveland Joan stayed at the YMCA; the cost of the trip was minimal. It all worked like a charm.

Our 1920s' semi-detached house (half a duplex) had belonged to a recently widowed older man who did not want to live there after the death of his much-loved wife, not did he want to have anything to do with the old furniture: we purchased it all for just $200, all good solid stuff if somewhat old: we were very lucky. Our new neighbor, married with two children, had bought the whole duplex at 2397 Woodmere Drive, Cleveland Heights; so he was our landlord.

All three children took to their new schools as ducks to water: the three loved their teachers. For us, the **Roxborough Elementary School,** just round the corner, was ideal for each of our children at such an important stage of their lives. The classes were small, for Jane just 20 students in grade 1.

The only thing that bothered them, particularly Caroline, was declaring allegiance to the 'Stars and Stripes' every morning. Most Americans thought that we would not return to Canada and many Canadians did not; thus, creating allegiance was the objective of that exercise.

The three children claimed they actually learnt things there, doing their home-work without ever being asked to do it. They worked quite hard, we thought, and they never complained, actually enjoying it. We never once had to tell them to go and do their home-work.

Miss Mannino, during the first year, said this, Miss Mannino said that: the continuous phrase. Jane loved her teachers. **Mrs Miller** during the second year taught her how to write: 'molasses shoe-fly pie' she remembers. She also spent some time in the corner one day. In the class weekly newspaper, known as the *"207 Press"* and published in Grade II, Jane wrote under the heading 'Comings and Goings':

> 'We got a new baby brother on Wednesday December 5th, 1962, *His name is Paul. He is a cute baby brother. He cannot do anything but cry, eat, sleep and play a little downstairs. He can even smile a little. In the summer, we can take him out in his pram and he will be able to say 'Good-bye'.*

One of Jane's friends at school was called, she thought, Anna Fussi. It took us a while to realize that the name was really Anne Ephrussi. Her father was **Boris Ephrussi,** *(Moscow 1901—Gif-sur-Yvette, France, 1979)*, a famous Russian born French Geneticist and a colleague of Jerome Lejeune (1926-1994) in Paris who had discovered that Down's syndrome was caused by the trisomy of chromosome no 21.

Dr Ephrussi had obtained a large grant at WRU to enable him and Dr Harriet Ephrussi-Taylor, an American scientist born in England, to further their studies centering on extra-chromosomal cellular inheritance. They headed a new Developmental Biology Centre at WRU, lived in a lovely large house close by. Joan and I were invited for an aperitif before our evening meal, with a Martini-Rossi, a first for us in North America, and a lovely experience. Little Anna is now a senior scientist at the European Molecular Biology Laboratory in Heidelberg.

Another friend of Jane's was Anne Schneiderman who became a neurobiologist. She subsequently became a lawyer specializing in Patent Law, her own law-firm based in Syracuse, New York.

Her father, Howard, was Head of the Department of Biology at WRU, my ultimate boss in Cleveland, living just around the corner. He was a brilliant scientist, teacher, administrator, and world expert on insect biology. He left Cleveland to become chief scientist and senior vice-president for research and development at the Monsanto Corporation in California. Born in 1927, three years after me, **Howard Schneiderman** died of leukemia in 1990.

Howard Schneiderman was a **"mensch"**, "a person having admirable characteristics, such as fortitude and firmness of purpose," a Yiddish expression that pays tribute to his personality.

I met these teachers at the meetings of the Biology Department and occasionally at their homes. I had never worked in such an impressive and competitive environment. Roxborough Elementary School was the best public school the children attended.

Jane received her First Holy Communion from Bishop Powers at Saint Ann's Church, Cleveland Heights, on Sunday May 12th 1963.

<u>Jane at School, grades 3&4, 1963-65: Antigonish, Nova Scotia.</u>

Antigonish (pop c4000), a county capital, has a small primarily undergraduate University (St. Francis Xavier, St FX), a Roman Catholic Cathedral (St Ninian'), the Coady Institute for International Development, and a Hospital that has been there since the beginning of the twentieth century, St Martha's. The yearly Highland Games are the oldest in North America. 80% of the people were Roman Catholic, and the number of children per family, eight, was the highest in Canada outside Quebec.

It is beautifully situated not far from Northumberland Straits, from the new Canso Causeway to Cape Breton, one of the most beautiful places on earth with its tidal indoor sea, the Bras d'Or Lake. The lovely long and narrow Lochaber is nearby.

During the XIXth century, Scottish immigrants would generally sail the Atlantic landing in Pictou, a small port 30 miles to the south: the Catholic Highlanders would mostly walk north to Antigonish and Cape Breton, and the Methodist Lowlanders south to Truro and Halifax.

To-day, the St FX University ranks first of twenty-one similar sized universities in Canada, quite an achievement.

Whereas school education was weak, libraries absent, films censored, the people were wonderful, hard-working, with much cooperative building of homes; being a small town, anyone knew everybody. But boys played cards at the back of the class and the children were all expected to walk to 7 am Mass at the Cathedral during Lent. Otherwise, one felt Antigonish was an integrated community.

We promptly sent Nicholas to the Dartmouth Academy as a boarder, hating the separation. Nicholas did well there but missed his family so much. The school superintendant in Antigonish was so pompous, so different from Cleveland's Professionalism, calling Joan, a university-qualified teacher with an MA (English and History) from the University of St Andrews in Scotland, plus a teaching diploma from Dalhousie University, Nova Scotia, a re-tread.

Jane and Caroline both sailed through school without effort. They made lots of friends, loving their time there, going on picnics, having parties, swimming in the lakes and sea, skiing on the little hill behind the house, visiting each other having a lovely time. Bird watching was very rewarding.

---

*   **Ninian** was a Welsh-speaking Briton from Cumbria, the first Bishop of the southern Picts. His centre was at Candida Casa 'White House' (Whithorn in Galloway).

Jane and Caroline always got on so well together, never quarreling. It was a really happy period for them both.

They were quite distraught when we left. Nicholas was of course quite delighted. Living at home in Kingston thereafter was 'like being on holiday all the time'!

Jane at School, grades 5-8, Sir Winston Churchill Primary School, Kingston, Ontario, 1965-69:

After our Cleveland experience in finding a home, we advertized in the Kingston Whig Standard (founded in 1834, the oldest continuously published paper in Canada) as soon as possible to find a house we could rent close to the school, opposite the tennis club; it reputed to be the best primary school in the whole of Ontario; we received just one answer, 24 Napier Street, very near the school and Queen's University where I would be working; after a few months, we bought the house ($22,000). We completed the previously bare basement: the house gradually became very comfortable. We had a lovely simple garden with lots of shade.

We were all happy in Kingston; the reason for leaving on September 1st 1969 was the offer of a better position with a better salary in a new Faculty of Medicine at *l'universite de Sherbrooke*, Quebec.

My French education would at last become useful; this was crucial for me. I felt that I had finally arrived at my final destination in the new world. It had taken over forty years since I left Ostend at the last minute just before the Germans had arrived there in May 1939 when I was nearly fifteen years old. A lot of water had passed under the bridge during that period.

On the 27th of May 1968 we all officially became Canadian Citizens.

Some of the highlights for the children occurred at school and on holidays:

Nicholas, at the Kingston Collegiate and Vocational Institute **(KCVI),** the earliest Public School in Ontario, founded in 1792 and one of the best, was chosen in 1967 by the Principal to be the only student at the KCVI to be a **Centennial Traveler,** a wonderful testimonial: two weeks trip by train to Vancouver where he stayed with a local family. This exchange of students was a massive

Canadian undertaking paid for by the Provincial and Federal Governments.

Caroline and Jane excelled at Sir Winston Churchill Primary School: they rarely needed prompting, were usually on time and participated in all sorts of activities:

On June 19th 1969, one could read in the Whig Standard a review of "HisMajesty's Pie", an operetta put on by the school: *"Pssst, do you see Jane? She plays the king". And she was an excellent king . . . a marvelous show"* (Brenda Pergantes).

We had some fabulous holidays without spending too much money:

= <u>Three nights in New York</u> flying from Syracuse, just a two hours' drive from Kingston. Joan had been there before arriving on the Queen Mary after the war, but for the rest of us it was a first. On Thursday morning March 21st 1968 we landed at La Guardia, such an easy flight in those days, staying at the Abbey Victoria Hotel, 7th Avenue at 51st street: the Statue of Liberty (climbing the stairs inside its arm up to the top), the Metropolitan and Guggenheim museums, the Empire State Building, the Zoo and Central Park, the stores and restaurants; That was a lovely introduction to the World's most vibrant City.

= <u>We had lovely family camping holidays</u>, **simple** ones in Cape Breton, Pennsylvania, Sharbot Lake in Ontario, and **luxury** ones in Vermont, with just twenty-thirty large wooded well-isolated sites with magnificent trees; they had to be reserved months in advance. This followed John Read's advice. Those sites in Vermont were where we slept and relaxed from days of excursion all over New England including Boston where we spent a whole long afternoon. The children all helped such a lot.

= The climax of our camping days was our <u>six weeks in Europe in 1969</u>: we rented a camper in London and went around Belgium, Holland, north-eastern France down to *Loches*, south of *la Loire*, then south-east England. We visited the three large Notre-Dame Cathedrals, *Chartres, Paris and Rheims,* plus Cathedrals in England, Ely, St Paul's, Westminster, St Pauls, plus University towns, Oxford and Cambridge. Paul was then 8 years old, Jane 15, Caroline 16 and Nicholas 18.

There was a beautiful evening in Blois, the first *Son et Lumiere* show we had ever seen. We camped in my old friend Charles Kyndt's garden near London, and near Pop and Granny's apartment in Surrey. It was the **Family**

Trip of a Life-Time. Camping in Europe was so cheap in those days. We paid about 430 GBPs for the economical well-appointed but small Hillman Camper for the six of us. It included a small tent to which I was relegated because of snoring! I cannot recall any unpleasant events on that beautiful trip, no pilfering, no rudeness, excellent weather.

Caroline and Jane had an exciting time in London: **Carnaby Street** where they spent their savings buying clothes, and the musical, **Hair,** the most important of its time.

We had lived in North America for just over ten years. It was the first time we had returned to Europe as a family. Many years later, my cousin Jan from Bruges told me that we had shown him for the first time an example of camping in a proper vehicle, a motorized camper; he had never heard of such a thing, it was a revelation. We were thankful for our decision to have left Europe.

It was also the last long holiday with all the family. During the summer of 1970, the girls attended a six weeks long course of French in Quebec City, and Nicholas went off to Europe and Morocco for four months with Kingston friends: they visited practically all the countries west of the Iron Wall plus Morocco, using the same transportation system as we had the year before. That left just Joan, Paul and I at home.

CHAPTER 50

A Historical Perspective of the Past Century's Primary Health Care in the English Speaking Western World: a Brief Personal Outline.

Of Mainly London, England:

1823- <u>Dr Thomas Wakley</u>, in London, was the first to coin the term 'General Practitioner'. He was one of them and had founded 'The Lancet' to inform his colleague 'General Practitioners' about the progress made by 'Specialists' in their various fields of endeavor.

c1870- <u>Alfred Krupp</u> (1812-1887) in Essen, Germany, instituted a comprehensive health care program for his steel workers; some were perhaps too frequently absent because of illness. Such a program might actually pay for itself in the long run.

c1902- <u>Dr Fraser Bromley</u> started his dispensing practice in a corner house on a residential Street, 124 Central Park Road in East Ham, London, England (140,000 inhabitants in the 1930s), a new working-class neighborhood with many retirees, two miles or so from the Thames opposite Woolwich. It was one of the nicest districts of this new town.

East Ham was characterized by three distinguishing facts: it had the biggest dock in the world, the Royal Albert Dock, the biggest gas works in the world, the Becton Gas Works, and what is now the biggest cemetery in Europe in Manor Park, in the north-west, the City of London Cemetery.

The new four bedroom house was extended from the start to include a consulting room, a dispensary and a waiting room with its own entrance from the street. There was also an air hose between the front door and the main bedroom through which a patient at the front door could talk to the doctor in his bed.

Dr & Mrs Bromley lived there for twenty years, going on holiday just once for two weeks. They had no children. They kept bull-dogs in the small concreted back yard.

The basement ceiling was reinforced during WWI by a length of railroad track beneath it, an added protection against Zeppelin raids. The large dining-room/library had a large number of books on the County of Kent, the Bromley's original home county. That was Dr Bromley's hobby. Mrs Bromley went to bed at 10pm and Dr Bromley at around 1 am. Behind a book was a bottle of Scotch. This surprised my father greatly.

The local corn chandler would come around with horse and buggy at two o'clock for house calls. Dr Bromley scrupulously kept notes and accounts, all in long-hand and beautifully written, some of which were kept until we left in 1956. I now regret so much that I had thrown them all away before emigrating.

Dr Bromley was very learned. A mature student, he wrote as a series six articles that were published in the first two volumes of the London Hospital Gazette (1894-96) the journal of the **London Hospital Medical College** we had both attended and that I now own, beautifully written:

MEDICO-LITERARY RAMBLES:

1. *WITH THE SPECTATOR.*
2. *WITH THE ANATOMIST OF MELANCHOLY (Richard Burton).*
3. *WITH THE CANTERBURY PILGRIMS.*
4. *WITH SIR THOMAS BROWNE.*
5. *WITH THE RESURRECTIONISTS.*
6. *WITH DEFOE IN THE PLAGUE YEAR.*

1904—Dr William Osler, Canadian born, left John Hopkins University where he was Head of the Dept. of Medicine to become Regius Professor of

Medicine at Oxford University (cfr Ch 3, and also the last page of this chapter).

There was a large difference between British and French Universities on one hand, and the new American Universities: scholarship was sought after much more in Britain, whereas early super-specialization, following the German model, was promoted in parts of the United States, particularly at the new John Hopkins University, very influential at that time in the USA[*]. This might have been a factor in Osier's decision to leave Johns Hopkins.

1911—Two major events in the health care field occurred in the English-speaking medical world:

Lloyd George (1863-1945), Chancellor of the Exchequer (1908-1915), introduced National Insurance in Great Britain. In a nut-shell, in the domain of health care, workers had to register with a general practitioner. He would receive a yearly capitation fee. A permanent record was created for each worker. Thus, general practitioners were guaranteed a small salary, useful particularly when workers were unemployed or on strike and hard-up. The same doctor would usually care for their families and charge fees for their services.

The Flexner Report on medical education in the USA and Canada was published.

The **American Medical Association** (AMA) was founded in 1847.

In **1904,** it created a Council on Medical Education (CME). What was the state of the medical schools: that was the question.

The AMA took advantage of the interest in education for the learned professions of Mr Henry Pritchett, President of the Carnegie Foundation for the Advancement of Teaching, founded in 1905 and chartered in **1906**

"to do and perform all things necessary to encourage, uphold and dignify the profession of teacher and the cause of higher education".

---

[*] *Marginal Man'*, the dark vision of economist Harold Innis, 1894-1952, by Alexander John Watson, Un of Toronto Press, 2008.

Mr Pritchett recommended **Abraham Flexner** (1866-1959) to find out.

Flexner was born in Louisville, Kentucky, of Prussian ancestry; he taught at the secondary school level for 19 years before qualifying with a doctorate in psychology at Harvard in **1906.** He then completed a month's reading as he had never entered a medical school before. All 167 medical schools in Canada and the US were surveyed, spending on average **1.1 day** in each; 50% were rated to be satisfactory, 30% as doing poor work, and 20% as unworthy of recognition. Within ten years, almost three-quarters of the lower two groups had discontinued operations.

After nearly a whole century, Flexner's work is considered to have been severely flawed*. He knew nothing at all about Health Care, his report based largely on the laboratory facilities available for teaching.

Hilliard Jason, a well known Medical Educator, stated in 1982 that **"during the subsequent several decades, most of the attention of the academic medical world was absorbed by the growing opportunities and support for research and by the rapid expansion of medical specialization".**

Thus, Blacks, Women, and the less-fortunate found it more difficult to enter medical school; some provinces/states lost their own and only school, such as Bowdoin College in Maine, where people from New Brunswick, Canada, could study medicine. New Brunswick and Maine still remain to this day the two only Provinces/ States not to have a medical school. Thus, Primary care, Social and Community Medicine, fundamental subjects in the study and teaching of health care, became ignored in the medical curriculum for decades to come.

1914-1918—World War I:

My Walloon mother Lucienne, 18 years old, came to London with her parents, leaving her younger brother, 16 years old behind. Her step-father, a well-trained physician, quickly found a permanent salaried government job, settling down after the war as a general practitioner near Croydon. My Mum spent the war years as an *au*

---

* Mark D Hyatt, *'The Amazing Logistics of Flexner's Fieldwork'*, the Medical Sentinel, 2000; 5(5):167-168.

pair young lady in English families around Barnet/St Albans, North London.

My <u>Flemish father</u> Joseph, 23 years old, a medical student with a recurrent dislocating patella which prevented him from being accepted in the Belgian Army, ended up as an intern for **three** years in Paris via London and Cork, qualifying after the war at his Alma Mater, the University of Ghent. He talked about noisy ambulances arriving day and night full of wounded soldiers, and one could hear the continuous firing of the 'Big Bertha'. All the Paris hospitals were permanently over-crowded with the wounded.

<u>My Dad as a child</u> had remained close to early school friends and their parents, many of whom worked at the Delva owned 'oil and soap' factory, the main industrial employer in Wervik, a town of 12,000 people on the Lys right on the border with France. Dad often talked about them. He had a happy childhood. The whole town, in no man's land during over 3 years, had been totally demolished

1918—The <u>first Minister of Health</u> in the British Empire was <u>Dr William Francis Roberts</u> in New Brunswick, Canada, followed shortly after by a Minister of Health in Britain. The flu epidemic was better controlled in New Brunswick than anywhere else. Smallpox vaccination prior to entering school became compulsory that year. He was thrown out at the next election, people not having understood the issues.

1921-<u>My Dad went to London</u>, bought Dr Bromley's practice, met and married my mother at the Church of '*Notre-Dame de France*', Leicester Square.

The cost of the practice was about one and a half year's income, about 2,500 GBP. My Dad rented the premises for quite a high price (200 GBP a year), Dr & Mrs Bromley leaving the property to the Delva family in their wills. Dr Bromley died shortly after WWII. He would return regularly as a locum, and was quite amazed by the income my father made. Within a year, it had doubled. Dad bought his first car, an expensive French 'de Dion-Bouton'.

1924 (June 3rd)—<u>I was born</u> in my parents' bed, delivered by Dad's best friend, Dr Modeste Kyndt, like Dad a Belgian immigrant from the University of Ghent, living and working two miles away. I was the eldest of three boys, the second, Andrew, found dead in his crib, three months old. This was very tough, particularly for my Mum. She felt so guilty and remained depressed for several months.

1926 (**3rd-12th May, 1926**)—There was a <u>General Strike</u>*, the worst ever to that date, with, at the start, the support of the Trades Union Congress. Before, there had been much social unrest: police strikes, a national rail strike, two national coal strikes, a two months ship-builders strike and violent demonstrations by the jobless.

> **Winston Churchill,** Chancellor of the Exchequer (1924-1929) was responsible for dealing with it; he was not exactly soft handed. He had re-introduced the gold standard in 1925; this caused the GBP to be too strong: exports dropped, interest rates went up and business had a tough time. Mine owners wanted to decrease the already miserable income of the miners.
>
> The workers felt the hard times experienced during WWI had not been worth all the trouble. <u>King George V</u> said *"Try living on their wages before you judge them"*. But they were forced back to work.
>
> Yet, one third of all houses built in the UK by 1939 had been built during the preceding twenty years: the building sector boomed.
>
> Thus, Dad had <u>problems that for him had not been foreseeable</u>. He had to obtain a sticker from the strikers for his wind-shield; thus, he could drive through the control posts manned by them to complete his many house-calls.

By 1930, over two million people in Britain were <u>unemployed</u> and remained so until 1936. In 1939 they still numbered one and a quarter million. That was the period when Dad became a socialist. East Ham town councilors all belonged to the Labour Party and many of them were patients. Dad was much affected by the prevalent social conditions. He would help people in need; when lending money 'never expect it back'. If you cannot afford to, do not lend it.

> Dad was <u>much appreciated by his colleagues</u>: his advice was sought particularly for children: he could hear chest noises with his stethoscope (bronchopneumonia or pneumonia) better than most. He would never seem to be in a rush. He was a good obstetrician; during his most productive years, he delivered over 300 babies a year at home; he charged 5GBP, prenatal, natal and postnatal care

---

*   The Canadian equivalent was the <u>Winnipeg General Strike</u>, (15 May-25th June 1919), dealt with the help of US advisors, when one person was killed and several unjustly imprisoned.

included. He was always extremely well-organized. He loved his work and he was good at it.

He had **three main principles** in running the practice: one had to live over the 'shop', always had to be on time as much as possible, and the patients had to know when he would not be working: within five years, he had a partner, another colleague from Ghent. From then on, Dad never worked on Thursdays and his partner on Wednesdays, and they each took a month's holiday a year. The surgery (office) was open Saturday mornings and evenings and on Sunday mornings until WWII.

After ten years, My Dad understood the working community of East Ham. He had become an intrinsic part of it: that was the nature of General Practice as I saw it.

1939-1945, WWII—Utter Chaos. The younger physicians were called up, the older ones taking over their practice temporarily for half the income, the other half for the doctor who was called-up, the salaries in the forces for national service people so poor. First-aid posts were allotted. My Dad, then 49 years old, was quite upset because he was asked to be responsible for the most vulnerable one in the middle of the docks. However, during WWI in Paris, he had gained some expertise in that field, so he was the best qualified for the job.

I will always remember his happy smiling face as he returned home after driving there following that first horrible bombing at **6pm on Friday September 6th 1940, the first real attack on British Soil since AD 1066:** it lasted forty-five minutes. Immediately after hearing the all-clear, he rushed there in his car, was back within 30 minutes: his first-aid post had been completely demolished. There had been no casualties, the docks empty of personnel at the beginning of the week-end. That was the end of a troublesome assignation. That first-aid post had never had to offer services and was not rebuilt.

That famous week-end, we all spent Saturday night in a hotel in Epping, twenty miles north. We visited the small antique dealer's shop and bought a beautiful French clock and two old Crown Derby candle-sticks for less than two GBP. Dealers were desperate to get rid of 'things' before the end of their world. Business people were spending their money as God only knew what would happen next. The end of their world might be just round the corner. Everything was so disorganized. There was a lot of drinking. That week-end was quite an experience. We were home within twenty-four hours.

Mothers and children were evacuated, so Dad's own practice dwindled. The older patients mostly remained in their own homes. John and I went to school at the **French Lycee** based in Kensington, London, but evacuated to Cumberland. I had two more years to do, John five. We had both had a Jesuit education in a Belgian boarding school until May 10th 1940 when Belgium was invaded..

For the next nine months, we rented a small duplex in Sawbridgeworth, a village half way to Cambridge. Dad would drive to East Ham for the day. German planes flew overhead on their way. When in difficulty, they would drop their bombs early: there was just as much risk living there as in East Ham.

Mum and Dad had a tough time during those war years. The climax of WWII for us was that first raid on September the 6th. It was a big shock, after which we became somewhat 'desensitized' and automated. Bombing is so dehumanizing. The practice recovered after the war.

1942-1947-I passed my premedical exams at the end of 1942, my preclinical basic sciences in March 1944, and my clinical years in December 1947, most of the time (1943-1947) living at home and travelling to and from the London Hospital Medical College daily. It was a grind.

January 5th to June 30th 1948: I obtained a License from the Royal College of Physicians (LRCP), and had become a Member of the Royal College of Surgeons (MRCS) and been accepted as a

- house-surgeon at the now Royal London Hospital to Mr Clive Butler,
- house-physician to the senior physician, Sir Alun Rowlands, each for three months.

I would then be called up for serve in the Royal Army Medical Corps (RAMC) for two years.

I was one of the last new doctors trained by the soon to be defunct London Voluntary Teaching Hospital System. The curriculum had barely changed for a hundred years. Those six months was a very happy period, although I only had one half-day off! On the last day of each month, we were given a fresh, large and beautiful large bank note, black writing printed on beautiful white paper with jagged edges, five GBP. They soon stopped being printed because they could be so easily counterfeited.

I felt I had lived in luxury for six months: a lovely large and well-furnished living room with separate bathroom, no telephones, awakened at night occasionally by a porter who gave you a little note with a question from the ward sister, full luxury service in a beautiful dinning-room around a large table with white linens, polished silver, newspapers and magazines readily available, billiard table and a tennis court. When I left on the Friday the 1st, my seemingly idyllic interlude suddenly came to an end.

Monday, July 4th 1948: the National Health Service was introduced.

Aneurin Bevan, the Labor Minister of Health, was Welch and one of 12 children. His father was a coal-miner.

He had ably split the medical profession in two: specialists had never been paid a bean for their work in the Voluntary Hospitals. They were now to receive sessional fees.

Nye was a charming and fantastic orator. At the last and only hospital Christmas show I attended in 1947, usually a very private affair for the Hospital staff and students, he had appeared on stage unexpectedly and talked without notes so admirably that most people clapped. Just a few booed. Several of the spectators were politically influential senior members of the profession.

General practitioner would be paid according to the number of people who added their names to their lists; it was just an extension of Lloyd George's Panel system introduced in 1911; originally, it was just meant to be to help general practitioners to survive a difficult period; now, it had become their main source of income.

Thus, the income of specialists increased, and that of general practitioners decreased.

Dad was getting tired that summer. He did far fewer confinements after the war. He had always smoked quite heavily, sixty a day, and coughed a lot. It used to drive my mother nuts, opening windows, particularly in the lavatory, initiating draughts. His office was invariably smoked out. Dad labored on. He started smoking small Manikin cigars.

I telephoned my ex-chief at the London Hospital in <u>September</u> after our month's holiday in Belgium. Within twenty-four hours, Dad saw a senior physician at the London. We drove up together. <u>In exactly half an hour</u>, X-rays were taken, **cancer of the lung** was diagnosed, a senior consultant in surgery of the chest judging it to be inoperable. Dad was advised to see his lawyer and get his papers and will in order. He could count on living for another six months. There was no need to return. They were very sorry, an efficient but somewhat heartless operation. I think Dad had guessed what was happening; he never talked about it. If only I could live another year he would say. At the beginning, we both thought this might be the case.

<u>**Thursday April 21st 1949: Dad died**</u> at the London where he had been operated three days before for a strangulated femoral hernia. He had been heavily sedated during those last three days. He had become so thin. He had worked in the surgery twice a day while I did all the house-calls until four weeks before he died. He never missed a surgery. His patients all knew what was happening. At the end, all he wanted to eat was peeled seedless grapes, with scotch and water, plus morphine. I must have skinned hundreds of those green grapes, expensive at the time.

My **first house-call** was for a child with chicken-pox, that first evening after our first and only visit to the hospital. My father hadn't felt like going! I recognized the condition but had no idea what to do about it, so I told the parents that I would ask my dad and return the next day. I would travel on my bike, as dad needed the freedom of the car and I the exercise. It was also much faster, not having to park and lock a car, my bag in a wooden box on my carrier.

That is how I learned my job. It was a tough period for Mum and I, but a fantastic medical opportunity for me. Dad was my best teacher. He would ask me for an extra dose of morphine during that last month, and I would oblige. I think I helped him. Friends who came to visit thought I was giving him too much, but I was not impressed. Dad was then 58 1/2 years old. What I learned most was about the care of the dying. The best time for a visit was late evening when the family anxiety was at its worse.

In the practice, two patients died a month, one suddenly, and the other like my dad. Thus looking after the chronically sick and the dying became second nature for me from the start. When there was a smog in East Ham, a couple of patients would die, and I rarely would know which of my many patients with chronic bronchitis and emphysema would go. That was horrible.

April 22nd 1949-December 15th 1956: from then on, I was one of two 'principals' in a large east London practice. It took me a while to understand what was going on. Our practice accepted all newcomers without any questions asked. I was my father's son and very keen. I loved the job. The patients all loved my Dad. We looked after over six thousand patients.

But I did not realize for the longest time that the system only pays its way when a practice is balanced with an average number of chronically sick patients. If you have twice as many chronically sick patients, you have perhaps three times more work, and the situation rapidly becomes untenable. Healthy people have no reason to look for another doctor. Those that desire to look for another physician are often the chronically ill. Specialists only treat people with a certain illness/sickness/disease, whereas general practitioners look after patients/families in their environment and ensure follow-up.

I married Joan Campbell on November 31st 1950, completed two years of army service in the British Army of Occupation of the Rhine (BAOR) from September 1951 to September 1953, a peaceful and agreeable interlude during which Nicholas was born on December 13th 1951, Joan arriving in Germany just three weeks before.

Back in East Ham, I was full of energy and optimism. Some of my older patients had been patients of Dr Bromley's, some had participated in the Boer South African Wars. One of them, an eighty year old tug master on the Thames was still working: his grand-father was forced into the Royal Navy and had fought at Trafalgar (1806).

However, I soon felt sucked-in by a vice that I could no longer control in a way that I could accept. I was putting on weight and suffered a lot of indigestion; then, one day, I had an intestinal hemorrhage from a duodenal ulcer that needed admission to the London and six pints of blood. We left East Ham six months later, on **December 15th1956.**

I was not sorry or even sad to leave the house where I was born thirty-two years before. I had always been very happy there, but the time had come for a radical change. Joan and I felt ready. By that time we had three children, Caroline, born on June 3rd 1952, and Jane on March 23rd 1953.

I had passed the **London University MB BS** (Bachelor of Medicine, Bachelor of Surgery) examinations (spring 1956). We were sorry to leave London, for us one of the world's greatest cities.

During the next eighteen months, we lived in Tunbridge Wells, a magnificent old medieval town in Kent: I took a three month's course in advanced medicine at the London where I met a future French Canadian colleague from Sherbrook, Quebec, **Dr Marcel Drolet,** traveling there three times a week. I did locums in various country and town settings, interesting, all of which, without doubt, confirmed our resolve to leave the country. I disliked doing locums though, because one does not understand the particular culture of the people you are dealing with, neither do they the temporary doc they had to deal with. I was offered several permanent jobs!

We had frequent pleasurable trips to the sea-side on the south shore with our three children plus their local friends.

Emigrating to a New Continent:

This is a difficult task for a family to undertake, particularly for a professional. However, we had certain advantages because our parents were immigrants: we had learned a lot from their experiences in their new country.

There were problems concerning the practice of Medicine for British new-comers to **Canada:** one

- had to be a Canadian citizen to be able to practice medicine in Quebec, five years.
- had to complete a one-year internship in Ontario or British Columbia.
- could settle down and earn one's living immediately in the other provinces just by registration.

We visited Canada House in Central London as early as the spring in 1951: the whole atmosphere was bleak and unwelcoming, enough to put anybody off, like a dusty railway station waiting-room in a middle-sized town. It improved over the years; after much hesitation, I answered an advertisement in the British Medical Journal.

A Scottish doctor in a small village, Glen Margaret, Nova Scotia, 40 miles from Halifax on the south shore, wanted to return to the UK. His two boys were being educated there: this was surprising for me. I later found that, at that time, it was a fairly normal thing to do for professional immigrants from the UK to the Maritimes. Such was my experience as a child, being sent to boarding school in Belgium; but Belgium was so close!

In <u>March 1958</u>, I flew over for an exciting trip leaving on Thursday 6th returning on Tuesday 11th, my first flight over the Atlantic: London-Prestwick-Montreal (BOAC)—Shearwater (TCA), a Canadian Air Force Base near Halifax on the North Shore. I left in the afternoon and got there the next afternoon, seemingly a 24 hour trip.

I had bought new wooly 'Chillproof' head to toe underwear that I jettisoned in the overheated Nissen hut waiting room in the still primitive Dorval airport. I had to wait there for six hours.

On arrival, our new doctor friend was there to meet me in his old extra large boat-like American car. He took me around, and I met lots of people. What a beautiful place it was!

<u>We all arrived on July 1st 1958</u>:

Glen Margaret, on Nova Scotia's south shore was as beautiful as most villages on the eastern seaboard of North America: no fencing around the houses, a rented small three-room surgery/office a stone's throw away from our new home, a rented Cape Cod cottage right on the large St Margaret's Bay with three bedrooms, a newly paved wide two-lane road in front, a new consolidated school a few miles down the road with new school buses, a small Catholic church in the village, St Margaret of Scotland, open during the summer. I was the only doctor serving a dozen or so small villages along the shore. As usual, the people were nice and responsive. Night calls were a delight whatever the weather: the views, the silence always spectacular.

There were important snags:

- the RCMP only displaced itself when somebody had died.
- an ambulance from Halifax would only come if paid immediately.
- there were quite horrible accidents because the new road was used as a racing track on Saturday evenings, three cars driving abreast.
- fishermen earned a lot of money during the summer but during the winter most lived on unemployment.

- here was very little cooperation between the doctors regarding work-sharing.
- many patients had no health insurance.
- many expected help to deliver their babies without any antenatal care: 'we will call you if we need you'.
- I hated the financial side, always having been salaried. In that first year I earned a respectable $12,000.
- funny things seem to be happening; for instance, the RCMP raided and demolished an illegal still on top of a small hill, leaving their cars unattended: when they returned, all their tires had been slashed. Everyone knew who did the deed; no-one spilt the beans.
- other misdeeds, such as break-ins, would be reported but known details not communicated when requested.

We loved the place and the work but did not see any long term future in this beautiful spot; by the end of the year Joan and I had planned a **massive change:**

- Joan would go back to study for a year at Dalhousie to obtain a teaching diploma to complement her MA, (English & History), St Andrews, Scotland. Thus, we could keep the home fires burning.
- I would 'specialize' in pediatrics. I was good at looking after the usual children's problems, but knew little about caring for the more serious ones. In addition, I had qualified over ten year before and felt the need for more training in North America. There was a two hundred bed Children's Hospital in Halifax advertizing for residents starting in July. The Royal College of Physicians and Surgeons* of Canada accredited the program for two of the four year program, although no residents had ever stayed more than a year.
- We would continue to live in Glen Margaret for a second year, working part-time with the help of a new emigrant doctor using the same process that I had gone through. For that second year's training, our

---

* **The Royal College of Physicians and Surgeons of Canada** (RCPSC, RC for short) was incorporated in 1929 to grant accreditation by examination in the various medical and surgical specialties. By 1945, the end of the war, there were 36 Fellows with four years' training with a right to vote, mostly University based specialists, plus several hundred certified physicians with three years' training working in the field with no rights: it remained a dreadful two tier system until the early seventies.

third in Canada, Joan would teach in Halifax, and we would live there in rented accommodation.

-   <u>Wherever we moved subsequently, we would stay for at least two years.</u>

"**By 1954,** general practitioners had become to feel like second-class citizens in the medical hierarchy. Specialists were seen as ruling the roost, and medical schools and hospitals were devoting less and less time and residency space to the field of general practice":

Thus, the College of General Practice of Canada was born, later renamed the **College of Family Physicians of Canada** (CFPC). The first examination, built with the help of trained experts in pedagogy, was as good or better than anywhere; it was held in 1969: there were thirteen candidates.

July 1st 1959—Everything went according to plan.

Joan had an excellent experience at Dalhousie, followed by a profitable year of teaching at Richmond Middle School, right next to the naval base in Halifax. We both worked very hard and learned such a lot, much on our own. I later learnt that few of the pediatricians were properly qualified. They were mostly General Practitioners with a year or two of training, a nice crowd, but the teaching was weak and boring. I spent three nights a week on duty that first year. The accommodation was primitive.

Dr Maureen Roberts, a graduate from the University of Edinburgh, worked there. Her husband was a senior physician in the Royal Canadian Navy. She helped revive my interest in Genetics. This had started in Cambridge. During my pre-medical year there (1942-43), Professor EB Ford from Oxford travelled every week for a trimester to give a set of fascinating lectures using his own compact textbook. It had just been published (1942) and I still have it.

Dr Roberts and I attended a series of lectures on Human Genetics at St Mary's University in Halifax by **Professor Hugh Soltan,** an immigrant from Poland, who had just obtained his doctorate in Biology at the University of Toronto. He married a lovely lady at St Margaret's Church in Glen Margaret that summer; his wife had been a student in the same teaching program as Joan. Her parents had a summer home near-by and we were guests.

Watson and Crick had just received the Nobel Prize in Medicine and Physiology (1962). It seemed like a good idea to spend two years in a really academic milieu. This plan was accepted by the Royal College. Four years of training was the preferred length for full accreditation.

In January 1963, I was notified that I had obtained a US National Institute of Health Grant administered through Dr Arthur G Steinberg (AGS) of the Department of Preventive Medicine at **Western Reserve University** (WRU) Medical School in Cleveland, Ohio: I was given a tax-free grant of $6,500 the first year, $8500 the second and subsequent years.

Dr A G Steinberg was Professor in the department of Biology, and Associate Professor in Human Genetics in the Faculty of Medicine. He had trained at Columbia. We promptly accepted: no more night work, Joan could stay home. We could rent a house in one of the best districts with the best schools.

Thus, for the first time in my life I would be exposed to a real academic milieu in an important world-class University. My clinical load would be minimal.

It soon transpired that my grant had been the last given to a foreigner, the new President, John F Kennedy, having decided that, because of the Russian Sputnik circling the earth, such scholarship funds should be granted only to US students. I had been very lucky.

September 1st 1963-June 30th 1965: the **USA**: two wonderful interesting years in the first medical school anywhere that tried to rethink and revamp the medical curriculum. In addition, it was the first and only Medical School that I have ever been involved with that was able to get everything written correctly about me in the yearly School of Medicine Bulletin (1962-63):

Peter L. Delva, L.R.C.P., M.R.C.S., M.B., B.S.,
Instructor in Pediatrics.
M.B.,B.S., (London University).

On Campus, great organizations amongst the best in the country, the Museum of Art, the Museum of Natural History, Severance Hall with Georges Szell and the Cleveland Symphony Orchestra.

John Schoff Millis, (1903-1988), a physicist, was the **President and Chancellor of WRU** (1949-1967).

It was a comparatively small medical school, with about 80 students per year, similar to what I had experienced, with several large teaching general hospitals, plus separate Children's and Maternity Hospitals (4,000 beds). The staff was distinguished, Benjamin Spock, Fred Robbins, a Nobel Prize winner, just two of many. The Head of the Department of Medicine was appointed Head at Harvard while I was there.

In a nutshell, the basic sciences, instead of being based on morbid anatomy (I had spent 1000 hours, mostly on the dissection of cadavers) were based on the study of a pregnant lady and the development of her child and her new often expanding family.

Right from the start, the new student had to follow-up a pregnant lady, do home visits, meet the father, accompany her when she had to have health care, attend the birth, study the growth and development of the new child in the context of its family; a wonderful idea but difficult to implement because it tends to disrupt the established time-table: one can study anatomy every morning from 8 am to 12 noon for a couple of years, but one cannot follow-up a family in a time frame. So some compromises had to be made in the program's implementation.

My headquarters were situated in the department of Biology, section Human Genetics, room 403, in one of the original main buildings, Adelbert College*, built in 1882, on the other side of the road from the medical school.

I was quite anxious at the start. How could I, 39 years old, compete with all these bright young keen students, many of whom were highly intelligent. I had never been in such an academic milieu. I need not have worried.

After three months, I was determined to ace Dr Steinberg's courses in Genetics which I did much to our relief, his lectures at eight to nine o'clock three times a week, the door locked at one minute past the hour, whatever the weather. On a bad stormy day, five students would attend. 'If I can get there, they can too' was AGS's motto. But those were the only courses for which I was examined. I

---

* The only College in the USA named after the first name of the dead child of the wealthy donor who had built it.

could sit through any lecture or conference that I wanted, statistics, grand-rounds, ward rounds, courses, conferences: how lucky!

I learned a lot of <u>clinical genetics</u>, Dr Steinberg having started a well attended service. He was very methodical, and I used his method until retirement. I soon realized that, with effort, you can persuade people to have their tubes tied for the prevention of an inherited horrible disease for instance; then it is your job to persuade your clinical colleagues to do the job, an unnecessarily long-term process where one's religion plays a large part. That is were a well-trained physician is a necessary component of a Genetic Service.

I also learnt <u>Pediatrics</u>. At Dr Steinberg's request, I freely volunteered my services for a weekly clinic subsidized by a Foundation for children with rheumatoid arthritis; this was a happy experience. I would send part of the blood samples I took to the genetics lab, one of them proving extremely useful for the research carried out there on the Gamma Globulins. Dr Steinberg had two large projects on hand, the second one on the Hutterite population in Canada and the USA.

Some pediatricians volunteered their services once or twice a week for similar activities. This was the difference between the care given to the poor and the affluent. The really sick poor had good specialized but different care. The USA is still the only country in the world with South Africa without a National Health Service.

I was agreeably surprised when I realized that the Head of Department in Pediatrics, a very learned person, would only look after two or three very sick children at a time: all his other clinical work would be delegated or postponed. His priority was limited to the urgent matters at hand. That would happen in the UK only when the King or Queen was sick.

Dr Sam Spector was deputy Head. He was short with a squeaky voice but tough. Every Saturday morning at 8am he visited each and every bed in the hospital to ensure that no child was there unnecessarily. If such was the case, he would become quite angry, discharging the child immediately: no excuses, no explanations. I accompanied him on these rounds for a couple of months: *"get them out of here"*.

I was <u>keeper of the flies</u> for year, a quite fascinating experience. Gregor Mendl (1822-1884), the discoverer of the Laws of Heredity, had used peas for his experiments, but these take quite a time to grow, whereas the common fruit fly, Drosophila Melanogaster, reproduces rapidly. **Thomas Hunt Morgan,** at Columbia during the 1920s, had started his famous studies using the fly, and AGS was a Columbia graduate. Thus, my training at WRU was traditional basic biological genetics with a clinical component. Most physicians had just clinical training, mainly at Johns Hopkins with Dr Victor A McKusick. At first, I envied them, but after a while I realized my experiences at WRU, while becoming unusual for a physician, corresponded better to my needs.

The flies were kept in those old half-pint milk bottles with card-board covers. I had to make the semolina-type food in a big pan, transfer the flies to clean bottles a quarter filled with food on Saturday mornings, making sure the flies did not meet thus retaining their different characteristics, eye color, wing shape, etc . . . . Thus, students could mate the flies and analyze their offspring. I was the lab instructor, delighted to meet so many young people. I cannot remember a difficult situation, although Genetics is not an easy subject to teach properly or to learn.

Interesting people visited the department, from England, France, Columbia University, elsewhere in the US, Japan, amongst them Rene Dubos, Theodosius Dobzhansky, and LC Dunn. It was an exciting place. Most of them asked you what you were doing, demonstrating real interest.

I was offered an interesting job: *Ralph Josiah Patrick Wedgwood*, a direct descendant of Wedgewood Potteries fame (founded in 1759 by Josiah Wedgewood) with a loud and deep English Voice, a Harvard graduate and a Markle scholar, had been appointed head of the department of Pediatrics in Seattle, Washington. He asked me one morning to accompany him. He loved sailing, one of the big advantages of Seattle. I had no desire for such a pursuit.

We knew a little about Eastern Canada and we liked it. We had serious misgivings about living in the US. The Vietnam War was starting, the racial situation had become dicey and Senator McCarthy's influence was barely over. So we did not accept such a gratifying offer; Joan and I have seldom regretted it.

In March 1963, we had to decide where to go for the next couple of years. WRU had finally decided to offer a new Professional Masters' degree and I would be their first candidate; but I would have to stay an extra year. My priority was to return 'home' to Nova Scotia and take the pediatric specialist examinations the coming fall, thus following our pre-determined plan.

Settling in the Halifax/Dartmouth area would expose me to an East Ham-type experience. I had done such a lot of primary care pediatrics there. What was the good of my four years of study. It seemed preferable to chose to settle in a small University town, sit the Royal College exams, thus becoming the first qualified pediatrician outside the Capital area in Nova Scotia.

We chose **Antigonish,** with St Francis Xavier University (StFX) and St Martha's Hospital, 220 beds (30 bassinets & 30 pediatric beds), and the first RC Bishop in the Maritimes since the 1830s. Antigonish had the highest birth rate in Canada outside Quebec. I wrote the hospital a letter; what followed was an invitation. I drove there for a couple of days, was made to feel welcome, with a delicious filet steak lunch at the Hospital. It was lovely being so close to the sea. I met the Professor of Biology, Dr Chiasson, the first Acadian I had ever met. Everyone seemed very congenial. We decided to move to Antigonish.

I told Dr Steinberg (AGS) of our decision; he was disappointed but he thought it was great going to Antigonish. He told me all about Father Coady; during the twenties, the fishermen were living in poverty, forced to sell their fish to middlemen who made a fortune: Father Coady organized unions which were able to sell the fish directly to the consumer. He established the first community bank in English Canada. Desjardins had done the same in Quebec 25 or so years before.

The <u>Coady Institute</u> was founded in 1959, and students from all over the developing world would attend a year's instruction about international development. Joan and I, new Canadians, had never heard of such things! For all of these candidates from poorer countries, Antigonish was the capital of Canada; those students were so easily noticeable walking the streets.

<u>AGS's first academic</u> appointment had been at McGill (c1939-1942); it was the unhappiest of all his appointments: there was a quota on the number of Jews there, three if I can remember rightly, and he and his family were not made to feel very welcome. AGS was a very learned person.

He once told us that Martin Luther King would give a sermon in a church close to where we lived; we had barely heard about him, and did not go: what a mistake that was. AGS invited me to accompany him to the yearly meeting of the American Academy for the Advancement of Science (AAAS) in Denver, the most 'high brow' meeting I have ever attended. He paid for me to attend the yearly Pediatric meeting in Atlantic City, the best I have ever attended in that field. I joined a bunch of Cleveland pediatricians, a most pleasant experience. We had a lovely lobster supper together one evening.

To my knowledge, I never once met a general practitioner in Cleveland. The word itself was never mentioned. I had a severe pain in my right shoulder on one occasion. The duty doctor at Student Health palpated my arm through my clothes, gave me some aspirin. I was in and out in two minutes. He might have been one. Previously, he might have been in the army.

Prior to our departure I spent four weeks with John Kennell, Assistant Professor of Pediatrics, who cared for sick young babies and children at the Hospital. During that month, I was able to reconnect with matters necessary for my new job: a truly wonderful and necessary experience with a truly wonderful person.

WRU proved to be an excellent place to spend two years, working mostly in a field that was marginally medical yet so fundamentally important, having the time to think about our own future: it seemed a luxury period in an increasingly rushed world.

Back to Nova Scotia for two years (July 1st 1963-June 30th 1965): we really felt as if we were driving home!

Five of us had arrived in the US two years earlier, but this time we were six: little Paul, an American citizen, was six months old. By necessity, we had exchanged our little Morris Minor which had transported us there for a new two-door Rambler, quite a lot bigger, favored in Cleveland by the University crowd. Paul would sit between Joan and I in the front, on a little seat that hung from the bench seat, the perfect observation deck.

That first day's driving got us to the Howard Johnson's in Ittaca on the New York Throughway, the second to the Howard Johnson's in Portsmouth via the mass Turnpike, the original capital of New Hampshire before the War for Independence, the third to Fredericton, New Brunswick, at the Lord Beaverbrook Hotel, and the fourth day at the old, soon to be demolished, George Hotel in Antigonish, Nova Scotia. At its border with New Brunswick, we were truly welcomed by a piper with a Nova Scotian tartan. It was an emotional moment after a beautiful trip that we all enjoyed.

I had negotiated a salary ($6,500 for the first year, increased to $8,500 subsequently) with 'The Antigonish Clinic', a group practice. Such an arrangement might ease my insertion and encourage cooperation, and I felt happier: there were four middle-aged general practitioners, an efficient general practitioner who restricted his field to internal medicine, a younger Royal College certified obstetrician, and myself, 39 years old, a trained pediatrician awaiting certification. One of the four doctors came from Lithuania. He had married a Scottish physician who, like Joan, attended St Andrews University. She no longer practiced. They had two young children.

In addition to the Clinic, there were three older General Practitioners who were nearing retirement age. One of them still did routine operations, appendectomies, hernias for instance. Another restricted his work to ear, nose and throat. The head or surgery came from Cape Breton, trained at the Royal Victoria Hospital in Montreal, and passed his Royal College examinations in Surgery becoming an FRCS. He had attended SFX and McGill; he was the success of the town and was treated with the utmost respect. He was an excellent general surgeon. A second surgeon was a qualified urologist and also came from Cape Breton.

The Polish anesthetist was very efficient and certified by the RC. Carvell McIntosh was the well-qualified, experienced and funny pathologist: I admired him a lot. His able assistant was a fantastic nun who supervised the laboratories. The hospital had its own blood bank, with its own list of donors who would appear rapidly and magically on request.

The radiologist was a very efficacious well-qualified Torontonian with a large farm with New Jersey cattle living on top of a hill just outside the town. He also had a large family. His undergraduate years were spent at St FX University.

A charming and efficient Irish psychiatrist completed the 'team'. Thus, there were four fairly recent immigrants, (two from behind the Iron Curtain, plus an Irishman and a Belgian/Britisher, and eleven Canadian-born): a potentially fantastic team.

We each had an office in the hospital, so we could easily cover the emergency room; access to the laboratories and to radiology was easy. On paper, this was a fantastic place in which to work. But how would it turn out, that was the question.

There was no Public Library in this University town. The Catholic Women's League censored many films, Dr No, the first of the James Bond films, being an exception. The quality of the teaching in the public schools left a lot to be desired, the boys routinely playing cards at the back of the class. Roman Catholicism ruled the town: during lent, Caroline and Jane would attend 7am mass, all the children having to walk to get there, supposedly good for them at that time of the year.

We decided that Nicholas should be a boarder at the Halifax Grammar School. It had resettled in Dartmouth. Nick had been there as a day boy three years before. This was disappointing but we never regretted our decision. We would go to Halifax to see him as often as we could. He never complained but we were all sad when Joan and I left.

St Martha's was a chummy place, each clinician doing his own thing and mum was the word. This did not appear to be sufficiently professional. We met for coffee at ten, exchanging gossip, perhaps local news or the stock market. We rarely talked shop. The work of the nurses was still considered as being totally based on the hospital wards and operating rooms.

Some **wonderful things** happened: at first, there was a lack of equipment for treating infants intravenously; this was quickly remedied, the hospital being very well organized in that respect and very keen.

That first summer, there was a **serious outbreak of infectious diarrhoea in Newfoundland.** It was caused by a bad strain of e-coli and many babies died. As was to be expected, some cases occurred in Cape Breton, and some of these (12-18) arrived at St Martha's.

It was a wonderful chance to put some order in the pediatric ward: it so often had a **95% occupancy rate,** children being admitted because 'it seemed the safest thing to do'. It was not unusual for a child to be admitted for the week-end for sniffles just when the rest of the family was off for a break. The nurses, mostly young students, were run off their feet. They looked despondent most of the time. So that epidemic gave us the perfect reason to limit admissions. From then on, it was unusual for the occupancy rate to exceed 60%, the nurses gradually becoming more efficient, relaxed and smiling.

What was more important was the **teaching** I had to do to instruct the **nurses** about the new mini-drops, the supervision of infants with a drip and so on. So every morning at 11am sharp I would discuss things for 30 minutes, Monday to Friday. The epidemic soon subsided and the teaching became a tradition. I would talk about the cases in the ward. Many interesting situations arose:

- the nurses were always talking about **heat rashes,** yet they had never seen anyone with an infectious disease such as rubella, or roseola, or scurvy (vitamin C deficiency) or rickets (vitamin D deficiency). All children admitted received vitamins with their first meal. Within six months we had witnessed several infectious diseases with evanescent rashes, cases of scurvy and rickets. Heat rashes had disappeared.

- **the treatment of the diarrhoea** is so simple: rehydration with intravenous fluids, no food by mouth, plus an appropriate antibiotic. Usually the child is discharged within four days. The only problem was that I was on call 24 hours a day. The nurses learned fast and were soon able to control the drips and make sure the needle was not getting obstructed. If that occurred, they would telephone and I would arrive within 20 minutes.

There was **a fatalistic ignorance about illnesses and their prevention** that I had not witnessed previously, and much faith in God and the medical profession. Here are some of the problems:

- a verbal message over coffee: *"Peter, can you just see baby X, five days old, getting yellow. I don't think anything can be done"*. It was a fourth pregnancy, the second had died, and the third was severely handicapped, a clear case of **erythroblastosis.** The mother never thought this one would survive and had not prepared for this birth. She had accepted the pregnancy because it was *'the will of God'*. We went ahead with exchange transfusions. At the start, the bilirubin level was over 25 mgms/100mlms, and I had to use one unit of blood every four hours for twenty-four hours (x6) before the bilirubin level came down to acceptable limits. We were all exhausted apart from the baby!. The blood bank had been superb. I received a picture of the little boy riding his tricycle in a very active way two years later.
- our neighbor had two children, a three-year old daughter and a one year-old boy. I noticed one day he was wearing a **truss for a hernia:** he had been unsuccessfully operated by one of the older GPs and a truss had been prescribed. By that time, the first trained pediatric general surgeon was working in Halifax; it took a year before the parents accepted my advice and go to Halifax. Trusses were first used in the early 13th century. I had never seen or heard of a one year old child wearing a truss.
- a boy of five died of **diarrhoea** after a week in hospital without consultation.
- a small baby was brought to emergency **apparently dead.** The duty doctor called me to see whether anything further could be

done. I thought he might just be suffering from hypothermia. I wrapped him in a blanket and rushed upstairs. By that time a small room on the pediatric floor had been transformed into a treatment room for infants. All the baby needed was a warm blanket and a small intravenous drip.

- our **head surgeon** had the habit of wearing his OR clothes in his office with his mask hanging around his neck. When he wasn't busy, he would stand in the doorway watching events. He was a good general surgeon but his skills in orthopedics were less well developed. He had no idea of the behavioral aspects when treating children, yet had four of his own. A child with a body cast would cry a lot, and he would respond by covering the sides of the crib with white sheets. All the child could do is stare at the white ceiling; depression might follow and thus the crying stopped.

- **no visiting was allowed in Pediatrics:** the children cried too much when their parents were leaving. After a few weeks, with the full support of our psychiatrist, I wrote to the Head of Pediatrics at Dalhousie. He soon published an article in the medical press about the necessity of free visiting. After a full year without ever being asked for my opinion, visiting was finally allowed between 1.30pm and 2pm on Mondays and Fridays when practically everybody was at work.

- there was an **immunization problem:** mothers would arrive with their children to be immunized. A screaming child would be sitting on her lap, held tightly, an arm bare: *'come on doc, just give it to him'.* I would refuse, then try and reassure the child as to my benevolence, *'it's just like a mosquito bite, and you never cry over that! I have some candy for you after'.* If that did not work, Mum and children would return later. Within three months that problem was solved.

- an infant developed **tuberculous meningitis.** With the internist, treatment was initiated rapidly and satisfactorily. Our young patient was transferred to the Provincial Sanatorium in Kentville following the regulations. It was the first child of a young couple living by themselves in a comfortable new home. Both parents worked, the mother a nurse. I was quite horrified when the sanatorium decided the infant could not return home until the age of eighteen months; I drove down an afternoon and had to threaten to write a letter to the Globe and Mail before they changed their minds.

Finally, the Famous Examination: it was quite a trek going to Montreal via Truro by overnight train. I failed my first attempt. We were just settling down after coming home to Canada. It had been a busy period and I did not feel well-prepared. The examiner, much younger that I, presented me with slides of the blood of a leukemic patient. I had not seen one for years. How ridiculous I thought, that is the job of the pathologist.

I telephoned Joan; she was always so supportive. We resolved that, during the coming twelve months, I would bury my head in books 2-3 hours a day week-ends included. I passed on the second attempt. I was examined by the senior examiner, an older man, Head of Department at the University of Manitoba, more oriented on community matters such as school health and immunization programs. Joan had come with me that **November 1964.** I was then 40 years old.

But, although I had completed four years of postgraduate work, I had not been allowed to sit for the Fellowship examination. Thus, I became a Certificant in Pediatrics (CRCP). It was most frustrating that every step of the way my past experiences as a principal in an old large and well-established practice for several years in a large London suburb had never been acknowledged.

In **January 1965,** the time was ripe to assess what had been accomplished and what was to be our future:

- professionally, the past two years had been well-worth it. I had much enjoyed the work. The student nurses had been a revelation. The Sisters of St Martha could not have been more helpful. Medically, the set-up, compared to that of East Ham, where total isolation of the GP was the rule in town working-class areas, was so much better. Yet the fundamentals had changed less: *each individual physician did his own thing.* There was little notion of the application of any management system in general practice. But at the same time, most medical schools throughout the Western world had failed to produce improved appropriate models in their teaching of primary care.
- the education of the children had not met expectations. We ruled out boarding schools for ever. Nicholas had done very well, but we missed one another so much.
- we determined to make a big effort to get a staff appointment in one of the twelve medical schools in the country. People in Antigonish thought we were nuts. I wrote a few letters to heads of department

most of which remained unanswered. One of them, an ex-Brit from Edmonton, was so condescending.

Our Shift to Ontario:

Luckily, Prof. Rudy Ozere, with a Belgian spouse, head of the department of pediatrics at Memorial University, St John, Newfoundland, had worked in the office of the dean at Dalhousie when I was working at the Halifax Childrens Hospital. He told me about problems Prof. John Read had in recruiting a fully qualified pediatrician to work full-time in his department.

John was a McGill graduate who had studied paediatrics at Ann Arbor, Michigan, where there was a Child Health Program (**CHP**). He then obtained a public health qualification from the Un of Toronto. He had recently replaced the retiring head of the University Department of Public Health at Queens University in Kingston, renaming it the Department of Social and Preventive Medicine. He and Mrs Read had four children, the six of them the same age as us! The CHP focused on the health of adopted children, foster-care children, and the children of students at Queens. John had been unable to find an Ontario pediatrician to take on this $12,500/year job.

I wrote, was invited to visit and was offered the job as Head of the CHP, starting August 1st 1965. A full-time very experienced Social-worker and a Queens trained RN, an experienced secretary and a receptionist were already on the spot. The program was subsidized by the Federal Department of Health and Welfare. What a wonderful chance! It was the last job I had to search for: I was later offered two jobs in the same department at the new University of Sherbrook (1969) and at the University of Montreal (1979).

I soon realized there were Administrative Problems in the Medical Faculties of the older schools (Kingston, Halifax, Ottawa and Toronto):

= many teachers had not adjusted to the new requirements of the RC, and had been appointed to the various clinical departments. Thus, new well-qualified Deans and Departmental Heads had been appointed to **"clear things up"**. That takes time.

= the old **'Public Health'** (clean water, proper drains, school health, immunizations and vaccinations) was being expanded to include more social and community issues, thus a change of name to **'Community/**

Social/Preventive Medicine'. This makes the presence of a clinical component essential for teaching.

= **much of the teaching was based on hospitalized patients.** Teaching in ambulatory settings was neglected. This was particularly true in Kingston. Most of the white-colored professionals lived and worked south of Princess Street on or near the Queen's campus near Lake Ontario, whereas most blue-collar workers lived on the northern side of Princess Street, with poor bus services between the two.

= Many doctors lived quite luxuriously near Lake Ontario. That was why the salary I had accepted was viewed as inadequate by pediatricians.

= **pediatrics had problems of its own:**

  - many school-aged children would chose to attend the doctor who treats their parents.
  - some pediatricians were starting to feel that family problems, so frequent, were better dealt with by family physicians.
  - I was starting to feel that primary care pediatrics belonged to family medicine.

= **"at a symposium sponsored by the Royal College at Queen's during the fall, 1965, Dr Donald Rice,** (executive director of the College of Family Physicians of Canada, and one of just two family doctors present) **listened with growing incredulity and apprehension to a position paper on training for the clinical specialties delivered with the effect, if implemented, of sounding the death knell of general practice":** internists and some other specialists would do the job better than general practitioners!

That fall, 1965, at Jones' Falls on the Rideau Canal, John Read had helped create the Canadian Association of Teachers of Social and Preventive Medicine **(CATSPM).** Our invited leader at that first meeting was **Wendell McLeod,** a McGill graduate and an internist, a great supported of socialized medicine and the founding Dean of the Saskatchewan Medical School in the 1950s. He had recently been appointed the first director of the Canadian Association of Medical Colleges (ACMC) in Ottawa. The universities of Ottawa and Toronto were not represented. Jean-Guy Bonnier, Medical Officer of Health for the town of La Salle represented the University of Montreal. I got to know Jean-Guy and Wendell well. Carol Buck represented Western.

That first of August, Helen and I spent a week at Harvard with **Joel Alpert,** a pediatrician, who had started a CHP there a few years earlier when John Read was in Michigan. That is how I was introduced to the Harvard

Medical School. Compared with WRU in Cleveland, I felt there was a lack of spontaneity of the senior staff when faced with questions: they seemed on the defensive giving textbook type answers.

Our own CHP worked so smoothly. It was a lovely experience. I did house-calls from the start. The parents were delighted, the Children's Aid society was delighted, the married students were delighted. Some of them became quite famous, such as Michael Onddatje. It was gratifying. We were soon giving parents advice on their own health concerns. The three of us shared the work and talked about our concerns.

John had organized **a monthly meeting** over a sandwich lunch **for local family physicians.** It was well attended, and I thought quite successful: we would present items that we judged useful: growth charts, Tanner's work on adolescence, medical records come to mind.

With the department of psychiatry, we had **a weekly three hour teaching cession** for the whole semester with third year students. It dealt with the growth and development of children and was problem oriented. I remember a cession devoted to 'the battered child' as it was then called. We invited guests, mostly involved community representatives, to participate. It was moderately successful. The students did not considerate it sufficiently 'scientific'. I decided in my own mind that it should have been presented to first year students.

But that was it: few students, interns or residents came through the CHP. They were not impressed. They had not been prepared for change and continued to develop in the old way. **The opposition of the clinicians** was there from the start: what had prevention to do with treating people: we had no right to prescribe medications: that was the clinician's job.

Dean Harry Botterell (1906-1997) taught neurophysiology at the University of Toronto (1936-1939), became the senior neurosurgeon to nol Canadian Neurological Hospital, Basingstoke, (half-way between London and Southampton) during WWII, Head of Department at the University of Toronto (1953-1962), then Dean at Queen's (1962-1970) with the difficult job of leading the ultra-conservative medical faculty.

Dr Botterell soon got complaints about us from some general practitioners as well as from the internists: on one occasion, I had given the mother of a child with an ear infection a sample of penicillin. Within 24 hours, the family physician had telephoned Dr Botterell in person to complain; John was summoned to see him the next morning! We had a good laugh about that!

It was early on that it dawned upon John and I that there might be other models for the execution of primary care that were different from the _conventional slavery_ model experienced by Dr Bromley, my father and I in East Ham. A _cooperative team approach_ model might be preferable, developed somehow from a CHP.

I also realized that there would be much more _freedom of action_ if, in the future, I remained in a department of social and preventive medicine rather than in a purely clinical department of family medicine or pediatrics. John and I talked about it quite a lot. We understood each other.

Dean Botterell took the bull by the horns, telephoned Dr John Stalker, one of his old students from the University of Toronto who had settled as an internist in Sudbury. John, a nice person, rapidly became Head of the new Department of Family Medicine (**c1968**). A Scotch friend, David Alexander, a pediatrician at Queen's who had trained at Johns Hopkins, joined him. David's father had been a well known pediatrician in Edinburgh. I was asked to join, but I did not appreciate an internist as my boss!

Dr Ernie Haynes qualified in Dublin in 1947; after working in England and Trinidad, he helped establish Family Medicine Teaching Units in Edmonton (Un of Alberta), and the Deaconess Hospital in Buffalo (New York State University). In **1973,** he accepted to become the first Family Physician to be Director of the Department of Family Medicine at Queen's.

Around the end of 1965, John Read was asked to write a section on _'The Physician's Records, Present and Future'_ for a new Textbook **"Ambulatory Pediatrics"**, edited by Morris Green (Un of Indiana) and Robert J Haggerty (Un of Rochester) and published by Saunders. It was to provide _'the conceptual and intellectual substance for health care of_ **"all non-hospitalized children"** (Julius Richmond), with 177 contributors, all from the US apart from 5 Canadians and 2 Brits!

John did not have the time to write it and wondered whether I would. I accepted immediately and was thankful for the opportunity, **Joel Alpert** was to write about _'research in ambulatory patients'_ and my great teacher from WRU, **John Kennell,** a marvelous chapter of 50 pages on _'infancy and early childhood',_ the best ever.

The book was published in 1968. In the meanwhile John had been appointed Head of the Department of Health Sciences at the new Faculty of Medicine in Calgary. That was the end of the CHP at Queen's as we knew it. It was finally incorporated in the Department of Pediatrics in 1969 when I went to work in Quebec.

There was a real Department of Family Medicine in Calgary right from the start, so that problem was settled as far as John was concerned.

John Read (1924-2002) was passionate and visionary: he loved all children, by far the best boss I ever had. He hated the word "accident", implying somehow the will of God, preferring the word "injury" which could and had to be avoided. I was so lucky to meet John. He achieved so much in his life, both professionally and privately:

= in Vancouver during the early sixties John analyzed 749 child pedestrian accidents.

= John would regularly spend a month or more during the summer as MO to a handicapped children's holiday camp. The whole family loved camping.

= John went to Bangalore for a few months' sabbatical, and when he returned I asked him all about it; 'never get involved in the administration of health services anywhere but your own country'.

= when John left Queen's in 1968, the first person he hired in Calgary was a medical sociologist. When he retired in 1989 there were around 50 full-time and even more part-time faculty people representing many of the paramedical and medical professions.

= in 1989, at the first _"injury in Alberta conference"_ John was awarded the first "John H Read award for outstanding achievement in the area of injury control".

= because of John, the Olympic Games in Calgary were the first **'smoke-free Olympics'.**

= his wife D (Dorothy Burden) was the winner of the downhill and combined events plus a third in the Slalom at the Dominion Ski Championships in 1948 in Quebec when she was 24. She qualified with a science degree at McGill. John was a hockey player, but changed his allegiance to ski after meeting D. They had four outstanding children, a daughter Jan, the three boys, Ron, Ken and Jim.

The world knows about Ken Read, the youngest athlete ever to win a world cup at the age of 20, now President of Alpine Canada's Alpin, the government body for ski racing in Canada. At D & J's insistence, Ken had completed his bachelor's degree from Western when he was 24.

= in Kingston, every winter, the family would leave for the ski hill every Friday afternoon and return Monday at noon. I thought this was great but some thought it was unacceptable. No medical school staff-member worked harder that John. D told me once that she was so busy in the winter, spending the whole week washing clothes and preparing for the next week-end!

= John looked after his staff who mostly loved him: he was concerned about my earnings. He heard that there was a need in the Provincial Government's School for severely defective children in Smith's Falls for a duty pediatrician during the week-ends: I could practically double my salary by doing 48 hour shifts every second week-end. I learned a lot there.

The effect of our published chapter at Queen's was limited to recognition by the archivist at the Kingston General Hospital. By 1968, Lawrence Weed at WRU had circulated a document that was later published. It introduced the Problem Oriented Record. I was asked to chair a committee at KGH, as the result of which KGH became the first Teaching Hospital in Ontario to introduce the Problem-oriented Medical Record.

> Prior to the publication of 'Ambulatory Pediatrics'; few textbooks ever mentioned medical records.

Dean Botterell did his best to encourage me to stay in Kingston. He was **interested in my career,** had read my CV, an unusual occurrence. He asked me one day who were my teachers at the London: George Riddoch and Russell Brain on the medical side and Douglas Northfield on the surgical I answered. He knew them all. I also mentioned Henri Souttar, a world famous surgeon who still sculled on the Thames during my rowing days. Rowing was dear to dean Botterell's heart, which I did not know at the time. I had somehow become a link with his war-time experiences.

> The faculty headquarters of the Medical School were situated in a beautiful Victorian house at the corner of Barrie and Stuart Streets on the Park.
>
> The Dean asked me whether I would take the minutes of the monthly Faculty meeting of Heads of Department. I felt I could not really refuse; thus I became **secretary of the Faculty.** There were no recording machines; I would take copious notes, edit and transfer them by hand in a large ledger. This was available for consultation, and I would read them at the next meeting. It was quite laborious. I

was given a small office next to his in that beautiful old house. I got to know and appreciate John Firstbrook, the Associate Dean; he left within a year or two to work at the Royal College in Ottawa.

A little later, the Dean asked me to be **Admissions' Officer** for the Faculty: this is a difficult job, especially in a small University town like Kingston where everybody knew each other. I accepted. I wrote a 4-5 page document regarding the academic achievements of boys and girls at school, how boys develop more slowly than girls so that girls often do better! He was very interested, asked me whether anybody had read it, and I said no. He then promptly tore it up: it would only complicate matters!

I always made it quite clear to Dean Botterell that I had not become a Pediatrician to become an administrator. I wanted to use my maternal language in my work and that I was interested in primary care. He understood that perfectly.

In March 1969, Dean Botterell asked me to represent the Faculty at the **yearly meeting of the American Association of Medical Colleges** (AAMC) in Washington. Joan and I flew there and stayed at Marriott's Three Bridges Motor Hotel for four nights. That trip was our first 'luxury' trip since leaving the UK: we rented a new Camaro two seater, and visited the area, Alexandria, Mount Vernon, the National Gallery of Art, the Washington National Symphony Orchestra, the White House, the Capitol building.

The highlight was **Margaret Mead** (1901-1978) at the Association dinner. One of the most famous women of her generation, she gave a remarkable talk, the highlight of our stay. I also met the dean of Hershey's Medical School and we had a long conversation.

Joan and I did two dangerous things, even 'insane' according to some, crossing the park and crossing the Potomac River by a bridge without sidewalks, both at night!

An amazing coincidence then occurred that spring. **The first meeting ever in Canada of all twelve admission officers for Medical School** occurred at the University of Toronto, a large oblong table with twelve comfortable chairs each labeled with our names in alphabetical order. My neighbor was none other than **Marcel Drolet** (cfr p 6) from the new University of Sherbrook, Quebec. We were doing the same job. We exchanged news regarding what had happened in each other's lives since our meetings at the London Hospital during that winter in 1957. We were delighted to see one another.

Marcel immediately insisted that I apply to teach in the new Faculty, inviting me to stay at his Chalet in North Hatley on a hill overlooking Lake Memphramagog in the Eastern Townships: three days with the whole family, his refrigerator full of French cheeses, croissants, fresh baguettes, bottles of French wine. We had a lovely time and discovered the beauty of the area.

My salary would start at $30,000/year. It would be a chance to finally use my maternal language and to sharpen my medical French which was not up to par. The conditions were better than those offered in Kingston and life would certainly be more exciting. I would rapidly be given the rank of Associate Professor. I accepted as of **September 1st 1969.**

Our last souvenir of Kingston was a dinner party for six at Helen's house, the Botterells, the Caves and the Delvas. We all had a lovely time. I had learned so much about the inner workings of the medical profession during those four years.

What was happening in the USA in Medical Education during that Decade:

On page 2, the reader was introduced to Abraham Flexner, and on page 10 to John Scott Millis. As Dr Millis puts it, in the 7th decade of the 20th century, the **AMA** has for the 2nd time **"again expressed its continuing concern by requesting an external examination of the internship and residency, the constituent parts of graduate medical education . . ."**

The **Millis report of the Citizens Commission on the Graduate Education of Physicians** was published in August 1966; over 100 pages long (5"×8"), it is thorough, learned and complete. Whereas the Flexner report was acted upon immediately and ruthlessly, the Millis report was not considered as meriting much urgency; although it covered the field, unfortunately there were no representatives on the committee of

Public Health/Community Medicine/Primary Care/Family Medicine.

On the other hand, **The Education of Physicians for Primary Care** by **Joel Alpert** (Boston) and **Evan Charney** (Rochester), both pediatricians, published during the autumn of 1973 by the US Department of Health, Education and Welfare was an electrifying effort. It was over 60 pages long (8"×10"), and was written while on Sabbatical in London, England, for a year.

Both of them had contributed a chapter in 'Ambulatory Pediatrics', and they both felt that primary care pediatrics was best dealt with by well trained family physicians. They spent their year with **Professor Margot Jefferys,** head of the Social Medicine Unit at Bedford College, University of London.

Joel I had met in Boston in 1965. I had met Professor Jefferys at Queen's. Sir John Ellis, of the London Hospital, was supposed to be **the** English expert on Medical Education, and we both agreed that he had insufficient experience or qualifications for such a reputation. We laughed together for a whole hour.

Recommendations for the future of the continuum of Medical Education (NEJM, July 14th, 1977) is a concise, useful but uninspiring document, a two page summary (William G Anlyan, Duke University). It fails to deal specifically with primary care.

The Sherbrook Period: (September 1st **1969**-August 31st **1975**.)

I had nothing much to do officially about family medicine at the totally new medical school in Sherbrook, the capital of the Eastern Townships.

It was the first medical school in Canada where the school, the hospital and the research facilities were integrated into just one building/organization, the **CHUS,** *(Centre Hospitalier Universitaire de Sherbrooke).* People seem to agree that this is the best model for an 'ideal' school. It was quite an achievement. Situated in the middle of a field, two miles from the town centre, it was in an area that was never to be integrated into the town itself, and it has so remained.

The reason for that was that the structure of the CHUS had been built as a large 1200 bedded psychiatric hospital of the old kind, isolated as was usual at that time in the countryside; it had become unnecessary: the unfinished structure was thus available and deemed to be ideal for a new large institution such as a CHUS. And it worked, although its start was perilous, with deans replacing one another at regular short intervals.

A Ministry of Education in Quebec was only created on May 13th 1964. A **Liberal Government** was elected on April 30th 1970, replacing *l'Union Nationale*. It's Ministry of Health, renamed **Ministry of Social Affairs,** followed in June 1970, and on December 24th 1971 **Law 65 on the Health and Social Services** was promulgated: local Community Health and Social Service Centers *(CLSCs)* with salaried staff would cover most of the province, and Departments of Community Services *(DSCs)* would coordinate them. The whole health care system in Quebec was being revamped in an exciting way.

As far as the health-care **staff of the CHUS** itself was concerned, most were **francophones,** mostly from Sherbrook itself, **just** a few from the Universities of Montreal and of Laval in Quebec City: others came from Acadia, France, Belgium, Switzerland, Catalonia, Central Europe, a few Anglophones from the rest of Canada, from **the** Mediterranean basin, the World Health Organization, the USA. To get everybody to work together was a feat in itself; it was similar to a thrilling roller-coaster ride. It had its ups and downs with two suicides amongst the senior staff.

The University had been started in 1955 by the Archbishop of Sherbrook and thus had a **Papal Charter.** The Archbishop had to promise the then prime minister, Maurice Duplessis, not to ask for government money for 10 years, thus the delay in founding the medical school itself.

The New Medical School was thus in a new location, separated from the rest of the University by the town of Sherbrook itself (population 65,683 in 1961).

An early Associate Dean, the only senior staff member who had a particular interest in **Medical Education,** died suddenly: he was never replaced.

At the start, the faculty was divided into three divisions:

= of the health sciences (sociology, psychology, anthropology, economics, statistics, epidemiology), its clinical arm being community medicine,
= of the basic sciences,
= of the clinical sciences.

The MD course lasted three years at first, with a short summer vacation.

Within three years, the whole organization had reverted to the usual hum'drum 24 departments, of which Community Medicine was the least important, one like all the others; the pay structure became 'normalized'. The length of the course reverted to the usual four years. Most of the staff of the health sciences' division resigned, including the economist head of the division and my boss, a pediatrician with a year in Public Health in California. He went back to the department of Pediatrics where his future would be traditional. He remained very active in the many committees.

The new young dean, a nephrologist from Verdun, a Montreal suburb, knew little about genetics, community/social/preventive medicine or the principles of teaching, but he was a good administrator:

His first year at University had been in Theology; he asked me
to be head of the department of Community Medicine, just at the

time when Dr Henry Morgentaler had won his battle and abortions had become legalized. The separation of Church and State became more of a problem especially for me, causing personal havoc. At the end of my first year, the dean asked for my resignation which I was pleased to accept. I was soon replaced (October 18th 1971) by an ardent Catholic working in Washington, DC; he was very nice, would not rock the boat, and knew little about the Canadian scene. This was also the period when I permanently stopped going to church and became an atheist.

Dr Louis Fortin (1920-2008), a family physician who had trained at McGill, started to work in the out-patient department of the CHUS in **January 15th 1970.** His office was right in the middle of the specialty clinics in the large out-patient department: he had to cope with all the health problems the patients had that the specialists could or would not deal with. <u>The employment of a general practitioner had become an early necessity at this early stage of development at the CHUS.</u>

Thus, Louis became the first family physician in Quebec with a University appointment (associate professor), thus satisfying the demands of the Canadian College of Family Physicians. During my mandate I asked the dean to promote Louis and he accepted, so Louis soon became a full-professor, earlier than any other general practitioner in the whole of Canada.

The physical site where he had to work at the CHUS was an ideal location for meeting medical students. That was an unplanned benefit for family medicine. Students all got exposed to a real working family physician early in their career. How lucky they were. Louis and I respected one another deeply; the students greatly appreciated his approach.

He was the founder of academic Family Medicine in Quebec. An official Department of Family Medicine developed soon after at the CHUS, but its location at the margin of the specialty clinics in this large building, several miles away and isolated from downtown was not an appropriate one. It took the best part of two decades before Family Medicine had gained a down-town location. The CHUS was not an ideal place for the Teaching of Primary Care.

Louis had moved from Godbout, a small paper-mill town on the North Shore of the St Lawrence. Baie Comeau, founded in 1935, is 35 or so kms to the west; 22,000 people live there to-day.

Godbout is much smaller. Ex-Prime Minister of Canada Brian Mulroney (b 1939) came from Baie Comeau. Two different ferries join Baie Comeau and Godbout to Matane (60 Kms) on the South Shore.

Most of Louis' income had come from the local industry. Thus, his apprenticeship as a family physician had been complete, ideal to help him understand the relationship between work and sickness, a perfect location for learning one's job.

Louis moved to Sherbrook when his children were growing up and needed to further their education. Marquis Fortin was one of them: he is now a senior staff member (Associate Professor) in the Department of Family Medicine at *l'Hopital Notre-Dame* in Montreal (now part of a future CHUM). He entered medical school at the CHUS soon after Louis got there. Marquis, one of my first students, was responsible for and played the main part in a successful recent weekly Health Education Program on Radio-Quebec Television. He was never seen wearing a stethoscope!

I got to know Louis well because I had asked him to help looking after Joan's father. John Walter Stewart Campbell, (Jack), nearly eighty, arrived by himself with just a day's notice at Dorval airport on February 27th 1970. He was very unhappy in the nursing home where he was living as Granny was unable to look after him. He was wheeled out of the plane, a tiny briefcase on his knees with his pyjamas and shaving kit. He had become so thin from an abdominal cancer; he died at home in Lennoxville, a suburb of Sherbrook where we lived.

After spending just two/three days in hospital under Louis' care to rule out any medical/surgical intervention, Pop came home and died. He enjoyed scotch, grapes and morphine to the end, just like my Dad. He kept saying how happy he was to be with us after his transatlantic flight: he had arranged it all by phone, by himself, at the last minute. Louis visited twice a weekly. Louis was an ideal model for students and he helped the Delva family greatly during a difficult period.

= **Julien Denhez** became a good friend. He was an experienced Public Health Medical Officer of my own age who had spent all his life in Quebec. He thus helped me such a lot to understand what had happened in that field in Quebec. He was intellectually quite brilliant although unrecognized by his peers. His salary had always been very much less than that of his clinical colleagues. He knew all about writing objectives and was good at it, a great help for me, particularly in the domain of the nursing program described below.

At first at the CHUS, salaries were all the same according to rank and years of service: this was all changed after the first three years, and the salary of doctors working in Community Medicine was actually cut when the department became one of the many others: I complained bitterly and that situation was corrected. So, my good new friend, who would never even think of complaining, was very relieved.

WHAT DID I DO at the CHUS?

=   **I taught Basic Genetics,** and I thoroughly enjoyed it, one hour a week for one semester. The library had few books and a decent budget, so I could purchase whatever textbooks and audio-visual equipment I liked. The librarian was so keen and efficient, everything arriving as if by magic and on time. But there was none of the clinical component because during the whole of my six year stay at the CHUS I was never referred even one patient for counseling. It was clear at the time that 5% of all newborns had possible problems that needed it; that just deals with newborns. I did more genetic counseling in Antigonish than in the CHUS.

=   **I did House-Calls** mostly for the children of staff-members, just as I did in East Ham twenty years before, and much enjoyed it: *"Peter, could you pop-in to visit Johnny with earache? Thanks a lot"*.

=   **The majority of physicians in Quebec took a holiday at the same time instead of going on strike,** the CHUS remaining open to cover emergencies.

I was asked to go to *l'hopital St Vincent de Paul* to see a very sick child who was just waiting to be admitted. **Mona,** aged four, had leukemia. Her Mum and her American Dad were teachers. I had the greatest difficulty getting her transferred to the CHUS. I continued to treat Mona, who lived in Windsor a few miles away, for over four years until I left Sherbrook. I gave continuing total care, at home and in out-patients. That was a wonderful experience. With the same nurse, in the same room at the CHUS, I was able to obtain all the samples of blood and marrow needed for proper follow-up, and Mona always accepted these horrible procedures without batting an eye-lid. We loved meeting each other. I never kept her waiting, and gave her little gifts now and again. We met once or twice a month for four years.

Mona had an older brother who felt somewhat neglected by so much attention being showered on his sister. Whenever Mona was suffering from the usual ailments of childhood, I would see Mona at home.

I soon found out that Mona's brother was likely to develop a streptococcal infection of his tonsils whenever Mona was unwell. I always travelled with test-tubes to take throat samples, so a 'scientific' diagnosis was readily made.

Her mother was very sensitive, and kept telling me tales, such as a neighbor wanting to lend her an adult-sized bed as Mona was growing up and it was not worth buying a new one. I suggested she write all these events in a diary, so that she might in the future write about it: she did exactly that, and "**Mona**" was published in 1979, over 200 pages: it sold over **12,000 copies** before being translated into English, a record. I wrote an unsigned two page addendum at the editor's request. Mona herself enjoyed the book. She actually lived for ten years after the diagnosis had been made.

I met her once in Montreal, a joyful event for Mona and a joyful/painful one for me. By that time, she had a younger brother. The beauty of looking after chronically sick young children is their unfailing optimism. Death is simply not in the cards.

= Before leaving Sherbrook to work in Quebec City, the head of the Division of the Social Sciences, an economist, was offered a contract by the Department of Health and Welfare in Ottawa to **train nurses for three months before their final posting to a nursing station in the Canadian North,** mostly around James Bay, in northern Quebec and on the north-east shore of the St Lawrence. Five such programs had been started around the country; this was the only francophone one.

I asked to lead the project and I was very happy to do it. That was exciting: six nurses, often married couples, would spend two months full-time at the CHUS before their twelve months' contract; during the third month we would visit them in their new work-stations for a few days to offer more practical support. It worked like a charm. The course gave them a lot more confidence. The big problem that arose was that after the completion of their contract, they quickly discovered that better remunerated jobs in better environments were available in the south, particularly in the new CLSC/DSCs. So after a few years, the Federal Government typically just abandoned the project.

An expert on education, CB Hazlett, PhD, Research Director and Workshop Chairman from the University of Edmonton, was attached to the program. He was methodical, enthusiastic and tough. He formed a *"Committee for Developing Validated Behavioral Objectives for the Clinical Training of Nurses Programs".*

The five centers worked and cooperated, meeting regularly, nurses and medical/surgical specialists together with the Medical Services Branch from Ottawa, often in Winnipeg because it was in the middle of the country. Each program had to write their own objectives, and these were circulated for discussion and adoption.

<u>The Manual of Clinical Skills in Primary Care Nursing</u> was finally published in **1977 by McGraw-Hill.** This was a fantastic and difficult achievement as far as I was concerned. I was happy to have been a member of that team. Nurses and specialist physicians plus an expert on postgraduate Education were responsible for the document. Unfortunately, there were no representatives of Family Medicine.

During that same period, the first edition of the **Terminal Objectives of the Undergraduate Medical Curriculum** was published in September 1977 by **the Department of Education of Laval University Medical School** in Quebec City, the first of all francophone universities in the world to do so and the first one in Quebec. Laval was the first Medical School in the Province of Quebec to have its own Department of Education. However, no general practitioner helped in the elaboration of the document although four of them were asked to read the finalized 600 page document before printing.

<u>The trouble about writing objectives</u> is that it encourages learning lists by memory and is <u>anti-primary-care</u> by definition: when seeing a person, patient or student, for the first time, you want to encourage communication and you avoid like the plague filling up questionnaires from lists. That is exactly what Louis Fortin and I had learnt by experience. Objectives are an important guide to be used to further ones' future experiences, but are of no help at all to encourage a positive interpersonal relationship. Who has ever filled up a questionnaire when one meets one's future spouse for the first time? That is what Flexner failed to understand.

= **A building was allocated in down town Sherbrook for use as a CLSC during the spring 1973.** I took a bunch of students and we sat on the floor in one of the empty rooms for a discussion. On one such occasion, the Minister of Health himself, **Monsieur Forget,** on a tour and alone, opened the door for an instant and promptly disappeared! There was much enthusiasm and spirits were high.

As soon as the local *CLSC* became functional, I asked the Dean whether I could work there two half-days a week: he was quite delighted at the idea; it was good for public relations; the income earned would be paid to the CHUS as my University salary precluded other sources of income.

Thus I did many house-calls with the nurses to visit some of the older poorer people in the area. The nurses gained confidence rapidly. They had organized volunteers amongst the younger old-age pensioners who would keep an eye on the older people in their own block. One of our young new doctors went there to work full-time that summer. It was just like East Ham where everybody knew everybody else. A great young team had started to develop. Another ex-student helped found a new CLSC in *Lac Etchemin*, a country area south of Quebec City, *'la Beauce'*, a beautiful fruit-growing/jam-making place; but it was a doctor-deprived area. Great things were starting to happen.

= **My relationship with the College of Family Medicine was ambiguous:** I emigrated from London to be a general practitioner. Then I thought I would further my education in my adopted country and specialized in Pediatrics. But comprehensive family care was my first love. I thought Ambulatory Pediatrics just for children to be unsatisfactory; a family physician knows all the members of the family: it was part of me as a general practitioner, I felt my specialist qualifications were viewed with suspicion by many family physicians. I knew all about the difficult examination of the College to obtain certification. I could not be considered an 'academic' family physician without it, so, with much trepidation, without telling anybody, **I took the CFPC examination without preparation just before leaving Sherbrook and passed at the 45th percentile.** I was happy about that. I was 50 years old, and it was the last exam I ever **took!**

This happened at the same time as **Dr Georges Desrosiers,** the first director (appointed in only 1973) of **the** University of Montreal's new Department of Social and Preventive Medicine asked me in March 1974 to develop a Family Medicine teaching unit at *l'Hopital du Sacre-Coeur* (l'HSC) in *Cartierville,* on the north shore of the island of Montreal.

Georges became a good friend. He had been a general practitioner in a working-class area of Montreal prior to switching to further study in Public Health and Hospital Administration.

During that time, he had spent six months at *l'HSC* as an assistant administrator during the mid-seventies. Thus, he understood the particular functioning of *l'HSC*. I would have half of the top 6th floor where young student nurses had been living plus $35.000 for transformation.

That is how I got officially involved in the **Teaching of Family Medicine. I finally felt ready to tackle that kind of job and was offered the opportunity to do so,** a rare occasion to do something that meets one's abilities and experiences.

I would never have heard of *l'HSC* if it had not been for **Dr Norman Bethune.** He had worked there for over three years during the thirties. The nurses in the teaching program in Sherbrook had given me a copy of Ted Allen's biography that had only recently been translated into French. I had been very struck by the life of Dr Bethune. That explains partly why so many French Canadians had never heard of Norman Bethune. The other reason was the attitude of the Roman Catholic Church towards Communism: just do not talk about it. Dr Bethune had become a Communist three years before he died in November 1939 at the age of 49.

The Montreal Period, 1: 1975-1980.

With the development of the Health Care System in Quebec, the Ministry of Health had become aware of the need for Teaching Units (four of them at the University of Montreal were in the works, all in locations in the periphery of Central Montreal) for the training of future Family Physicians. However, the Medical and Surgical Specialists in the Medical Schools controlled the pre-and post-graduate Hospital Based Medical Education. Academically I had become one of their elite! So I felt empowered to a certain extent to do just something like that.

I was interviewed prior to my appointment to the staff of the hospital; the Chairman, *docteur Andre Proulx,* a quite charming and intelligent senior cardiologist, asked me why, with my qualifications, had I chosen to lead such a project, implying I might be wasting my time; I answered that the reason I had accepted was because of my background and qualifications: I believed passionately that the success of the project would be easier to accomplish because I was better officially qualified. I would be able to speak my mind more easily and resist pressure. I also thought I had my own ideas on how it could be done.

In a nutshell, *l'Hopital du Sacre-Coeur* (HSC), was built on its present site in the 1920s specifically for treating patients with tuberculosis. It had started by *les Soeurs de la Providence* during the 1890s in a house in down-town Montreal as a refuge for the dying, moving a mile or so further east to larger quarters which burned down. Tuberculosis was an enormous problem particularly after WWI, so during the 1920s *l'HSC* was rebuilt in *Cartierville* on the North Shore of the Island of Montreal as a sanatorium, specifically for the care of patients with tuberculosis, with wide corridors, large open balconies and over 600 beds; it was situated on a large plot of land nicely landscaped.

Such Institutions had two priorities pertaining to surgery: establish orthopedic units as tuberculosis can affect the bones of the body, and chest surgery. Norman Bethune was the first Chest Surgeon to be appointed after his ignominious dismissal from McGill in 1932. L'HSC eventually became a full-blown University of Montreal Teaching Hospital only in the early 1960s.

To-day in 2009, *l'HSC* is an extremely well-oiled and well-administered institution with a vision: it is the referral centre for the whole of North-Western Quebec with well-over a million inhabitants. Its Trauma Centre, just down hill from the Laurentian ski slopes, is the best in Quebec. The large Family Medicine Centre is situated right next to the largest emergency centre in the Province and there is much cooperation between them. Over 50% of the emergency physicians there are now fully accredited family physicians. The headquarters of Bombardier are in *la ville de St Laurent*, with a large multi-ethnic population and which lies immediately to the south of the Hospital, and with *la Cite de Laval*, now the second largest City in Quebec, immediately to the north.

By January 2007, at *l'HSC,* an advanced care University of Montreal General Hospital with 670 beds, Family Medicine had become responsible for 30 geriatric beds, 40 beds for long-term care, 20 beds for acute care and 12 beds in palliative care. Fifty % of births were delivered by Family Physicians. The teaching program for prospective Family Physicians respected the philosophy that I had introduced in 1975.

The HSC is sufficiently isolated from the very complicated politics of the down-town Montreal Hospitals; it is entirely French speaking, but many patients of Italian origin who often speak only English go there because it is a Catholic Institution. Teleconferencing was developing there in the 1970s. *Les Soeurs de la Providence* possess the hospital: it is rented by the Ministry of Health, half the rent being reinvested by the Sisters in basic research in the hospital itself.

I planned the Family Medicine Unit in 1974 carefully with several innovations; it was situated as far from the front-door of the hospital as possible with a single small rickety elevator; this location caused me some anxiety but I need not have worried; a large residents' room where each had a little desk of his/her own and a little library, a large waiting/teaching room with tables that can be joined together to make a circle so that 12 people can sit together around it. Single offices for each staff member, four clinical offices to see patients, each with decent upright scales and small desks against the wall so that the patient sits close to the physician. Two offices with a one-way glass partition with a video-camera on one side.

After a long discussion with the hospital **records librarian,** it was decided to use the hospital record with a separate family medicine section: thus our record was available for any staff person to see when needed: <u>one patient, one record, one institution.</u> The wide corridors of the hospital were used by tri-cyclists with large baskets to distribute records as required day and night throughout the hospital, a very efficient operation. We also had a small treatment room, and each resident took the necessary blood samples or performed other procedures as required: this was easier for the patients and it was often a first experience for the residents. It increased bonding of relationships.

The staff included **Marielle Beauger,** a Haitian lady with a Master's degree in nursing, two school-aged children, whose husband taught high-school mathematics in Laval, and **Yolande St Germain,** a first class experienced social worker and a keen follower of Virginia Satir in California, the mother of Family System Therapy: *coping with problems* was her important message. Yolande would disappear for a week or two during the winter to go to California.

The three of us went off to Miami to participate in a seminar by Hilliard Jason and his group at 'The National Center for Faculty Development': *"Being an Effective Clinical Teacher",* March 3-7 1980: an excellent experience for the two dozen or so participants that reinforced what we were trying to do. I had attended a similar one with Dr Richard Nelson, a young general practitioner who had joined the faculty, for a long week-end while in Sherbrook, and we had been struck by the excellence of the experience. Unfortunately, Richard moved to the USA shortly afterwards.

As in Kingston, **I allied myself with Psychiatry.** But Psychiatry at Queen's in Kingston and at *l'HSC* was quite different: the first French Psychiatric Teaching Hospital was opened during the 1920s just around the corner from *l'HSC*; it is to-day incorporated within the HSC complex. Prior to the 1950s, all French speaking psychiatrists had to leave Quebec for training, in Paris &/ or the USA (usually Boston).

Dr Camille Laurin, of Bill 101 fame, finished his training in Boston/Paris during the 1950s. He was immediately appointed Head of Psychiatry at *l' U de M.* His first project was to institute a program for training French-speaking psychiatrists so that they no longer had to leave Quebec.

He was very much influenced by French Psychiatry where some of the fully-trained Psychiatrists sub-specialize in Psychosomatic Medicine*, and that is what Dr Laurin introduced in Quebec: to-day seven of them are on full-time staff at the HSC, more than in any other hospital anywhere in North America.

Dr Jacques Monday was one of them. To-day, he is Head of the Department of Psychosomatic Medicine at *l'HSC*. He had been a general practitioner before becoming a Psychiatrist/ Psycho-somatician and quickly became an essential member of our teaching team.

Psychosomatic Medicine was thus an intrinsic component of Family Medicine at the HSC. It took me several years to understand all this; thus serendipity played its part. At Jacques' suggestion, we purchased ten two-inch foam mats, and on teaching days we would all spend ten minutes on them learning the Jacobsen technique which we could then pass on to our patients.

Jacobsen, (b.1888) a reputed scientist with a PhD working for Bell Telephone in Chicago during the early twenties coined the term. He discovered that muscular exercise promotes the production of endorphins with itself improved immune responses. He subsequently obtained an MD degree.

= **The Philosophy of the Unit** was new in Canada: at the U of M, the medical course lasted five years at that time, so the students were a good deal older than those in Sherbrook where the course lasted at its start just three years: our priority was to encourage an early exposure of the resident to the patient, the excellence of the doctor/patient relationship **(bonding)** being the top priority. I also remembered my experiences at the London Hospital: students were treated like morons until they got through their finals, then, from one day to the next they had become experts and treated with dignity. We always tried to treat our residents **with dignity.** We gave them a home and they loved it.

Until we came on the scene, young doctors could enter general practice after a one year long internship in the various specialties with no specific introduction

---

*   *psychosomatic* means relating to, involving, or concerned with bodily symptoms caused by mental or emotional disturbance (Merriam-Webster); the word itself is mentioned in the *Larousse* and the *Robert*. There is no mention of the word in the Oxford Reference English Dictionary. *Psycho* refers to mental processes and activities; *Somatic* means 'of the body'.

to general practice/family medicine. They were just cast out of the faculty to make a living without further ado. **In our program, they started caring for a new patient by themselves within a week or so of starting their residency without direct supervision,** but we were available for consultation at all times and we tried to create an environment that encouraged communication.

Thus, the residents immediately felt responsible for their patients. They were empowered for the first time the day they saw their own first patient within a week of starting their residency. At the end of their training they could go on looking after their patients if they did not settle down too far away. If they settled outside town, they would introduce each patient to a younger resident colleague. The patients were thus attached to their doctor rather than to the institution.

= in the same way, we never routinely examined the **residents' records:** we took it for granted that each resident was able to do it. But we discussed record keeping a great deal, the problem oriented chart and flow charts included. One resident produced an excellent audiovisual slide/tape show about medical records that was distributed to all the other Family Medicine units. Three or four times a year, each resident had to produce a ten minute tape of the recording of an interview they had had. They might tape several interviews, being able to choose whichever one they wanted.

= **our mistakes were there for all to see and talk about:** I suffered much from my own! But everybody realized mistakes happened to everyone and we tried to talk about them.

= the unit soon became cohesive, with marriages, births, family problems and broken relationships amongst the residents, so much that at one point they seemed to melt with the real patients, a great but surprising and un-planned experience for the staff!

= once a week, the unit offered a <u>catered snack/lunch</u>: as the residents did most of their other rotations in the hospital, it was an occasion where we could all meet and talk shop: very soon, many of the residents would bring sandwiches on other days which they ate in the unit.

If one of the patients they looked after on the ward on one of their rotations had no Family Doctor, they could suggest a follow-up in the unit with an explanation of its function.

= two or three times a year the unit organized an afternoon or even a day off: we could reserve the use of a university-owned <u>riverside mansion with a tennis-court</u> free, usually a property left to the University in a will. All residents in Family Medicine from the hospital would be invited. We would all have lunch together, talking shop or not. Jacques Monday invariably participated in most of these informal meetings.

= none of our <u>residents</u> ever left the program: we had four in the first year, four in the first plus four in second year, increasing to eight in each year within a few years. What did we do? We discussed a great deal about what to do after their two-year stint:

They all took the national family medicine examination and they all passed, just one or two on their second try. This was a first in Quebec. We kept stressing the stupidity of examinations, measuring someone's capacity to do something for the rest of his/her life in such a short time without any knowledge of the person being examined apart from some knowledge accumulated from sheets of paper. But certain national standards had to be reached, and exams were the only way to do it. The quality of the CFPC examination was the best available anywhere in the world; failure is no dishonor. One just tries again. A friend in England, the senior pathologist for many years in Warwickshire in the UK and quite brilliant passed his fellowship exams in England on his 7th yearly attempt! He never took it too seriously.

We talked about where and how to start a medical practice: in a working-class or a middle-class area, the countryside or the small/big town, living over the shop rather than travelling to work, taking note of the necessity of educating a future family and the needs of the spouse: my own experience helped in that regard.

Further studying in adjacent areas was an important topic: two of our residents are now senior founding physicians at <u>*l'Institut de Geriatrie de l'UdeM*</u> after two years extra training in Community Medicine. One went off to Stanford for two years (the second year at my insistence) where he acquired an MSc and eventually a PhD at McGill in the field of Health Care.

Claude Baudouin, one of the original four who had to repeat his final examination just once obtained a grant to obtain a PhD at *l'UdeM:* '<u>the Impact of Family Medicine in Health Care</u>': he quickly became head of research in Family Medicine at *l'UdeM*. He was a heavy smoker and unfortunately he died at an early age of cancer of the lung; he was a much loved, honest and sincere person: he was missed by everyone.

Marielle Beauger obtained a PhD at *l'UdeM* on the study of a <u>family-based **health record**</u> to be given to the parents of new-borns. It had always struck me as incongruous that when one purchases a new car one is given a beautiful book on its maintenance, whereas a mother is in and out of hospital in the shortest possible time with perhaps a sheet or two of instructions as to the immediate care of her new-born. Marielle's booklet included Holmes' list of normal events that could lead to a break-down in family health.

= there were three <u>basic texts for discussion</u> that we used all the time: the *Kerr-White square* summarizing the epidemiology of health care, *Holmes' study* on the effect of situations in life that can lead to a breakdown in health, and the *Alpert and Charney* study mentioned above.

= the <u>head of the new *department de santé communautaire*</u> at *l'HSC* had an office on the same floor. <u>Rachel Parent</u> was his quite fantastic head nurse. She and I understood one another well, and she would whenever she could be very supportive. But her boss was of the old school of Public Health, and kept advising me to work with the local general practitioners, some of whom were old class-mates: *c'est du bon monde* he used to say. He never really understood what we were attempting to do.

= I had retained contact with the Federal Ministry of Health regarding the care of isolated **Indian settlements** and was asked to look after a settlement on an island just north of *St Michel-des-Saints*, a three hour drive. One had to take a plane for a ten minutes' flight. I accepted on condition that residents could come with me. This was not a problem as the plane rarely carried more than two people. Thus, all our residents in turn could spend a few hours there. They loved it. The flight was occasionally quite stressful, fog and wind. Joan (my wife) accompanied me on one occasion; she had to use a paper bag for the only time ever. She has never forgotten that windy trip.

= I met a few local medical-practitioners; some had children studying medicine, some in our own program: these were enthusiastic about what their children were doing. They all had busy practices and none of them understandably ever suggested helping. Thus I never sought the help of any of them in the teaching unit. Some volunteered help by accepting students in their offices as an introduction to family medicine. That is why one of the original four young newly qualified Family Physicians who had trained at *l'HSC*, **Jacques Trudel**, was able to take my job over when I became **head of Family Medicine for the University in 1980**. All future heads of Family Medicine at *l'HSC* had completed their training there: thus a young new team had been established and continuity could be guaranteed.

The University had recognized Family Medicine as a separate Department of the Faculty of Medicine **before** the Faculty of Medicine itself! *L'UdeM* did not tolerate cross appointments, so I opted to be the first GFT Full Professor of Family Medicine in the new University Department of Family Medicine, the faculty only agreeing in 1978.

Other Pertinent Teaching Activities were introduced **during the five undergraduate years**: one cannot expect a new student to be enamored with family medicine if, during the five years' training, he or she is never exposed to it. It so happened that the first year would soon be eliminated. So there was a dearth of valid experiences for first year students. Likewise, teachers were not so interested in teaching during the first semester of the second year because of the so-called 'immaturity' of the students.

So, during the first year, I volunteered to organize an elective, *"Introduction to Family Medicine"* or some such title for a maximum often students. We would meet once a week for a couple of hours for three months to discuss the subject. One or two students at a time would accompany me on house-calls once a week. I would collect the student/s and we would drive to see the patient, thus I was able to introduce the visit:

= an 80 year old widow came from Baltimore and told everyone she did not like French Canadians. She lived by herself on a second floor apartment in a dwelling with an outdoor staircase. Her husband had been a purser on the Queen Mary, and her pension was paid in GBP. She had diabetes and both legs had been amputated. Every morning she would put on her artificial legs but never walked on them. She lived in a wheel-chair with her dearly loved canary who sang constantly. Her cleaning lady helped a lot. She read a lot of Harlequin Romances. She was just about able to look after herself and refused to enter an institution. Two or three times a year, an ambulance would turn up to take her to see her internist, and two attendants were needed to carry her to the ambulance in her chair down the narrow staircase. So many questions arose:

- why not in a home? She doesn't want to.
- why not on the ground floor? There was no sun-shine and her canary would not approve.
- why not take a blood sample at home? Is there a need to see a specialist at a considerable cost to the Health Care system?

Now and again, she would crave for some ice-cream and would telephone before my visit to ask me to bring some. I would bring a small container and the ice-cream would last a couple of days.

= an older professional couple lived in a pleasant well-furnished apartment: they were a typical 85 year old couple with the usual problems, hearing loss, cataracts, difficulty in moving around, fatigue, insomnia, coping with stairs, hardening of the arteries, wanting to stay in their home for as long as possible. They each had about three or four different specialists looking after different parts of their bodies: dentists, ophthalmologists, cardiologists, urologists, gynecologists, hearing specialists, rheumatologists with pills and creams and eye drops etc . . . .

It was a different way of looking at health problems. There was not one of my patients who refused to have students accompany me. Older patients were delighted to break the monotony of their lives by welcoming such visits. The students were quite delighted and disseminated their experiences. Within a couple of years, third year students visited older people at home in pairs, one with a small video camera. *L'UdeM* had a good audiovisual department with a lot of equipment students could borrow. They would record part of the interview and then show us the tape and talk about their feelings about the interview. The tapes were immediately erased after use.

My most important contribution in the teaching of the new **_Community Medicine_** started in October 1978, the first semester of the first new four year curriculum, **_"Child Abuse and Neglect"_**. This replaced many lectures: four three hour periods on Monday mornings, new students, one month after their start. Details of the course can be found in Chapter 43.

Emphasis was placed on sending the 157 students out in 15 groups to interview professional workers of all kinds, plus <u>NGOs</u> such as the Home for Battered Women, the Children's Aid Society, the Provincial Medical Society, *Centre-Aid,* very important in Montreal; and <u>GOs</u> such as the CLSCs and the DSCs plus lawyers and the Police. The secretary of each group would have to report what happened and submit a one sheet summary. Thus we had a 30 pages' long account written by students. We tried to stress prevention, *primary,* before the onset, *secondary* soon after the onset, and *tertiary,* after the condition is fully developed.

Students cannot be exposed to Family/Community Medicine in a class-room: **the Medical School must include the City** and **the <u>City serves as the Laboratory</u>** for **<u>Community and Family Medicine</u>**. A take home exam followed; it stressed prevention. Most of the students approved of the formula.

It was much harder to organize than to give a set of dull lectures repeated year after year.

Within three years, nine other problems were presented in similar format, one in each semester during the first year, and two in each semester during the second and third year, the whole thing organized by colleagues in Family Medicine, Community Medicine, and Psychiatry:

= Industrial Accidents.
= Learning Problems at School. = Loss of Autonomy associated with Ageing.
= Road Accidents.   = Teenage Pregnancy.
= Alcoholism,   = Depression.
= Sexually Transmitted Diseases = Approaching Death.

Thus, students were exposed to Family/Community Medicine every semester of their first three years in medical School. What a change! At the end of those first three years the students had a pretty good idea of medical priorities and of the distribution of family physicians in the City, a good introduction to Family and Community Medicine as well as to Psychosomatic Medicine.

We soon discovered a poor area in Montreal with **37,000** people and no physican's office, *__la Paroisse Rene Goupil__*, north of *le Boulevard Metropolitain* on *Boulevard Pie IX*. There were no green spaces. So I obtained a line of credit for $22,000 from *la Banque Nationale,* rented a ground-level apartment and transformed it into a doctor's office. It soon proved to be damp, so we moved to a first floor round the corner.

With voluntary personnel and a paid secretary, we soon had a successful operation with the help of an ex-resident who ultimately became a child psychiatrist. He continued to work there after qualifying as a psychiatrist. I worked there for two cessions a week, and as soon as my debt was paid off, after about five years, when the operation was functional, I left. It was not suitable for residents, as they were not allowed to practice without the presence of a teacher, but it was very useful for undergraduate students. There is now a *CLSC* in the parish.

I did house-calls there. In the whole of England I had never heard of such a large population without a doctor's office. It was there that a patient, a lady, a very loving person with a sad background, had become angry and disillusioned. I encouraged her to write her story. It was published in 1982, *'Une Fille comme Moi'*, by the same publisher as **'Mona'** mentioned above, *Heritage+plus,* St Lambert,

Quebec. The mental health of the two authors was much helped by the experience.

I had the funny experience at arriving at the patient's door at the same time as the local television crew who had heard that I did house-calls. It was a disaster because of a total lack of preparation: they had telephoned a couple of hours previously, and I had stupidly accepted their presence. The patient had a chronic condition and was house-bound. His wife was quite devoted to him.

My last patient in *la paroisse* was a postal worker with a terminal cancer who was in a home for the terminally ill; he was very unhappy, and convinced his wife to look after him at home if at all possible: she made me promise that I would personally help, and I estimated he would live another 6-8 weeks. I had no need to leave Montreal during that period and accepted: I visited him at home three times a week increasing to once a day during the last two. He was so happy at home surrounded by family and friends. I would load a syringe or two of morphine so that his wife could give him an extra dose as necessary. He died one late evening; I visited the family and met the undertaker that night, taking the bus, a first experience for a house call: it was snowing, my last house-call before my retirement.

On the first of June 1980 I was promoted to *'professeur titulaire plein-temps geographique dans le department de medicine sociale et preventive' a l'UdeM*. At *l'UdeM*, there was as yet no official department of family medicine, the five units for its teaching administered by *le department de medicine sociale et preventive*, that had been officially created only in 1973. The University did not accept cross-appointments; so, when the University recognized Family Medicine as a Department, I had to choose to which department I would belong, and I chose Family Medicine.

Family Medicine

Principles and Practice

The First Encyclopedic Textbook edited by a Family Physician, 1365 pages, with a foreword by

John S Millis.

Edited by

Robert B Taylor
Department of Family and Community Medicine
Bowman Gray School of Medicine
Wake Forest University

Springer-Verlag, 1978

I was very proud at being asked to choose and write a Chapter in this volume, the first ever attempt by a Family Physician to **document Family Medicine:** chapter 19, **The Years from Birth to Puberty,** by Pierre L Delva and Louise Seguin.

The editor and four co-editors were all Family Physicians, with 128 contributors, of which there were only five Canadians and two Brits.

The Montreal Period, 2: 1980-1984: Head of Family Medicine in an officially non-existing

Department of a large Medical School, l'Universite de Montreal.

That first year, 1980-1981, was difficult. I had an office in a building on *la cote Ste Catherine* that housed the Faculty of Nursing and that of Music. A part of the top fifth floor housed the Department of Social and Preventive Medicine. I shared a secretary. Most of the Faculty was housed just under the tower on the top of Mount Royal, several blocks away. We were very isolated.

Within a year, **the Dean, Dr Pierre Bois,** had a **brainwave:** I was promoted to Assistant Dean and a suite of two adjoining rooms was made available right next to his own office with an experienced secretary, Mme Marie-Jeanne Dorval. Our door was left open a lot of the time; thus, the many visitors that came to meet the Dean could not fail but notice that Family Medicine really existed. As Assistant Dean, I was automatically a member of the Board of the Faculty. It really was the first time that most of the senior staff of the large downtown Hospitals actually became aware of our existence.

Pierre Bois was straightforward, honest, liked people; he was ethical, very patient and determined. He had a most difficult job, far more so than both Dean Botterell at Queen's and Dean Pigeon in Sherbrook. I admired him a lot. He never summoned me to his office. In the three years that I worked there, I received but two visits from him:

= when I first arrived, he came in to tell me he knew nothing about Family Medicine; should he have a problem in that domain he would come to see me; he insisted that I send him monthly minutes of the department and program Family Medicine Committee meetings. This lasted just two minutes.

= he came to see me just one second time. He had just returned from Toronto where he had heard that Family Medicine was being considered as an option and not a prerequisite for practicing Family Medicine*: what did I think? Has the teaching of surgery ever been considered an optional subject? And that was that. That meeting lasted two minutes.

= we communicated in another fashion:

The Dean and I filled our cars at the same Shell station nearby, very clean with an attractive little bench to sit on. People might sit there and have a puff. The affable manager/owner was much appreciated. He had won a large new Nissan in a raffle around that time, and his customers were happy for him. It was a congenial place the likes of which have now disappeared.

So one morning when we were both filling up, the Dean told me the story of the son of the owner: he had developed a brain tumor which was removed at the Montreal Neurological Institute (MNI) of Dr Wilder Penfield fame. He had been very sick, losing most of his hair from the chemotherapy. He had obtained an MD from the *l'UdeM* and was in the middle of a post-graduate program in Oto-Rhino-Laryngology (Ear-Nose-Throat). He had been unceremoniously sacked from the program without notice, and was at present despondently recovering at home without any prospects of an occupation. Every time the Dean filled his car with gas he

---

* That option, supported by Professor **Ian McWhinney** from Western University in London, Ontario, followed the British pattern developed over centuries. Dr McWhinney is a sensible intelligent and cooperative person who had passed his membership of the Royal College of Physicians of London (MRCP), the first step in order to become a medical specialist in the UK; after some bright academic work, he was invited to become Head of Family Medicine at Western in 1968, the second such appointment in North America, just after Nebraska. He had settled in Stratford-upon-Avon in Warwickshire where his father was a well-respected senior General Practitioner. In Canada, such a new country, we do not need to import such centuries' old traditions. Professor **Carol Buck,** an outstanding forward-looking person I had met in Shaffey's Lock in 1965, Head of the Department of Epidemiology and Preventive Medicine at Western, had been largely responsible for Ian's nomination.

was kept up-to-date as to the lack of progress of the young man. Finally, after briefly telling me the tale he asked me so nicely and apologetically by the pump whether I might suggest a course of action, not once mentioning Family Medicine and not talking about this strictly non-academic matter on University grounds: just let me think about it for a few hours*.

I talked to **the Head of Surgery** the next day, an older pleasant man who stuck to his decision: he might develop seizures during an operation, no question about it. I then changed the subject to 'the place of women in Surgery': no, women are meant to stay home and look after the family; a surgeon's life is far too difficult for them. At most, they might perhaps work two half-days a week in General Practice. We then talked about the weather or some such matter and parted in excellent terms.

---

*   I interviewed the young man, and soon realized that he had not been seen by Professor **Brenda Milner,** PhD, who worked at McGill, the first scientist outside the United States to receive the National Academy of Sciences (United States) 2004 Award in the Neurosciences. She was then 80 years old, had been there 50 years and was still working. So I telephoned her to ask whether she could see our young friend. He was assessed within the week. This evaluation proved to be crucial for his rehabilitation. Dr Milner had found that his auditory memory had been severely affected, but that his visual memory was practically normal. What a crucial piece of information this was: it was far better for him to avoid lectures and conferences relying on reading and looking at movies, video-tapes, photographs. With his consent, I suggested a plan for a gradual return to 'academia', two half-days a week to start with, increasing gradually to full-time work in a Family Medicine program; what a fantastic experience that was for the unit, rehabilitating one of their own! I submitted the plan to *la Corporation;* it was accepted immediately. I thought it would be easier for him to further his education at the CLSC in Pointe-aux-Trembles at the eastern point of the Island of Montreal: it was staffed by residents and staff of his own age, and there were just a few of them. It worked like a charm, and a year later, our friend invited me for lunch in a nice Outremont restaurant!

It is a well-known fact that sick doctors and dentists often do not get the best treatment available, especially in the area of rehabilitation. This is not a subject that is frequently discussed or studied. Our head-surgeon's decision is in no way uncommon. Having served in an artillery unit for my military service, it seems that decisions taken in Surgical Units are similar to those taken in Artillery Units.

Likewise, doctors who become chronic alcoholics, drug dependant or affected by psychiatric/psychological problems remain largely unknown.

I talked with **Dr Jean Mathieu,** Head of the Department of Medicine, a strong supporter of Family Medicine right from the start. He had become quite frustrated with some of his senior staff and was looking forward to his retirement. He told me once that he was very worried about one of his internists that I knew: he thought that he was contemplating suicide. He always seemed pleased to talk to me.

I talked several times to **Dr Jean Morin,** Professor of Pediatrics, but never in his or my office. He had started a large Department of Obstetrics at *'l'hopital Ste Justine pour enfants'* just down the road. Several times I suggested that a Family Medicine Teaching Unit should be incorporated at the Children's Hospital: he just listened politely. I was never asked to be involved in any of the teaching of the Department of Pediatrics. Some of the younger pediatricians were always enthusiastically helpful in teaching activities in our field, Community and Family Medicine. With Jean Morin, I felt I was talking to a brick wall.

I met **Professor Jacques Genest** a couple of times: he was the founder of *l'Institut de Recherche Clinique de Montreal,* and one of the founders of the study and management of Hypertension, the best-known researcher at *l'UdeM.* He was very interested in Dr Norman Bethune, and had told me he had asked *la reverende Mere directrice de l'Hotel-Dieu* why Dr Bethune was refused an appointment there after his ignominious dismissal from the Royal Victoria Hospital next door: Dr Archibald, Dr Bethune's ex-boss, had actually come to see her as soon as he had heard that Dr Bethune wanted to work there to forbid her from offering him the job. That was why Dr Bethune went to work at *l'HSC.*

I soon realized that I had a lot of support amongst the senior staff who themselves thought I had a difficult job; our main antagonists were the senior staff of the three main teaching hospitals, *l'Hotel-Dieu, Notre-Dame* and *Ste Justine pour enfants.*

On the Home Front, I had two priorities of my own:

=   Our five teaching units, four of them hospital-based and the fifth in a *CLSC,* were widely separated and each had its own characteristics. We now had the opportunity to exchange information for the first time. In order to encourage cooperation, I scheduled our monthly meetings in each unit in turn so that every participant had the opportunity at least to see what was done such as the use of space, equipment, as well as meeting other members of the staff. We met one morning a month, one two-hour departmental committee meeting followed by a third hour for the program committee. Nobody volunteered to be chairman or secretary, so I accumulated the four jobs. It was a heavy load; there was no easier alternative. I was considered by many of my Family Physician colleagues as a specialist which I was of course. But it is because of my specialization that I got such an easy passage as an Assistant Dean.

= The progress of the residents was assessed by the regular completion of individual pink sheets completed by local supervisors that ended on my desk, over eighty at a time, every few weeks. I soon got *Marie-Jeanne* to weed out those with less than 70%. I would then visit the unit to interview each of those residents to find out exactly what had happened. It was imperative at that particular time that residents should count on the support of the head of the department. I realized early on that a poor assessment was usually associated with a personality conflict that was easy to settle. I never once summoned a student or a teacher to my office.

One unit wanted to dismiss the only lady-physician on the staff there. She was very bright and spoke her mind. I was surprised by the behavior of her colleagues.

Some colleagues made me feel a bit like a pariah. I thought my defense of the residents was most important: ensuring fairness of the evaluation process in those early stages was fundamental to the success of our program.

Dr Robert Bourret from Verdun was the most famous of the staff members of Family Medicine. We got on well together. He was President of the College in 1983; we had dinner together in Singapour. We were both attending the WONCA* meeting there. I asked him why he did not chose to become a full-time University Professor in Family Medicine? "To meet our commitments, pay for our childrens' education, our summer cottage, our two cars plus our winter holidays, we need $250.000 a year; the university pays a quarter of that for a full-time job.

By the end of 1983 I felt I needed a break and sent in my **letter of resignation as of June 1ˢᵗ 1984. Dean Bois'** mandate finished that same year. I had spent ten years, from 50 to 60 years of age, working for a cause I really believed in for which, in many ways, I was better prepared for than most. Joan and I felt quite liberated. I really had thought that one of my colleagues would volunteer to take over, but that had to wait another three.

After my Sabbatical, I concentrated my teaching activities to undergraduate education. I was continuously harassed by my new and first boss who insisted

---

* **WONCA, W**orld **O**rganization **o**f **N**ational **C**olleges and **A**cademies of Family Doctors. The Canadian College played a crucial role in the founding of WONCA.

that I 'teach' in a new CLSC, two cessions a week, in the _Bordeaux/Cartierville_ area. But did not feel comfortable being parachuted there. It was not my way of doing things. I tried to tell her that my undergraduate teaching efforts were far more productive than postgraduate ones to no avail. In fact, she might very well not have wanted me in that area at all. I had the feeling that my new boss had never read my CV.

By that time, as past President of the Norman Bethune Foundation, I was seriously implicated in an exchange program with the Bethune International Peace Hospital in Shijiazhuang, Hebei Province, and with the Bethune Medical University in Changchun, Jilin Province, Manchuria. I negotiated a $10,000 a year allowance for each of the five first years of my retirement to help me with the project. My last visit to China occurred in 1995.

Post Script : 2009.

I have read the CFPC report of the evaluation of Emergency and Family Medicine _UdeM_ programs, dated April 2008. There were 286 medical students that year. Family Medicine has 13 teaching units with 213 residents. 40.1% of the students chose Family Medicine as a career. The average in the rest of Canada is 30%.

There are 26 residents at _l'HSC_ and they complete most of their specialty requirements there, disliking the pediatric rotations at _l'hopital Ste Justine_. Their rotation there does not meet the objectives of the Department of Family Medicine and fails to promote the value of Family Medicine.

As was stated earlier on, Family Medicine at _l'HSC_ is responsible for 30 geriatric beds, 40 longterm beds, 20 short term beds, 20 palliative care beds, and 50% of deliveries. It seems clear to me that such patients are better cared for by Family Physicians largely because they are better prepared for the job and because of their links with the families of the patients.

It is just a question of time before the _HSC_ model becomes "the norm" throughout the country; it will take another 50 years. Thus, family physicians and consultants will look after their patients in and out of hospital. The slavery issue for primary care physicians will have disappeared. Most Family Physicians will work in a hospital. In cities with medical schools they will look after hospitalized patients in University Hospitals and will participate in medical education during the whole of the curriculum.

In **1988,** I was honored by the College of Family Physicians of Canada by being given the yearly **W. Victor Johnson Award for an Outstanding Contribution to Family Medicine.** My address was published that year in

INFOMED, the Journal of the Faculty of Medicine, (sept-oct 1988, vol. 12 no 1) and was entitled **Man Adapting,** with apologies to Rene Dubos.[*]

On June 10th **1996,** on the 25th anniversary of the Founding of the Department of Social and Preventive Medicine, I was given one of two plaques, both recipients chosen by members of the staff, for an '**Outstanding Contribution to the Development of Family Medicine and of Community Medicine'.**

On Friday Mai 9th **2008,** Joan and I were guests of honor at a fantastic Evening of Celebration, *'Plus d'un quart de siecle',* with the present Dean Jean L Rouleau and Dean Yvon Gauthier, who succeeded Dean Bois when I resigned my job in 1984 and their wives, plus of course the present head of department and his wife, Francois and Ghislaine Lehmann. The dinner/dance was at Club St Stephen, 1440 Drummond, Montreal. There was a lot of entertainment, music, songs and dance, all by the guests!

At present at *l'UdeM* Family Physicians take part in 50% of the clinical teaching during the crucial first three years of the curriculum.

Francois and Ghislaine had visited us in Kingston on February 1[st-1908]. A short interview was taped and was shown that evening for everybody to see. He asked me two questions: why did I resign, and what were my priorities when I was head of department. It was a lovely evening and Joan and I felt quite grateful and honored.

What did William Osler think about the Flexner report, a fundamental issue. He had become Regius Professor of Medicine at Oxford University. *All the medical students from Oxford and Cambridge went to London to learn about clinical medicine and medical research in the London Voluntary Teaching Hospitals.*

Harvey Cushing wrote his Pulitzer award winning biography of Osler, two volumes, 1500 pages, published in 1925: two important events occurred in 1911,the Flexner report was published in the late spring, and King George V was crowned in July, following which a list of Coronation Honours was published: Osler became a baronet. He had been very busy that summer, went on holiday (August 11th to September 6th) at Llanddulas, a tiny village in North Wales where he caught up with his correspondence, including reading the Flexner report.

What follows is a facsimile of page 293, volume 2, of the biography: the laboratory issue is just a small important item that had to be considered in the

---

[*]   Man Adapting is the Title of a book by **Rene Dubos** which gave me a lot of pleasure (1965). Mankind Evolving also, by Theodosius Dobzhansky, (1962) both published by Yale University Press. Both should be required reading for all thinking people.

report. **The London Voluntary Teaching Hospitals offered, at that period, the best clinical teaching and research in the world.**

Under the same date, September 1st, he wrote this much-treasured letter to the Librarian and staff of the Surgeon-General's Library in Washington:

Dear Friends, Among the 1000 telegrams and letters which I received not one touched my heart more closely than that which you all so kindly sent. Not a little of any success I may have had is due to the enormous stimulus which the publications of your department have had in my work. You who are part of the machine that pulls the profession along little realize the amount or importance of your labours. I dare say the next generation will be able to appreciate better what you have done. I can honestly say that no one of this generation has had a more grateful sense of his obligations than your sincere friend & well wisher, Wm OSLER.

To Lewellys F. Barker.   Llanddulas, N. Wales,
                                                                              2nd [September]

. . . Yours with enclosure has just come. I wish I had had it earlier as I have just sent off to the press the revise of a letter which I am sending to Remsen on Whole-time Clin. Professors. He sent me a letter a month or two ago, & with it Flexner's Report. Kelly had sent his copy some time ago but it came when I was very occupied & I had not a chance to read it until a few weeks ago. It never should have been permitted to go out in its present form. You will see what I say & think of it. I am sending the letter to all the Trustees & the teachers of the school, as I believe most of them have had an opportunity of reading Flexner's Report tho not for circulation. Your address will do good & it puts the clinical problem in its proper light—and it must be solved by clinical men not by the pure laboratory people who know nothing of it—as F's Report clearly shows . . . . We are all well, enjoying the peace of this lovely spot, after a horrid racket. A baronetcy is a worrying honour—but fortunately it does not make any changes in one's sensations or in the general outlook on life. Love to Miss Humpton. I have fortunately lost my plantigrade secretary—I did *not* kill her tell Miss H., though often tempted. Revere 11/2 in. taller than his daddy—a sweet lad, but no student . . . . I shall not be out this year. I am trying to revise the text book—very hard—It should be rewritten. Miss Humpton could do it! I am getting McCrae to help. We expect them next week. By the way, since I last wrote we had a delightful visit from the Müllers. M. as you will see by my letter is strongly opposed to the whole-time scheme—His evidence at the Lond. Univ. Commissn. was most interesting. It will be published before long—I will send you a copy . . . .

CHAPTR 51

Staff Exchange Programs in North China with the Bethune International Peace Hospital, an affiliated Military Teaching Hospital (there are four Military Medical Colleges in China) in Shijiazhuang, the new Capital of the Province of Hebei (1989-1995).

At the Montreal end, it was a cooperative effort between McGill University and *l'universite de Montreal,* mainly the Royal Victoria Hospital (April 1928-December 1932) and *l'hopital du Sacre-Coeur* (January 1933-Spring 1936) where Dr Norman Bethune had worked for just eight years.

We had received a $300,000 Canadian Government grant for a five year project starting in January 1989.

Introduction: Dr Norman Bethune had two senior important medical teaching institutions named for him in China:

The **Bethune International Peace Hospital** (BIPH) is an Affiliated Teaching Hospital of the "People's Liberation Army" on the main road (circa five km long) of *Shijiazhuang,* the new capital of the Province of Hebei, 200 km south of Beijing; the words International and Peace are there because of a financial gift from Britain during earlier hard times. It was **affiliated** **to one or more of the four Army Medical Colleges** in China. Thus, young doctors from the one or more of the four schools would attend to complete their training.

At first, Civilians and Military personnel were treated on an equal footing, just as would have occurred when Dr Bethune was around. In 1986, the BIPH had 873 beds and 20,000 adults were admitted; there were 339,000 out-patients; six and a half million tests were processed by its laboratories; 60% of all patients were civilians, 40% army personnel. There were only about 500 nurses and just a few less doctors, about 400. There was a national shortage of nurses. The BIPH was a busy place.

The **Bethune Medical University** (BMU) is in *Changchun,* the capital of Jilin, the middle Province in Manchuria, with Heilongjiang (capital Harbin) to the north and Liaoning (capital Shenyang) to the south. Jilin's southern neighbor just on the other side of the famous Yalu River is North Korea. Chairman Mao's best troops were North Koreans; many of them still live in Jilin province.

Changchun was the Capital of the Japanese State of Manchukuo (1931-32) after the Japanese invaded Manchuria. It was soon renamed The Empire of Manchukuo, with its own Puppet Emperor, Pu Yi, (1932-1945) and its own Japanese Medical School. Changchun is divided into three sections, Chinese, Japanese and Russian, the Chinese the poorest for many years.

As a child, Pu Yi (1906-1967) had succeeded the empress dowager Ci Xi (1835-1908) as Emperor of China. In 1912, he was replaced by Dr Sun Yat-sen, the first President of the Republic of China.

Changchun and Jilin Province as well as the whole of the Empire of Manchuria thrived during the Japanese occupation. Manchuria was Japan's breadbasket for 15 years.

Immediately after the end of WWII, the Russians invaded and occupied the whole of Manchuria; all heavy machinery from the many factories was dismantled and sent to Russia by rail. It was only in 1959 after Chairman Mao had taken over that the Russians accepted to gradually leave Manchuria: this took about three or four years. Mao and Stalin rarely agreed, but pretended to get on because of their political orientation.

Incidentally, the Province of Jilin is of the same size as the Province of Saskatchewan, with soil of the same quality and with the same climate. They were both settled and developed at the same time historically; to-day Jilin has a population of 23 million people, Saskatchewan one million. In 1980 when I first went there, Jilin was self-sufficient for food with little mechanization of its agriculture.

Also incidentally, the BMU replaced a Japanese Medical School. Many Japanese professionals stayed behind when the Japanese were defeated: they had lived there several years and their country of birth was in a dreadful state. Many became Chinese citizens.

The curriculum was entirely changed mostly by the now world-famous Minister of Health at the time, **Dr Qian Xinzhong**: he had been at one time director of the BIPH and would visit the BMU and the BIPH periodically. He subsequently introduced the one-child Family to the World. He talked about six languages fluently, was affable and of such easy access. I met him several times, once for a whole hour with his aide-de-camp after he had retired.

The BMU has an intake of **600 students a year for a three year course, thus one of the largest if not the largest in the world,** from all over China. Much of the teaching was in English. Acupuncture required a further three years of study. Thus, young doctors specializing in acupuncture have to study for six years.

The **first President** of the BMU, Dr Ho Yun Qing, had been on the Long March and had attended Dr Bethune's Funeral. I met him several times: he was soft, polite, funny and tough.

I had met and knew well the **present dean,** a microbiologist. Joan and I had invited him to our house in Montreal: he had spent two years in Quebec, at the University of Montreal and at Laval University in Quebec City, each for twelve months.

He had a tough time in Quebec, his very nice advisors having assessed him as inadequate as the dean of a new Medical School: they had failed to understand the essence of postgraduate training, a **time for thought. He had no desire for a narrow training in a particular subject.**

Shijiazhuang lies at the railway junction between Beijing and Southern China on the one hand, and the railway lines to Shanxi Province to the West and Shandong Province to the East. When we went there first in 1980, the town was comparatively small with perhaps 350,000 inhabitants. Before the building of the railway at the beginning of the 20th century Shijiazhuang was just a village. The last time I was there in 1995 the population was over five million, and that of Hebei Province over 63 million. I once met the Minister of Education of the Province, and told him I had never met a Minister of Education responsible for 61 million people, such an enormous task: he immediately laughed and said "not 61 million but 63".

The town, so new, is rarely on the visitor circuit. It was very poor at the start, the peasants in the area earning the lowest income in the country, under $65 a year. To-day, it has become a large industrial city: the manufacture of heavy machinery, electronics, textiles, a large pharmaceutical industry, the most important in China, cigarette manufacture, plus many others. It has many tall buildings, wide boulevards, many bars and excellent restaurants. It is from Shijiazhuang that the new TGV, built by Bombardier, starts its long voyage to Lhasa, the Capital of Tibet. Its population is gradually and thankfully getting older.

Shijiazhuang was the first town in the Province to be liberated by Chairman Mao's forces when they descended from the hills from the north-west in <u>September 1948. Thus, it has become a symbol of success in the recent history of Communist China.</u>

A major problem with any new town for me is the absence of older mature people: the few noisy and boisterous bars and restaurants seem to be uniformly patronized by people under the age of 45; for a 65 year-old visitor this is not too welcoming.

However, some aspects of living there were for me quite exciting. For instance, every Saturday morning outside one of the four largest post-offices in the country on the main road with a wide side-walk, enthusiastic stamp collectors mostly young would meet to exchange and/or sell stamps, one of my hobbies since childhood. I started to look forward to my occasional visit there. On one occasion, a young man with an air-force uniform rushed up to me in a BIPH corridor, and gave me a first day cover of a Kotnis (Bethune's successor) stamp in exchange for my signature on his own Bethune first day cover, a 15 second meeting. He was not supposed to do such a thing!

I would catch the invariably clean bus outside the hospital for a five minute ride, much to the concern of the hospital senior staff who always used a staff car with chauffeur. The local people in the bus always treated me with the utmost courtesy and some amazement. They would notice me and start chattering amongst themselves, a chummy ride. Rarely, a passenger would try and practice talking English. I might also borrow a bicycle, but thought it more harrowing considering the thousands of cyclists around me. We had to cross the busy railway line and the gate seemed closed much of the time. A bridge was subsequently built.

I would enjoy waiting in the bus for the trains to pass.

The Sino-Japanese war (1937-1945) followed the 'incident of the Marco-Polo Bridge', near Beijing, where shooting occurred between Japanese and Chinese soldiers: **China declared war** and the whole of North-Eastern China right down to Shanghai was occupied by the Japanese; the Marco Polo bridge is just outside Beijing on the road to Baoding; it is beautiful, wide, with sculptured marble walls. I have crossed it many times.

The Japanese built a small hospital in 1937 near the railway station in Shijiazhuang. Thus, part of the structure of the BIPH was built by the Japanese; in 1945 it was under the control of the Nationalists under General Chiang Kai-Shek (1887-1975). **In September 1948 it became the BIPH.** Thus, when I visited it first with Joan in 1980 (Ch 45-46), it had survived three quite tumultuous periods in its' forty-three year history.

The BIPH itself:

I had first gone there in 1980: it was the most extraordinary Hospital I had ever seen, in many ways it seemed like a Medieval Fairyland. A wide tall three km long wall surrounded a rectangle.

Over 3000 people lived there in five or six-floor blocks of apartments, each one quite small, about 500 feet square. There was a large (2,000+ people) meeting hall for shows and meetings.

There was a farm with cattle and a lovely orchard; since the Cultural Revolution (1966-68) until Chairman Mao's death in the 1975, the doctors would look after the farm in the afternoons. The farm supplied food for the patients and the people living there. There was also a lovely large rock-garden and a large botanical garden; beautiful large well-kept trees lined the more important and not so narrow tar-covered roads in the compound.

A beautiful Museum/Memorial Hall, devoted to Dr Bethune on the left and Dr Kotnis on the right, had its own building. The meeting room there was superb, with paintings of Dr Bethune, some on horse-back, some coming out of a cloud, comfortable chairs, a lovely large carpet and nice heavy curtains.

The Director was an excellent painter, **Mr Jin He De,** middle-aged, who was very knowledgeable of the whole field of Chinese Art, old and new. He taught me such a lot. His assistant was Xiao-Ji, really her name being **Ji Jun-me.** Xiao—is a term of endearment for young people, Lao—for older people. I might be called Lao-Delva. They both had Army Rank. Clinicians were officers but were not ranked.

Next to it was a small two star hotel where Joan and I stayed, in a small suite with a sitting-room, a large bedroom and separate bath-room on the ground floor. The large double bed was very comfortable. A new pack of cigarettes was always on the table, as well as lovely covered tea-cups, tea-bags and an electric kettle. The food was simple and well-prepared. The head-cook had senior qualifications, a very important rank in China.

The head of the hospital, **Dr Lu Ruling,** acted as mayor of the compound. The Head Surgeon, **Dr Zhao Po,** lived in a Japanese built bungalow. Perhaps a quarter of the whole area was devoted to the hospital itself.

It took me a few years to be invited to enter an ordinary living quarter: two small bedrooms, a small kitchen, a living room, a toilet and a small vestibule. There was a primary school and two hair-dressers on the premises. I would have my hair cut there (13 cents): men and women, boys and girls, a very efficient operation except that the hair accumulated on the floor until the evening when it was all swept up and put in big bags. What happened to it I ignore. There were also public baths for the men and showers for the women, at a specific time four cessions a week. At my old school, we had a quick shower just once a week.

Most industries, schools and colleges had the same kind of arrangement, people living and working in the same kind of compound. Married couples might work in different places: in such a case, a bicycle would be used by the person working elsewhere.

The wards were very simple: the narrow metal beds close together, a small chest between them, with clean unbleached sheets, two floors without elevators, a ramp to wheel stretchers or equipment up and down to and from the 7-8 operating rooms, the radiology department, laboratories or the adjoining road. A mother had to sleep and look after her child under the age of twelve and they shared a larger bed.

At the official entrance of the compound, there were guards and open gates, a large statue of Dr Bethune surrounded by flowers. There were a few other unofficial small unguarded doors around the periphery and a guarded utility double gate, but within a few years the small doors were all locked because a couple of burglaries had occurred. At the start, burglaries were totally unheard of anywhere.

We were all awakened by martial music from speakers at 6.30am (instead of 6am for me at my Jesuit boarding school, by a hand-held bell) and at 7.15am sharp everybody walked to work in their work clothes, the army doctors with white coats and hats. There was a one hour break after lunch when everybody went home for a nap.

At first, following the old tradition of the Long March, the only thing that distinguished a soldier from an officer was the quality and the number of pockets in the uniform; officers had no 'pips' to show rank and no decorations. Clinical PLA doctors had no rank. The PLA prided themselves as friends of the people, and Mao always insisted from the start that any damages that occurred to civilian property by the Army had to be compensated; the Kuomingtang invariably pillaged along their way. Thus, a very important friendship was promoted between the army and the civilian population.

The uniforms changed shortly after our first visit in 1980 when the army suddenly looked like any other. For the same work, the pay of army personnel was 25% more than a civilian counterpart. Older personnel who had joined the forces prior to Chairman Mao's victory in 1949 received an extra regular allowance.

Down the road half a mile away is the North China Revolutionary Martyrs Cemetery, a beautifully kept park where the main attractions are the two beautiful tombs of Dr Bethune and Dr Kotnis with their own statues. Participants in the Long March are buried there. It is very impressive.

There are five statues of Dr Bethune in the whole world as far as I know, two in Shijiazhuang, one at the BMU in Changchun, one in down-town Montreal at the corner of Guy/de Maisonneuve, and one more recent one in Gravenhurst, Ontario, where he was born.

There was a period during the 70s when China was building a railway in East Africa. The BIPH supplied medical personnel. When the project was completed, several members of the BIPH delegation refused to return, much to everybody's astonishment. Black students have the toughest time in China.

Baoding, the old Capital of Hebei:

Baoding is a beautiful and civilized old city a day's horse-driven coach ride to the south from the Forbidden City. It is about half-way between Beijing and Shijiazhuang. I spent just a few hours there on two separate occasions: my interpreter at the BIPH was **Dr Sun Hui-Chen,** a very bright pathologist who specialized in electron-microscopy. He spoke perfect English. He came from Baoding where his father had been an ophthalmologist.

We had a very civilized lunch in the largest dinning room in town, resembling in every way a large railway restaurant in old Europe, anywhere between Ostend and Munich: people of all ages having lunch together with twirling fans hanging from the ceiling and older experienced staff. It was quite a discovery, clean and comfortable, just a little shabby, with excellent simple food. There was a continuous rumble from the many conversations that were taking place, but no loud laughter. We then walked around the city gardens that seemed as old as they really were, perhaps a few hundred years, with a lovely lake, water lilies, little bridges and rock gardens.

Throughout the centuries Baoding was the capital of Province of Hebei and later the home of one of the two Military Colleges in China, the other near Canton in the South. They had both been strongholds of the previous Nationalist government led by General Chiang Kai-Shek.

Chairman Mao insisted on leading his government from the old Palace area in Beijing instead of shifting it to the north a couple of miles away to a new town as suggested by a committee of experts; in a similar way, by one stroke of the pen, he decided that Baoding would be decapitated and all its institutions, (colleges and universities, most government offices, large national businesses and the army's northern headquarters), apart from the very large prison with very tall old red brick walls, reputed to be the largest prison in China, were moved to the new Capital, Shijiazhuang, which had to take everything over. How long would that take? All those new organizations in Shijiazhuang were at that period in the slow process of reaching maturity.

Thus. Shijiazhuang became the Northern Headquarters of the Chinese Army, and one of its first components had been the BIPH. Three provinces came under its jurisdiction, Hebei Province, Shanxi Province to the west and parts of Inner Mongolia to the North, an enormous area.

When I first went there in 1980, I was totally unaware of any of the above. I then spent 15 years visiting Shijiazhuang twelve times, spending about six months there altogether, four of them in 1989; I got to notice a little of what was going on: there was a Chinese Air Force Unit around the corner, with its own Hospital, and Russian-made fighter planes flying over. Up the road half a mile away the new Army Headquarters became obvious, with guards at the gate and nice flowers lining the road inside.

I heard unofficially that its Head was a Major-General, the son of Deng Xiaoping, chief of General Staff, the most influential man in the whole of China.

I was very impressed by the members of the Army Signal Corps, who, in three or four days had beautifully and cleanly installed cable TV in all the apartments and hospital locations so very efficiently. They all seemed so young and keen. That is how I started watching Chinese TV productions which could be quite spectacular.

The soldiers in the Army seemed all to be young adults (18-24 years old), surely coming mostly from the Province of Hebei, from within a radius of one hundred or so km around Shijiazhuang, mostly from peasant families who were the poorest in the country, a nice bunch, very polite, clean, and in good health. One of them regularly drove us around, very amusing, made me think of those funny Shakespearean characters: a breath of fresh air, he was always laughing; I liked him very much.

The town soon had its own beautiful large zoo with pandas and lions, and a most beautiful park designed by experts from the South, both within half a mile from the BIPH.

The BIPH itself built a beautiful little park for patients and families, with little bridges over lovely small rock ponds with lilies and other plants.

The first new large well-organized medical building was a six storey out-patient department with elevators, a long structure with access in the centre. Its two elevators were the talk of the town. It was built in the mid-eighties and served as a referral centre for the town and as a primary care center for the adjoining rural community.

There was nowhere in Canada with such a large out-patient facility at that time.

Its new equipment included a CT scan, the two technicians speaking English with a Dutch accent (they had spent two months in Eindhoven), a new radiological machine for cardiac catheterization and an emergency room with a few beds, one of about forty such emergency rooms in the Province. A doctor with his bag would accompany the barely equipped ambulance when called out for an emergency. A fifth year resident would sleep on each hospital floor at night.

Cardiology including nephrology had about ten dialysis machines and four monitors in intensive care. A 'Cardiology Dictionary' had just been published by the hospital which brought kudos from Beijing, selling 10,000 copies. However our Chinese cardiac scholar to be was not too impressed.

When I was there last in 1995, there was talk of building a new hospital, a tall square structure, a tower. *The Chinese are master-organizers: in order of priority and in sequence, since arriving in Shijiazhuang in 1948 they had:*

1. *provided water and electricity to every spot in the Province and developed primary care with barefoot doctors working in teams of five, each with two to four months training in one of the following areas:*

   - *communicable diseases,*
   - *sanitation,*
   - *children and women's health including midwifery,*
   - *first-aid and treatment,*
   - *administration.* providing at the same time secondary hospital care for simple hospital-based procedures (appendectomies, hernias, pneumonias, broken bones and accidents etc . . .).

2. *started to provide tertiary specialized care to the whole population 40 years later.*

   Such a lot had been accomplished in such a short time in such an enormous country with 20% of the world's population.

I also realized some of the differences between people living in the south of China and those living in the north, the wide Yangtze River completely cutting the country in two. People often visited relatives in the south, or just went there on holiday; on their return they would complain about the rice: three crops a year in the south and usually just one in the north, the taste not being the same; and it was far too hot down there, such a horrible climate.

By this time, I started to think that I was very lucky to be able to observe and participate in the development of the new Capital of Hebei Province, over 200,000 square Km, the size of England, Scotland and Wales put together, with 63 million people, just 5% of the population of the whole of China, in the most populous country in the world, the third in size after Russia and Canada.

Dr Zhao Po was the senior surgeon. He qualified at the best school in China, the Peking Union Medical College, in 1948. I had qualified at the best school in England, the London Hospital, that same year. He was then 22 years old, short and slim, two years younger than I. He immediately married his sweetheart, a co-student, and they both immediately joined Mao's army. She became an anesthetist. They were a fantastic couple, so idealistic. They had two children, a girl and a younger boy. *They have lived all of their lives at the BIPH since its beginning* and were approaching retirement age.

We really understood one another. Dr Zhao led our first group of seniors in Montreal arriving on May 29th 1989. We liked the same foods (ice cream and Mars bars): he told me Mars bars sold in the store around the corner from BIPH were better than the Canadian ones he had bought in Montreal. The ones bought in China came from Australia! He had introduced me to those in China. I introduced him to Laura Secord icecream in Montreal and he was very impressed. He would buy one surreptitiously at 9am. He was a soft person, so unlike the average surgeon who is so much more assertive and spoilt. In his small cluttered office at the BIPH, at least fifty certificates of merit were hanging on the walls, all of the same size and color, duly signed, stamped and framed, the only reward for good work in Communist China.

He worked in a 'MASH' type organization in the Chinese Army during the Korean War. "We saved many niggers with bleeding livers": Joan promptly explained he should have said Black or Afro-American: he never used the term again! He then explained that ruptured livers were due to high explosives that created severe abdominal injuries and deaths from ruptured livers that bled heavily; he had found that, by using mattress sutures with very thick catgut, one could actually sew up the brittle liver and thus save lives. One used a large non-cutting curved needle and took deep wide slices of liver with the stitching fairly close, about 1 cm apart.

That was a major contribution to the treatment of abdominal wounds in wars.

Dr/Mme Zhao Po, his wife was just as impressive. She was petite, frail looking but tough. **She was in charge of the blood bank,** thus following the Bethune tradition. She had been doing it for over 40 years. The system she used I had never seen before: in a small waiting room with two or three chairs, there was small hole in the wall at the level of the waist through which the donor put his arm on a table on the other side of the wall where the small blood bank was: thus he could not see what was going on and could attend with muddy shoes: a clean easy operation ensued at little cost. When I left there for the last time in 1995 the BIPH was still the only hospital in Shijiazhuang (five million people) with a blood bank and a list of donors. Blood was available to any hospital on request, just as Bethune would have done fifty years before in China on an individual basis.

Mme/Dr Zhao fell and broke a hip: China had no such things as screws and pins to join the bones together, so the Head Orthopedist, very pleasant and efficacious but so assertive, treated her in the old fashioned way with ropes and pulleys; she had to lie flat on her back for several weeks. Many people die in that situation, often of pneumonia or of the injury, but she recovered with a permanent quite severe limp. I visited her in hospital: by then, there was a new simple building for sick senior staff and guests, with about 100 quite large rooms with a nice view without any built-in equipment, just a bed or two, a small locker and a couple of chairs. Mme Zhao had lot of help from the physiotherapy.

The BIPH had an excellent very large **physiotherapy** department, just as good as anywhere. It included acupuncture and moxibustion (heating the needles) and T'ai Chi. We joined a group in the mornings at 6am for a while. There was no psychiatry in Shijiazhuang, most depressed patients ending up in physiotherapy, which could be quite beneficial. If you had schizophrenia, tough luck; but this was the norm at the time in most parts of the world outside North America and Europe. For psychiatric care one had to go to Beijing where there were just a few psychiatrists, a very difficult enterprise.

On my 1993 visit to the BIPH, I was asked for supper in Drs Zhao's small retirement apartment, on the top floor. The children had prepared a lovely meal. At the end, much to my consternation, Mme Zhao insisted on walking down those several floors of stairs to see me off for the last time. I felt like crying, such a sad ending for me. With the same predicament, Norman Bethune at first would have complained and complained, as he did when he had developed TB! But during his last year of life he had become much more patient and philosophical. He never complained during his last illness. He just wrote his will and died a couple of weeks later at the age of 49.

I had a very painful meeting with Dr Zhao and his daughter one evening: they had come to see me in my own room just to talk. She suddenly started to talk about her own past. She was married with one child. Because of the effects of the Cultural Revolution her whole education had been messed up, and she had never finished her University courses whereas her parents both had:

"All you have to show after your years of first-class service and hard-work is a whole pile of useless bits of paper hanging in your office for all the work you have done during your life-time, and your daughter has not had the chance of a University Education"!

She continued like this for a whole hour, and Dr Zhao just nodded his head in agreement. She was so angry. Her father hardly opened his mouth. He was so soft. He did not even appear upset.

What happened to her subsequently? Dr Zhao's daughter went back to University in Beijing, qualified as a psychologist with a Masters degree, ending living in California with her husband and child.

Our first of two visits to China in 1989 (Sunday, Feb 19th-Sunday, April 16th).

Joan and I, both in our mid-sixties, travelled through London: my mother was 93 years old. Thus we could see her on our way to and from China. We had a stop in Bombay for a couple of hours at around midnight and were struck by the poverty: children selling trinkets at that time of the day in dark corridors. Sunrise was so exciting as we travelled eastwards crossing the whole of south-east Asia before turning north to Beijing via Hong-Kong. The visibility was perfect.

Our Work:

About the Administration of the Bethune International Peace Hospital (BIPH), a People's Liberation Army (PLA) Hospital: talking with the Director.

Dr Lu Ruling was the Director, and a Commissar (not a physician) was co-Director. I had many meetings with Dr Lu and we got on very well together. He was very frank. I got to like him very much. I never met the Commissar; I would just see him walking around, middle-aged, dark hair, quite slim, a bit round shouldered with his arms clamped behind his back, as I always imagined a commissar would look. I had never seen a real one before. I had heard of them before in Russian tales: it was quite thrilling to see one regularly even without ever speaking to him.

There are three large departments at the BIPH:

- = of <u>political</u> affairs with about twenty people; the commissar was not a member.
- = of <u>medical</u> affairs with its three divisions, Pharmacy, Logistics, and Medical, itself with 30-40 services.
- = of <u>logistics</u>.

There are three statutory meetings a week:

- = Saturdays, Political Affairs, three hours, for all heads of service.
- = Fridays, Heads of Services.
- = weekly meetings of each service, usually three hours, exceptionally 1-2 hours.

<u>Our discussions</u> centered mainly on three subjects:

- = the younger doctors, all at least 30 years old, who would study in Montreal for—a year; they would be attached to a particular service, some in an English environment, some in a French *milieu*. This caused some concern. The students had to face the fact that

Dr Bethune worked perfectly well in both languages! Although never speaking French or Spanish, after a few months in China he spoke quite a lot of Chinese. We established a selection process. The young students all had to promise that they would return to the BIPH: they all did, which was very unusual and possibly unique as I discovered later. They would start to cross the Pacific Ocean in 1999.

= older doctors would come for a four week visit; they each had to submit suggestions as what they would like to see, a certain lab, a service, a head of this, that or the other, and I would arrange a meeting in advance. They would start this coming May.

= we would eventually establish a permanent Sino-Canadian Centre at the BIPH for teaching **Research Methods in Health Care:** this is what intrigued Dr Lu most. It was to be a long-term cooperative project requiring permanent outside financial help:

health is determined by a variety of factors falling into four divisions: life-style, the environment, health care organization and human biology (Laframboise, 1973); the BIPH had to be interested in all those aspects because the care it provides involved all three levels of care, primary, secondary and tertiary.

I wrote a four page document with general and specific objectives plus something about methods.

The Teaching of English as a Second Language (TESL) by Joan

two hours a day six days a week. Joan was extremely well prepared, with a MA (St Andrews, Scotland), a Teaching Diploma from Dalhousie University in Nova Scotia and a TESL certificate from Concordia University in Montreal; her teaching was a revelation, particularly for the Chinese teacher of English; he had never heard of TESL nor of the specific Teaching of Medical English; he taught the old-fashioned way by rote two hours a day; he was very receptive and met Joan several times, photocopied all her stuff, and attended whenever his duties allowed.

'English in Basic Medical Science', OUP, Joan Maclean,

(from the series 'English in Focus', editor, JPB Allen & HG Widdowson).

The course was compulsory for the younger doctors and the nurse who might be going to Canada for a year. The six seniors who would be coming in the spring also attended; a few others attended occasionally. The whole book was covered. The size of the class was ideal.

Joan much enjoyed the experience and the whole course was much appreciated.

The Seniors would come in the Spring.

four women and two men, all card carrying Communists for many years. It goes without saying that they all revered Dr Bethune. They knew a lot about his Chinese experiences but little about his past. He was on the battlefield in China for just over eighteen months, such a short time.

Dr Zhao Po, the BIPH senior *surgeon,* mentioned above, was the leader.

Mme/Dr Li Xifa started working at the BIPH in the mid-nineteen fifties. Senior pediatrician and second senior member of the medical staff, she he did her best under quite trying circumstances. The equipment available to me in Antigonish, Nova Scotia in the mid-sixties, such as mini-drops for rehydrating infants and young children, were just not available. Yet she worked and worked. She was the first to describe an unusual-looking newborn with a unique chromosomal anomaly and wrote it up for the National Medical Journal. The hospital had a chromosome lab. She had an enquiring mind and was very kind.

I found her one day with a dying scrawny baby in her arms: what can we do? She asked. I just sat with her for a while. She really suffered when that happened. I had never seen a pediatrician behave like that before.

She was in charge of the hospital library, a dark spooky place with a few tables with a single low neon bar light over the tables. She was most impressed with the Library at *l'hopital du Sacre-Coeur,* so clean and bright. When I returned, the whole BIPH library had been repainted and the lighting much improved: 'come and see our library' was the first thing she said with a smile when we met again a few months later.

There were two young children in the BIPH compound with Trisomy 21/Down's syndrome: they were both well integrated and well-accepted by everyone. They ran around like all the other kids and attended school like everyone else. The kids rarely seemed to bully one another.

Mme Li was a staunch communist. I felt she was politically unwavering. We never talked about it. She had one married daughter who had a child who died in childbirth at the BIPH: she was quite angry about that, implying that things might have been better managed.

Mme/Dr Meng Cangzhe was younger, perhaps in her late-forties, the Head of the large Department of *Obstetrics and Gynecology,* tall, elegant and chic, frank and open-minded. She listened intensely and talked little.

Four thousand babies are born a year at the BIPH. Oral contraceptives were not available at that time. So one day I asked Dr Meng how many abortions were performed? *Twenty-nine a day* she immediately answered. How did the young ladies get there? *Their mums bring them by the hand.* In China one lives at home until marriage. So, whereas in Canada there was at that time a ratio of one official abortion for three live births, the ratio in Southern Hebei Province was five to one.

Mme/Dr He Quina, (internist-intestinal tract), was short, funny and talked easily, the soul of any party or meal.

Mme/Dr Cai Jinxian, (internist-lungs), was sociable and easy to talk to. She had family in Singapour.

Dr Gue Quan, (cardiovascular surgeon), was the enigma. Whereas all the others had chosen to visit several different services (specialized labs, geriatrics, different libraries for instance), he had chosen just cardiovascular surgery at the Royal Victoria Hospital. He hardly ever uttered a word. The English he spoke was poor. He was very lucky because a resident at the RVH was Chinese and of great help.

It transpired within a few months that an exchange student from the BIPH had already been accepted at the Royal Victoria Hospital for a year in heart surgery, thus avoiding our selection process. It also happened that the only scholar to have problems was that young-man: I had to insist that he be allowed to finish his year in Canada, it being an absolute disaster for him had he been forced home early. He was such a nice and able person. Cardio-vascular surgery was just not his bag.

Our Spare Time was spectacular:

XIBAIPO: we visited this small village about two hours away, by a narrow road to the hills north-west of Shijiazhuang, close to the border with Shanxi Province.

Mr Jin He-de, an Army Officer in charge of the Bethune-Kotnis Memorial Hall, was our guide. He was an artist who himself painted; he knew such a lot about Chinese painting. For instance, those large black Chinese characters on the special white paper they used are meant to last one thousand years. One has to have just enough paint on one's brush to complete the letter: if one uses too much the paint runs; if not enough one gets a blank space. This takes a lot of experience. Chairman Mao was good at it.

When the revolutionary war resumed at the end of WWII in the summer of 1945, it became clear that Chairman Mao's headquarters in Yenan might become susceptible targets from attacks from the air. They chose Xibaipo as their temporary headquarters between 1947 and 1949. Chairman Mao himself moved there in 1948, probably just after the 'liberation' of Shijiazhuang.

Thus Xibaipo became a kind of shrine. Its original location was spectacular, near a small river, the Hutuo He. About ten small houses were erected; from the air, the site looked like any other village.

During the fifties, a reservoir was built close to the village. All the small buildings that made up the Headquarters were dismantled and reassembled on the crest of a small hill prior to the flooding.

From the ceiling of those peasant houses bare bulbs hung on wires, some with a white glass shade. The furniture was just as simple, with small oil-lamps on small tables in case of electric failures. Chairman Mao had his own house with a leather armchair as did all the other important people. One room was permanently locked, that was the *operations room,* itself with two tables and about ten chairs, with maps on the wall. General Nieh Jung-Chen had the only key. He had been Dr Bethune's commanding officer.

The meeting room, like a small church, had about 12 pews that could sit perhaps thirty people comfortably. All the important decisions were made there.

Joan and I had never thought it possible that such a powerful group on the eve of victory could possibly live so simply. After all, that small group, just a few months away from total victory, without any artillery or Air Force, had in forty years

= unified China for the first time in over a century.

> = got rid of all foreign invaders from Europe including Russia, plus the USA and Japan.
> = had beaten the Chinese Fascists headed by General Chiang Kai-chek, heavily subsidized by the USA.

Changang/Xian: Joan and I, plus Dr Sun Hui-chen our interpreter, guide and friend spent four nights away including two nights in the Capital of Shaanxi Province, from Friday March 31st at 11:30 am to Sunday April 2nd at 8:30 pm: the most concentrated visit lasting 57 hours to which Joan and I had ever been exposed.

The **train trip** was in itself an adventure: the economy class sleeper and the food were very good. The distance was similar to the Halifax-Montreal run.

What was new to us was the change of locomotives: a large steam engine for the first part, travelling east from Shijiazhuang to Taiyuan, the capital of Shanxi Province. The station there had a large metal/glass domed roof as in pre-war Europe. We had not travelled in a steam train for years apart from a short tourist train trip one summer in New England. It was even exciting putting one's head out of the window to enjoy the smell, the steam and the soot.

A large diesel-electric engine took over in Taiyuan travelling due south.

In Fenglingdu, just before the bridge over the wide Huang He River, an electric engine with overhead wires took over to take us through Shaanxi Province to Xian, three hours away due west.

Dr Bethune had passed through Fenglingdu on the same line travelling north on his way to Yenan in 1938, just forty-one years before.

CHANGANG itself dates from 2,500 BC: situated at the **Eastern End of the Silk Road,** it was totally rebuilt as a rectangular walled city during the sixth century AD following a geometric plan with straight wide streets, surrounded by a four-car lane wide wall on which people walked. It became one of the two city homes of the Tang Dynasty **(618-907)** and renamed **XIAN**. Three million people lived there in the 7th century, probably the most populous city in the world.

The second home of the Tang Dynasty was Luoyang, the Capital of Henan Province and founded in the 12th century BC, four hours away by train. It was to become an important Buddhist

Centre largely located in Cave Dwellings. Henan lies immediately south of Hebei and east of Shaanxi Provinces.

(=) **Buddhism** (Buddha, c.563-c483 BC) was introduced in China for the most part by <u>Xuanzhuang</u> (600-664). He was born in <u>Chenlu</u>, a few miles north of Xian. In 629, he walked to India, via the Gobi Desert, Xinjiang province in the Chinese North-West, Afghanistan, the Valley of the Indus River (now Pakistan), where he stayed for a couple of years.

He then visited all the major historical sites in North India, journeyed 140 miles to the South and returned by sea via the East Coast, <u>carrying on his back 150 pieces of Buddha's body, 657 books, and the recipe for making sugar</u>. He arrived back home in 645.

By 652, the five storey **Davan Pagoda,** (later increased to seven storeys), was completed for the scholars who had to translate all those books. A brick structure with arched doors on each side and a wooden staircase inside, it is shaped like a square pyramid 64 meters high. By the front door are two beautifully inscribed Steles (upright stones) designed by the Tang Emperors themselves and truly beautiful.

It is claimed that the Chinese translation of the famous texts is easier to understand than the original ones.

(=) The **social occasion** we remember most clearly was a lunch the three of us had on the terrace of a small Moslem cafe. Xian is the home of people of many different races. There are 80 minorities in China and eleven million Moslems. We each had a plate of delicious Jiaotzi (dumplings) with a large bottle of local beer, one dollar per person: the weather was perfect, and watching everybody pass by so exciting.

(=) I am not going to talk about the fabulous **"Museum of the Pottery Warriors and Horses of Qin Shi Huang's Mausoleum" (246BC):** we took the bus there, and I took a beautiful photo surreptitiously with my Leica with a wide-angle lens, a fast film without a flash.

(=) The **Shaanxy Provincial Museum** is the most fantastic museum we had ever seen. <u>80% of the exhibits *come from within 20 miles of Xian*</u>: jade carvings, glazed pottery, some of it multi-colored, gilded copper, painted clay, marble carved heads, agate, gold and silver. It is recognized by UNESCO as one of the top fifty museums in the world. A whole wing is devoted to a **Forest of Steles,** all on wheels and rails so that they can be stored in a relatively small area yet studied easily, the largest such collection anywhere.

Just as we were leaving to go home, Dr Lu Ru-ling told us about a telegram that had arrived two days previously to advise us that my <u>mother had had a stroke</u> and had been hospitalized. Her retirement home had a small sick-bay, so she just had to move to another floor. As we were leaving anyway and that changing bookings on airplanes at the last minute was difficult, he felt that it was better to delay telling us the bad news.

We were both sick during our stay, Joan in bed for a couple of days and myself, laryngitis for a day: we were so well looked after, Joan with massages. She always loved massages.

Beijing: we left Shijiazhuang by car on our way home with Jin He-de, Hui-chen and Xiao Ji at 8.30am on **Tuesday April 11th,** all our students being there to see us off; we stopped at the Baoding Provincial Guest House for lunch. We walked around the lovely old park noticing many steles that we had not seen before, then drove across the Marco-Polo Bridge to the PLA Guest House in Beijing. We arrived at 5:30pm. We were able to telephone for news about my mother's health: she seemed to be improving.

There were three sterile visits in Beijing: Marilyn Colette, attaché, at the *Canadian Embassy,* the pretentious *Peking Union Medical College* that I wanted to see with my own eyes, a 1916 Flexnerian copy of the Johns Hopkins University School of Medicine totally financed by the Rockefeller Foundation, and the *CIDA language school.*

A visit to the National Gallery: Li Jungqi was born in 1943 in Heilongjiang Province and taught art at the College there. He had just painted a **Scroll of Famous Chinese Poets, two meters high and 170 meters long** with more than 500 paintings/drawings of poets and scholars from the earliest periods to the present. Attached to each of the pictures of the 500 poets was one of their poems. The scroll was being exhibited in Beijing for the first time. The young artist was there and signed our program. We had never seen such a large, new and beautiful work before. Jin He-de had strongly recommended this visit and came with us. The four of us had our picture taken by Sabastiao Salvado, quite a well-known Brazilian Photojournalist who happened to be there.

The Beijing Zoo, founded during the rule of the Ming dynasty (1368-1644), must be one of the earliest. The Public was only allowed access in 1908. The attendance, many of them children, is now over 10 million a year (over 35,000 a day). It is beautifully kept.

We revisited the **Temple of Heaven,** built in 1420 AD, to my mind one of the most beautiful structures ever built. It is supported by four enormous trees recently replaced by British Columbia Cedars. It is so light, peaceful, and beautifully decorated, with its own Whispering Gallery as in the Dome of St Paul's in London.

We spent a morning with our old friend at the Headquarters of the Friendship Association, **Lu Wan-ru.** She was an active participant in our Bethune Conference in Montreal in 1979 with **Ma Hai-de,** *alias* Dr Georges Hatem, a Lebanese-American who had been Dr Bethune's boss in China. He had joined the Communist Party in Shanghai in the thirties and looked after Chairman Mao during the Yenan period. The two papers they presented at our conference were published in our book, including references to Chairman Mao's writings.

The Friendship Association was housed in the Old Italian Embassy, a beautiful large old building down-town. **Rewi Alley,** a New Zealander, had survived WWI in France and immigrated to Hong Kong in the twenties. He lived there in his own apartment and had died on December 27th 1987 with **Georges Hatem** at his side. The two of them were great friends. Wan-ru, who worked in the same building, had known Rewi quite well and had been busy sorting his papers; she had just finished writing his biography: she gave us a copy. Geoff Chapple had written one in New Zealand in 1980, its third edition in 1989 after he died. Wan-ru took us around Rewi's spacious apartment and we sat in his comfortable soft chairs.

Rewi Alley was an incredible larger than life person. He introduced the Gung Ho Industrial Cooperatives in China in 1938 amongst so many other things. On his last 90th birthday, just a few days before he died, Zhao Ziang, the General Secretary and Li Peng, the Premier, came to visit him in the morning.

Unfortunately, Georges Hatem died shortly after in 1988. He had long-standing prostatic cancer.

Soong Ching-ling (1893-1981), the second of three rich and famous sisters, became secretary to Dr Sun Yat-sen (1866-1925) and married him in 1915. She 'loved' China. Sun Yat-sen, a physician, had become the First President of the Republic of China in 1912.

The eldest one, Soong Ai-ling, 'loved' money and married the richest man in China, a Banker and an Industrial tycoon; the youngest, May-ling, married General Chiang Kai-shek and she 'loved' power. Ai-ling and May-ling were at one point the two richest women in China.

That week-end, we visited Soong Ching Ling's home, an old modernized imperial domain with a Rain Listening Hut in the beautiful garden. It was very comfortable. She had lived there since 1963. Her official rank was Honorary President of the Chinese People's Republic.

Mme Soong, Rewi Alley and Georges Hatem were great friends. According to Lu Wan-ru, the authorities were always wary of making decisions that the group might view with concern; thus, the group had a considerable influence on important decisions; this had evaporated at the end of the eighties after their deaths.

Lu Wan-ru herself was an exceptional lady:

(=) during the Cultural Revolution, she was sequestered for two years in a poor country village, separated from her son and husband. The village was close to the quarters of <u>Kathleen Hall</u>, from New Zealand, the Methodist Minister who had been so helpful to Dr Bethune during the last year of his life helping to purchase much needed medical supplies. Wan-ru got to know well the peasants in the village and learnt to appreciate and accept their judgment: Bethune, a white man with a long nose on a white horse, would arrive at dusk and leave at dawn. The peasants all knew Kathleen Hall, and there never was any doubt in their minds that they were lovers.

(=) she was an excellent interpreter, writer and actress: in 1979, she had accompanied the violinist Isaac Stern during his visit to China. One of the results was an Oscar-winning documentary, **'From Mao to Mozart'**. Wan-ru had a quite large role in that marvelous film. Stern had asked her for a helicopter to move a Grand Piano from somewhere: *'we do not do things like that in China'* replied Wan-ru.

(=) I was invited to supper one evening in 1993 with her husband. They had two boys one of whom lived next door: he had schizophrenia and did not feel like coming. We had a lovely time. Her husband was quite a senior journalist who eventually was posted to Hong-Kong. They had quite a lot of music records, eastern and western, plus gifts of violin records from Isaac Stern. We ended by having a lovely glass of French brandy, our last meeting.

(=) Because of her work, she knew about China more than most: where to buy things, what to visit, where to stay, the history and geography of the country, its culture. She never talked about the political situation. She never talked about Chairman Mao. She thought Chou En-Iai was a great man. She never mentioned where she had gone to University, what degrees she might have. She was happy that her husband had a new job in Hong-Kong. Her son, with bouts of acute schizophrenia, must have been a great burden: this was never a subject of conversation. Joan and I thought she was a great lady.

The Gate of Heavenly Peace (Tiananmen), a massive stone column, was built in 1417. The square around it was enlarged four times and finally cemented over in 1958. On the west side of the square, the Great Hall of the People, a gift from Russia, completed in 1959, houses the National People's Congress with room for 10,000 people and a Banquet Room for 5,000.

The square is the largest in the world, 880m from north to south, 500m from east to west, with room for one million people. It is always a busy place with several hundred people milling around several times a day. For several centuries it has been a place for demonstrations of all kinds, particularly in April and May, the end of the winter.

The April 5th 1976 Movement is an example: after much loved Zhou Enlai's death in January, a mass protest took place in the whole country culminating on April 5th in the square: probably a million people commemorated Zhou Enlai and protested against the 'Gang of Four'. The crowd had to be forcibly but comparatively harmlessly removed from the square.

What triggered Tiananmen protests on Saturday, April 15th 1989, the eve of our return home?

Hu Yaobang (b Nov. 1915), fought alongside Chairman Mao and became head of the Communist Party under Deng Xiaoping. A 'relative' liberal, he was blamed for supporting students who were demonstrating for more reforms during winter in 1987 and he lost his job. His death that April

15th 1989 sparked the Tiananmen Incident: *students brought wreaths to the square* and *stayed to demonstrate.*

Our Chinese friends thought nothing of it: it would last a short while and evaporate without further ado. European students demonstrate far more often than they do in the UK or the USA: it is a normal activity for them, a part of student life, a part of their political experience; the same seems to be true in China.

Hu Yaobang was finally exonerated and the 90th anniversary of his birth officially commemorated on Friday Nov 18th 2005.

Bibi, my mother, lived for another two weeks:

We arrived in London at 7.30 am on Monday morning April 17th, rented a car and drove to her abode, Kekewich House, Marie Fielding Guild, in Highgate, a residential home for the elderly, with just 65 residents. Its Victorian name was the 'Working Ladies Guild', at first a heavily endowed institution mainly for retired Nurses, extremely well-organized. Senior nurses were so badly paid during the period of the Voluntary Hospitals. Bibi had lived there for several years. She was in the sick bay having suffered a stroke. She improved as the day wore on. There were a couple of rooms there where relatives could stay at a very moderate cost. She was able to walk around with help, and we spent nice hours in her own quarters, just a few minutes walk away.

We were so happy to see one another. We stayed in London for exactly one week. We saw her lawyer and realized her will had to be updated: this was promptly done and everything was settled. Bibi seemed to have reached a plateau. Her friends came for visits. We returned home on Monday April 24th

On Thursday 27th, she had a relapse. I immediately flew back, arriving the next morning at 9am: she had died at 4am London time, and was buried in the cemetery in Golders Green. Joan flew over on May 1st, having completed the income tax returns that same morning. As they were a day late, we were fined. I returned to Montreal on May 4th and Joan on May 8th.

We saw my brother John daily and would drive him home. He lived in Leytonstone, about five miles away. Alfred Hitchcock was born there. The large and efficient Whipps Cross Hospital, just round the corner from where John lived, has now become an annex of The London Hospital in Whitechapel where I trained. When John had health problems that required specialized care, he would be admitted there, and there he died on January 11th 2003, 75 years old: he had developed a bacterial infection in his urinary tract that did not respond to antibiotics. He had had bouts of acute schizophrenia.

It was always nice to be in London, my home-town. But Joan and I had few regrets about leaving the country in 1958. From then on, we had to replace my mother who did so much for John: he had no relatives in England, just a few friends; we went to England to see him twice a year for a few days from then on and we would go on a trip. He came over for a two week visit and he met all the different members of his Canadian Family.

The Senior Doctors' Visit to Canada, Monday May 29th-Saturday June 24th 1989.

Introduction:

It was usual for 'students' visiting Canada on a grant to receive a bimonthly allowance that could be spent at their discretion. That was the way for our own long-term students from China. I felt it was not appropriate for the visit, lasting four weeks, by our six seniors 'students' that Joan and I knew so well, apart from one of them, the chest surgeon. We had planned several visits, to **Niagara Falls in Ontario,** four days out of town, via Ottawa and the Chinese Embassy, Algonquin Park, Gravenhurst (Dr Bethune's birthplace), Toronto, Niagara Falls, returning via Kingston were lived my son Nicholas and his family, then to the **Sherbrook** area for the day where the Faculty of Medicine had offered us lunch at lovely Hovey Manor by Lake Massawippi near North Hatley, and finally to **Quebec City** for two nights.

This was quite a lot of travelling: it would be cheaper to rent a van with eight seats that I would drive during the whole four weeks. It would save time and money. I would also be able to collect our friends to and from the airport and show them Montreal itself. We would stay in Journey's End Motels, (a Canadian chain at the time), or an Accor (French owned) hotel, and usually eat in the cheaper chain restaurants, McDonald's, Suisse Chalet, Kentucky Fried Chicken, St Hubert Barbecue, Marie-Antoinette, Pizza Hut, hot dog stands, plus restaurants in Chinatown (usually the 'Poon Kai'), with occasional exceptions.

Chinatown was within easy walking distance from their new, cosy and reasonably-priced Arcade Hotel, with very good fresh croissants and a nice restaurant, on old Dorchester Avenue, opposite *le Complexe Desjardins.* Our visitors would also share rooms in the hotels and be given some pocket-money on arrival. Whatever money was left at the end of the trip would be split into the six of them: thus, they might buy things before going home.

This was discussed and they accepted the plan enthusiastically. They were relieved not to have to make those choices themselves individually. It fitted their life-style at home. It was also so much simpler: they would give me their checks which I would cash, pay all the bills, keep all the receipts, making a tally every evening.

Martial Law had been declared in Beijing on Friday May 19th; horrible events in Tiananmen Square started two weeks later on June 3rd at 10.30pm. I will cover the first ten days of our colleagues' visit in some detail, as those horrible events occurred during that time. The time in Montreal is the same as in Beijing but twelve hours later.

It was easy talking with them. It was wonderful having met them all before, just treating one another as old friends do. Dr/Mme He Quina would arrive two days from now. We drove them to their hotel. I returned to China that coming September for nine weeks and was confronted with many unforeseeable problems. Thus, the second half of the year was just as eventful as the first.

I had found **Mr Yu Ning, an excellent interpreter,** a senior Chinese student who was studying law at McGill. He was happy to earn some extra money and was available whenever necessary. We never talked about politics.

The arrival of our guests on Monday May 29th at Dorval airport was so easy: we knew each other well as friend do. They were happy and relaxed. The trip had been uneventful.

On **Tuesday May 30th,** in Tiananmen, the students erected the Statue of the Goddess of Democracy.

We went for lunch at the Poon-Kai close-by. **We drove around town,** pointing out the various sights, the St Lawrence River, the Bridges over it, the two Universities they would deal with, the Mountain with its lake at the summit, the Parks, the beautiful Churches, the Olympic stadium, stopping periodically. Montreal is a really beautiful city. It was all so restful.

On **Wednesday 31st,** Joan and I picked-up Dr He Quina and drove her to the Hotel.

Thursday June the 1st was spent at *l'hopital du Sacre-Coeur,* with an absolutely delicious lunch with about thirty guests, so informal. We toured the hospital. Everybody enjoyed themselves.

On **Friday June 2nd** we spent the day at the **Royal Victoria Hospital:** a formal baronial-style Victorian building with turrets completed in 1893, with a large mahogany table and chairs plus a grand-father clock in the board-room. Lots of nice food was on the table. There is a beautiful marble statue of a young Queen Victoria in the entrance hall: I have a photo of our Chinese Communist Doctors standing next to it.

That board-room and its furniture always makes me think of my house-staff days at the London Hospital and its two hundred year-old board-room after WII in January 1948: we had to parade there at the beginning of our cession with future chiefs sitting around the large mahogany table with all our dossiers scattered on it: photographs were not available so each one of us had to be recognized. It was quite intimidating.

On June 2nd the use of the military is approved to put an end to what was going on in Tiananmen Square.

On **Saturday June 3rd**, my 65th birthday, we set off on our four day drive. Our first stop for the night was Ottawa. We travelled along the north shore of the Ottawa River, stopping several times, a beautiful trip. The weather was lovely. Our guests were getting anxious about the development of events in Beijing. They had been watching television and were looking forward to their visit at the Chinese Embassy: we had been invited there for breakfast the next morning, Sunday, June 4th at 9am. That was the first time that I recollect that the problems at Tiananmen problems were mentioned.

We had the buffet lunch at the log-made **Chateau Montebello,** a Fairmont Hotel on the edge of its own large estate by the Ottawa River; 3,500 laborers completed it in only four months in 1930 as a private club. It was made of 10,000 logs, 500,000 hand-slit cedar roof shakes and 166 kms of wooden moulding, all from British Columbia; built around a six-sided stone fireplace it rose twenty meters to the roof, the largest log building in the world. The scenery around is superb. There are over 200 guest rooms.

It is the site for many International summit meetings, the G7 in 1981 and NATO in 1983 amongst others.

The buffet food was excellent, and our guests like all visitors there could not get over it. We walked around the lovely grounds for a couple of hours before leaving for Ottawa.

We spent the night in the outskirts of the town in a Journey's End Motel.

On Friday June 3rd, 300.000 troops enter Beijing. At **10.30pm** fighting breaks out in the roads leading to the corners of the square. Many stones were thrown and many shots were fired.

At **1am** on Saturday June 4th the army finally reaches Tiananmen Square. The students were told to clear the square before 6 am and **they left at 4am.**

The Chinese Red Cross reported **2.600 deaths.** The Chinese Red Cross was told to adjust these figures: the official figures were 241 deaths and 7.000 injuries.[*] Exact numbers are unknown to this day.

On **Sunday June the 4th** I knocked on the door of the **Chinese Embassy** in Ottawa at 9 o'clock sharp: _there was no answer,_ so I kept on knocking: after about five minutes, the door was opened a couple of inches, a chain keeping it from opening altogether: an older man who was crying, still in his pyjamas,

---

[*]   red ink writing indicates quotes from the Globe and Mail, May 30th 2009, pages A14-15, by Mark Mackinnon.

hair uncombed, regretfully told us that we could not possibly see anybody. That was horrible news for our guests. They might be unable to go home. What was going to happen next? What had really happened at home? I tried my best to be reassuring: Canada might be the best place to be for them during the next few weeks.

Thirteen full-time members of the Chinese Embassy staff subsequently refused to go home.

As everybody was climbing back into the van, one of the ladies suddenly said **'there is nothing left to do but pray'**; two others agreed; it transpired that the three ladies had gone to private schools run by Catholic nuns when they were children.

We had a sad breakfast down-town and visited the **Parliament Buildings,** but the mood was upset. We drove past the building of the **Royal College of Physicians and Surgeons,** and a sad photograph was taken of all of them on the door-step of the College under its crest.

We then drove for 400 kms to Gravenhurst via beautiful **Algonquin Provincial Park** on route 60; at its entrance one has to register one's car: the attendant told us moose were by the road and to take care. It was a beautiful day. There was nothing to see except nature, streams, lakes and wild-life for miles. Apart from the road itself the area has remain unchanged for centuries. Such a drive would be very unusual in China. I had new dollar coins in my pocket, 'loonies'. So I promised a new one to the person who first saw a moose. 'What is a moose?' 'A big dark horse with a hump on its back and large antlers': 'ha-ha' said they unanimously.

That new exceptional scenery cured the doom. He Quina, sitting in the front next to me won the gold-looking dollar 3 miles or so down the road, 'Moo-moo!' said she, pointing her finger. We stopped and all got out to take pictures.

Another mile or so **a beautiful pristine large curved S-shaped lake on the edges of the road:** 'stop here' says Li Xi-fa. We all got out and Li Xi-fa walked off in the lake with her shoes and stockings on. They all followed suit. The water was so clear, clean, refreshing, for them so unusual. From then on, the horrible problems of the day seemed to have been shelved. Smiles returned.

We went to our Motel in **Gravenhurst** and spent the evening at the home of the young **Director of Bethune Memorial House** and her staff. There were about twelve of us having tea, biscuits and cake around the small low table in her living room, a quite intimate, informal, easy and enchanting private occasion.

On **Monday June 5th** we drove around beautiful Gravenhurst and visited **the Bethune Memorial House:**

'It was built in 1880 as the **Knox Presbyterian Church manse.** The family of Rev. Malcolm Bethune occupied the house from 1889 to 1893 and Dr Bethune was born there on March the 3rd 1890. The house was restored to the 1880 period and is operated by Parks Canada'.

John Knox (1523-72) founded the Church of Scotland in 1560. It remained the official Church in Scotland for two centuries. John Knox had been influenced by **John Calvin (1509-64),** his **Church of Scotland** being more democratic and decentralized.

We then drove about 100 miles to the **Doctors Hospital** at 45 Brunswick Street, Toronto, a smaller down-town hospital that became incorporated in the Toronto General Hospital Complex in 1997. It had a large out-patient department and dealt with many accidents and injuries. The Doctors Hospital had approached the Bethune International Peace Hospital suggesting some form of cooperation, and Dr Lu Ruling, its director, had asked me to visit if at all possible. We were very nicely received; a fine example of a cork carving in its glass case was presented by Dr Zhao to the director.

That afternoon we motored towards **Niagara Falls,** crossing the whole of south-west Ontario along the western shore of the Lake, 120kms, arriving at **St. Catherine's** where we spent the night, just a few miles west of the Falls.

On **Tuesday June 6th** we spent all morning at the Falls, looking and listening to its roar. We had breakfast in a restaurant overlooking **Horseshoe Falls.** All I had ever learned and remembered at school about Canadian geography was a textbook photograph of Horseshoe Falls, and the same is true of all schools in the world. It is the first choice for a 'must see' magical experience for visitors to Canada. The Falls are

= second only to Victoria Falls in Africa;
= 188 feet high and 170 feet deep where the water falls; its rim measures 2,200 feet.
= where 4-6 million cubic feet of water fall per minute;
= where a sixty-three year old woman and her cat were probably the first to go over the Falls successfully in a barrel in 1903;
= where there are 50,000 couples on their honeymoon a year, a world record.

I was somewhat concerned when Li Xifa climbed on the top of the stone barrier at the edge of the falls to sit on it! That was so high! She just sat there. She had been working at the BIPH since the mid-fifties.

We motored half-way to Kingston before lunch; I thought we would stop for an hour or so at **48 McDonnell Street in Kingston** where our eldest son Nicholas, a psychiatrist, lived with his family, Dianne, a family physician, and their three children, Luke, Adam and Amy (8,5 and nearly 3 years old). Their parents were both at work. I wondered how the children would react, their house suddenly invaded by their grandfather with six adults from China.

I needn't have worried: He Quina immediately noticed the piano, sat down and played a tune. Luke and a friend of his age soon took over to demonstrate their skills. I went to Winston Churchill Primary School (one of the best in Ontario) just round the corner with Zhao Po to bring Amy home: she had just finished her kindergarten class. He was very impressed with the school, so clean and orderly with so much equipment. When we got home Li Xi-fa played with Amy as if she had known her for years.

On one occasion during that trip, I drove the car in an automatic car cleaner not telling them what it was all about: they all got scared and subsequently had a good laugh.

We finally reached Montreal at about 8pm: a fantastic and unpredictable nine days since our friends landed; for them, a traumatic period that caused much anxiety and concerns which would mark their future.

Ten Days for our guests to meet various health professionals/hospital departments of their choice:

= Dr Cai Jinxian, lung diseases: the Royal Victoria Hospital, *l'hopital du Sacre-Coeur, l'institut de Geriatrie.*

= Dr Gue Quan, cardiovascular surgery: the Royal Victoria Hospital.

= Dr He Quina, gastro-enterology: the Montreal General Hospital, *l'hopital St Luc, l'hopital du Sacre-Coeu,*(endoscopy, laboratory, radiology).

= Dr Li Xifa, pediatrics: the Montreal Children's Hospital, (respiratory diseases,biochemical genetics,intensive care of newborns,out-patients); *l'hopital Ste Justine*, (cytogenetics, intensive care of new-borns); the Royal Victoria Hospital (intensive care of newborn babies, operational research in the delivery room); *l'hopital St Luc* (vitamin D research and the liver).

= Dr Meng Cangzhe, obstetrics and gynecology: the Royal Victoria Hospital, Montreal Children's Hospital, *l'hopital St Justine*, (child birth, diagnostic radiology, amniocentesis, gynecological operations, chromosomal genetics).

=   **Dr Zhao Po, Head of the delegation, Head of Surgery at the BIPH, having worked there since its inception in 1948:** *l'hopital du Sacre-Coeur, l'hopital St Luc,* the Royal Victoria Hospital, (diagnostic radiology, endoscopy, surgical operations), *l'institut de Geriatrie.*

The seven of us met most evenings to talk about their experiences and to adjust their schedule as needed.

The Last of the ten days was devoted to a seminar **'an introduction to research'** at the University of Montreal. The last two hours on the **'writing of objectives'** for a hypothetical post-graduate doctor who might come to Montreal for a year's study.

The Faculty of Medicine at the University of Sherbrook invites the group for Lunch on Sunday June the 11ᵗʰ:

There were three reasons why I was happy to go on this trip:

(=) that was where I had taught Human Genetics, did a lot to introduce the teaching of Family Medicine and for a year had been head of the Department of Social and Community Medicine. I had never been back since my departure in 1979 when I was invited by *l'universite de Montreal* to start a teaching unit of Family Medicine at *l'hopital du Sacre-Coeur de Cartierville* where Dr Bethune had started working in 1933. That was how I got involved in the originally McGill-based Norman Bethune Foundation eventually becoming its third President. This would be my first visit with my old colleagues in ten years.

(=) I would meet an old colleague M Bernard *Longpre,* a hematologist there. *Mon cher Papa* (that was how he always called him) was a general practitioner in a poorer area of Montreal who had started a free clinic in a doctor-deprived area during the depression in the early thirties, just as Norman Bethune had done. During the sixties he had been invited to visit the BIPH. Dr Li Xifa remembered that visit. He had been given flowers by a young nurse who was now head of the Department of Nursing; he visited the Revolutionary Martyrs Cemetery to put a wreath on Dr Bethune's tomb. Bernard sent me a picture of the event. The Head of Nursing actually came over for a month in 1990 as part of our program, but we did not visit Sherbrook.

(=) I met Nigel Spencer there. He taught English literature, drama and film at Champlain College (like a CEGEP in francophone areas), in Lennoxville, Quebec. I knew of him. In 1981, he had written *'Louis Riel and Norman Bethune, a Critical Bibliography',* a document written mainly for his students that was published in the Moosehead Review (volume three No1). It was very helpful. Thus, in English-speaking areasof Quebec, Dr Bethune was mentioned in College syllabuses during the eighties.

Hovey Manor is to-day a five-star <u>"Relais et Chateaux"</u> Inn, situated at the northern end of Lake Massawippi, perhaps twenty Km long, surrounded by hills, one of the most beautiful locations one can imagine. We met there. The southern end of the lake is in Vermont, USA.

The gardens of Hovey Manor, with chairs and small tables, line the lake. It is most comfortable and luxurious. Dean Pigeon, the dean since when I was there (1969-1976), was chairman of our meeting. We all had a delicious three-course lunch with wine, sitting around a large table. There were about twenty four of us.

An Associate dean then presented the development of the medical curriculum at the University of Sherbrook, the most important of which was the *elimination of formal lectures.*

Nigel Spencer was an able and pleasant person. Unfortunately, we did not really have a chance to have a good talk.

Meeting those old colleagues made me feel quite sad; it was an unusual personal academic experience. I never thought I would reconnect with old colleagues in such an extraordinary way. I felt really grateful for what was done that day. My old acquaintance Bernard Longpre was so happy to meet representatives of the BIPH on his own turf and talk about his Dad with them, an experience he never thought would be possible.

We all had such a lovely time. <u>On the way home</u>, we stopped half-way at a Pizza Delight in **Brome:** the scenery from the window next to where we were sitting had a lovely view of the ski-hill. Brome was also the sight for the Equestrian Event of the 1976 Montreal-based Olympic Games.

<u>Five lesser but still important events before returning home on Saturday June 24th at 7:30 am:</u>

On **<u>Thursday June 15th</u>** we <u>invited our guests plus our daughter Jane for dinner at home</u>: we had moved to a renovated old apartment on the second of a three floor duplex with an outside staircase, a typical home on the plateau of Montreal; it was built before WWI. We had moved there just a year before as my retirement was approaching. We had kept as many of the old features as possible, but the kitchen area was modern with a beautiful efficient grill. It was quite an intriguing place. The size (1,200 square feet) was more in tune with their own housing, usually less than half that sizeI We had a lovely cold buffet with nice desserts as I recall. It was an informal evening with everybody helping out.

On **Friday the 16ᵗʰ,** Joan and I plus our six guests set off for two nights near Quebec City, **a World Heritage Site:** we lodged on the south shore of the St Lawrence in *Levis,* cheaper than in the City itself. I always thought that arriving in the morning in Quebec City from Levis by ferry is the most beautiful and unexpected experience: our guests agreed.

We walked around the streets of the beautiful old walled city, the only one in North America. The present walls were built by the British around 1825. We visited old churches.

We stopped at the **Chateau Frontenac,** originally a Canadian Pacific Railway Hotel built in 1893. Winston Churchill and Franklin D Roosevelt met in Quebec in 1943 to discuss strategy for WWII, **the Quebec Conference;** most of the staff stayed there. We walked around the hotel having a drink in the beautiful main bar.

We drove east to the *Montmorency Falls,* so-named by *Samuel de Champlain* in 1613 in honor of *Henri II, duc de Montmorency,* who served as viceroy of New France (1620-1625). It is higher but so much narrower than Niagara Falls.

At 7:30pm, we went to a Motocross in the *Colisee de Quebec,* a first for all of us! We all much enjoyed it. We then took the ferry back to our motel in Levis.

The next morning we returned to Montreal. At around noon we took a side road towards the river to a small town and stopped outside a restaurant advertizing a Sunday brunch. The food was ***absolutely delicious, everyone spoke French so unlike downtown Montreal. We felt that nobody there*** even understood any English. Nor had they any reason to.

On **Tuesday June 20ᵗʰ,** the **Norman Bethune Foundation** invited our six guests with a dozen or so members and other guests for dinner at the Poon-Kai. Our oldest member who was there was **Dr Wendell McLeod,** 84 years old, who had known Norman Bethune so well. They had worked together on the multi-professional task force created by Dr Bethune during his period at *l'HSC* to suggest changes in the administration of Health Services in Canada; many features of that report were incorporated in the **Hall Commission's Report on Health Services** published in 1964. It was a wonderful evening.

In a nut-shell, Wendell's father was a Methodist minister in Montreal; he would accompany him to his visits to the Bordeaux jail as a child. As a teenager, he sold brushes for the Fuller Brush Company during the summer in St Stephen, New Brunswick. He had to pay for his own medical education at Mc Gill. That was where he met and was much influenced by Dr Bethune, working on his famous committee on Health Services. He became an internist, served as a medical officer in a destroyer in the Atlantic during WWII, was the first Dean of the new medical School in Saskatchewan, became a great supporter of the National Democratic Party (NDP) right from the start, became the first Director of the Association of Canadian Medical Colleges and received the Order of Canada: **Dr Bethune had influenced Wendell's career.**

Our Chinese Friends could not get over meeting him.

On **Friday June 23ʳᵈ,** we had a lovely fish supper at one of the two or three best fish restaurants in Montreal, *'Chez Pauze':* shrimp and lobster and a bottle of white wine. It was quite delicious.

On **Saturday June 24ᵗʰ,** our friends returned home, catching the 7.30 am flight to Toronto. They had each received about $150, the left over money from their allowance. I know that Li Xifa, always so practical, had bought a food processor!

Second stay in China in 1989, from Friday September the 8ᵗʰ to Tuesday November the 14ᵗʰ.

An extraordinary nine weeks that can be divided into four:

= the <u>fifteenth</u> anniversary of the <u>Bethune University of Medical Sciences</u> (NBUMS) in Changchun on September 12th. It was also the 50ᵗʰ anniversary of Dr Bethune's own Medical School in North China: within a few days of its opening it was demolished by Japanese bombs.

= the <u>40ᵗʰ anniversary of the People's Republic of China</u> (PRC), Shijiazhuang, September 30ᵗʰ-October 1ˢᵗ.

= the <u>first Congress of General Practice in the PRC</u> in Beijing, November 2ⁿᵈ-8ᵗʰ.

= the <u>50ᵗʰ anniversary of the death of Dr Bethune</u>, Beijing and Shijiazhuang, November 9ᵗʰ-13ᵗʰ.

I must introduce you to **Sister Jacqueline Villemure,** in Chinese <u>Wei Jei Ling</u>, of the order of the *'Sisters of the Immaculate Conception'.* The Mother House is in Outremont, near where we lived in Montreal. Sister Jacqueline was for many years the Administrator of the Chinese Hospital in down-town Montreal; she had on her own raised the funds and doubled the size of the Institution. She was a University graduate including obtaining a Masters in Hospital Administration; Sister Jacqueline then decided to enter a doctoral program in Administration of Health Services (Chinese Culture) at the University of Montreal (HEC). The subject she chose was to analyze Administration in China and compare it with that in the Western World.

To do this, she had to find an Institution in China where she could study its Administration. This was difficult; her supervisor had heard about our project and suggested that summer she ask for my support. I immediately thought it was a fantastic idea to have an experienced administrator on one's side. Her thesis: *"les particularites du management Chinois"* was accepted in 1993. That thesis flows from her experiences at the BIPH. For instance, we talk all the time about ad hoc & standing committees and take them for granted: in China, few people understand what that means. She helped me so much. She came from Timmins and was thus a Franco-Ontarian. Dr Lu Ruling, the Director of the BIPH offered a crucial help. Jacqueline's father was a widower: his health was precarious and this concerned her a great deal. She was an only child.

By 1995 I was the only head of a CIDA project one of the components of which was a PhD thesis on hospital health administration in China.

I flew to Hong-Kong and spent the night there, then caught the 7.30 am short flight the next morning to **Guangzhou**. From there to Changchun the flight lasted about 2 ½ hours. I was very surprised by the two or three attendants who, at no cost, were putting loads of tape on the large parcels travelers were going to carry on board. What was going on? The plane was packed, people having those large parcels on their knees. As soon as the wheels left the ground, all the parcels were thrown in the alley! Thus, they had to be safely packed. I later gathered that the parcels contained clothing made in and around Guangzou that was sold at a market in Changchun, a much wealthier town. Air transport is relatively cheap in China.

I was met at the airport in Changchun. They were quite delighted to see me.

The fifteenth anniversary of the NBUMS in Changchun September 12th 1989:

> I was the only Canadian present; nobody was there from the Canadian Embassy. There were about twenty Japanese guests: they were building a new hospital, and the dental school had been Japanese since the early thirties when the whole of Manchuria had been annexed by Japan. The Japanese wanted to maintain their influence in 'Old Manchuria' as much as they could. They were building a new hospital and the Dental School had been the continuation of the old Japanese one.
>
> The Medical School held its celebration meeting in the city forum with 4-5,000 seats. There were two hours of speeches,

followed by a concert lasting an hour by the workers and students of the NBUMS; the orchestra was professional. I thought this second part was excellent. I was asked to give a speech. This I had not foreseen. I worked half the night:

Dear Friends,

It is a great honor for me to be here to-day!

Fifty years is quite old for a medical school. But that it would have been started by Dr Bethune himself is what makes it unique in the world. He is an example for us all and the behavior of each one of us must reflect his ideals. He fought in three wars; in the first world war, he was wounded, like a dog, carrying a stretcher; he then established in Spain the first mobile transfusion service in the world; **"go to the wounded and the sick, do not expect them to come to you"** *was his motto, and this must always your motto. This is what we can learn from him. He thought of himself as an artist, and this is, as you know, with considerable justification; what follows comes from an article he wrote in Madrid during the Spanish Civil War:*

"the function of the artist is to disturb, rouse the sleepers and shake the complacent pillars of the earth. The artist reminds the world of its dark ancestry, shows the world its present, and points the way to its new birth. He is at once the product and the preceptor of his time. After his passage, we are troubled, and made unsure of our too easily accepted realities . . . He is the creative spirit working in the soul of man."

I must now bring you greetings from the two Canadian Institutions in Montreal with which Norman Bethune was associated, l'hopital du Sacre-Coeur and the Royal Victoria Hospital; and from the two Universities with whom they are affiliated, l'universite de Montreal and McGill University.

Also from le college Rosemont, a French-speaking College with which links were established last year: a very successful experience for us all; one of your professors spent six months there teaching Acupuncture.

I also bring you wishes from the Norman Bethune Foundation, particularly from **Irene Kon** *who knew him well and whose father Louis was so influential in shaping Norman Bethune's political ideals, and from* **Dr Wendell McLeod** *who worked with Dr Bethune to produce one of the first attempts in North America to* *introduce a National Health Service: the Montreal Group for the Security of the People's health published a report which was sent to all the important figures in Quebec in 1936.*

The Canadian International Development Agency has asked me to be their spokesman in wishing you all the best for the next half-century.

An finally Dr Potvin, Dean of the Faculty of Medicine at Laval University, sends his deep regrets for not being able to be here to-day; he was admitted to hospital in June for some weird infection and has not yet fully recovered. An important project between Laval University, the oldest in North America, the Canadian International Development Agency and the Bethune University of Medical Sciences is under study. It stands a very strong chance of being approved within the next few months.

This leaves me with one final sentence: I wish you all the best for the next fifty years. May this University flourish, I am sure it will. Never forget its founder, Dr Norman Bethune.

A senior medical student, a nice young lady, translated: she worked all morning at it; I would read my English paragraph and she would read her Chinese one. She was not that happy with her translation, a good sign!

I had a chat with Mr Tetsuya Furuya, of Kitasato University in Tokyo. He had never heard of Norman Bethune and was interested by what I had said.

That same evening, I was invited to the banquet given by the vice-governor of the province of Jilin in a restaurant in the town, a large table with twenty-four guests, informal, pleasant with delicious food and drink.

The next evening, I was asked to attend a lovely dinner in the corner of the schools' cafeteria. Around the round table was the President, Shu Zheng Liu MD, Dr Cheng, an old acquaintance who had spent two years in Quebec and was now secretary-general of the party at the University and just one or two others, quite a delightful evening. The food and drink was just as good as that of the night before.

By that time, my old friend born in Baoding, now an electron microscopist at the BIPH, Dr Sun Huichen, had arrived in Changchun to help me travel back to the BIPH in Shijiazhuang by train. It was nice meeting him again. We left together the next day to Shijiazhuang by train.

Staying in Hebei Province and Beijing, principally at the BIPH in Shijiazhuang,

(Friday, September 15th-Tuesday, November 14th 1989).

Introduction:

Since June, <u>individual freedom</u> has been more restricted: one has to have permission to travel between one town and another, even for an Army truck from place A to place B, with accrued security in airports and railway stations.

<u>Television news</u> became more limited: a news program often seemed to be divided into four segments: receptions for seniors many of whom were taking notes; a senior member of government welcoming guests from an African or Central/South-American pro-communist country; this is followed by a clip of people working very hard before the revolution compared with to-day when people watch television or work on their computer; finally, a light program about animals such as pandas, a zebra or circus animals. There is little news from the rest of the world.

There was a lot of <u>anger</u> when France officially welcomed some of the Chinese students from Tiananmen, and even more when the Dalai Lahma received the Nobel Peace Prize.

<u>Within the walls of the BIPH</u>, doctors cannot invite foreigners such as myself to their apartment without the written consent of the director; the demand must be made a week in advance. This was always so. This might not stop one of them to cook a meal and come and eat it in one's hotel room unofficially! Or, more officially, they might cook a meal and eat it in the Hospital Cafeteria with the director as a guest.

As far as <u>mail</u> is concerned, one can only send a letter to a person's work-place. Any letter from abroad might end up in the hands of one's boss.

A surreptitious early visit to Beijing: something of what had really happened at Tiananmen.

I soon learnt that the seniors who had just visited Canada had refused to make an official report of their visit to Canada as they were supposed to do. The most likely reason was that they did not want to broadcast the failure of their embassy in Ottawa to meet them. The Director, Dr Lu Ruling, would agree with such a proposition. The result for me was the impossibility of meeting them officially during the whole of my stay. I was so looking forward to meeting them after our lovely time together.

As Mark MacKinnon put it, as early as May the 20th PLA convoys were sent into Beijing but were blocked by protestors: those troops left the City on May 24th, unable to even reach Tiananmen Square. Thus the government including Deng Xiaoping himself had been severely humiliated by the PLA itself.

There were no special units in China to cope with such non-violent outbreaks. Most countries in the world at that time were in a similar situation. Police Emergency Response Teams (PERT) are all relatively new in Canada as in most other countries. Neither the Fire-Brigade nor the Police in Beijing could be relied on to control such events. They had never been trained for it. So the government was in a very sticky situation. Only the Army might cope. That had been tried, one of its own experienced Senior Commanding Officers based in Hebei Province having given up and his troops withdrawn on May 24th. So, what next?

Deng Xiaoping (1904-1997) was the senior politician in the country: he was 85 in 1989, and held the two most important positions in China. He had Parkinson's disease, often associated with impaired cognitive, memory and psychomotor performance. He was a most influential person (politician/ military), more so than any other in the whole world at the particular moment. His actual positions were:

1) **Chairman of the Central Military Commission of the People's Republic of China,**

   (1983-1990): Political Office.

2) **Chairman of the Central Military Commission,**

   (1981-1989): Party Political Office.

In early June, he was succeeded in the second position by **Jiang Zemin** (b **1926**), the ex-mayor of Shanghai, but he maintained much of his influence; Jiang Zemin had ably succeeded in defusing a similar situation in Shanghai earlier that year without any violence. Deng kept the first position until the end of the year.

Then an **extraordinary event** happened to me, an unofficial day-trip to Beijing in mid-September (that I never officially mentioned) during which I learnt a little more of what happened at Tiananmen Square on the night of June 3rd 1989.

Dr Lu Ruling told me he wanted me to meet some-one in Beijing. Dr Lu comes from Beijing: his daughter had married the son of one of the few rich owners of one or more large department stores in down town. They had a few private cars. His son-in-law would be at our disposal for the day to drive us around, meeting us at the railway station. By 'us' I mean Sun Huichen and I. We would travel by train, returning that same evening. I had no idea what it was all about. We arrived in Beijing at around 9:30 am and caught the train home at 5pm.

A nice, polite, intelligent young man met us at the station with his small four-door car and immediately drove us to meet the Colonel in the Army who was in charge of communications between the PLA and the rest of the world on the night of June 3rd-4th. We stayed there for two hours.

The Colonel and his wife, a Nurse who worked in one of the many small hospitals in the immediate neighborhood of Tiananmen Square, lived there in a small apartment; she was also on duty that night. We talked for two hours around a small table between two small settees in their small living room, just the four of us. We drank a lot of tea and ate a lot of peanuts; there were lots of paper handkerchiefs around.

The Colonel told us that

> 'Deng Xiaoping himself had telephoned his son probably on May the 25th: his son was in Command of the Military Forces in Shijiazhuang. He was ordered to Beijing with his armed forces to deal with the protests in Tiananmen Square'.

In China, one is taught to obey unconditionally only two people, one's Father and the Emperor: his son had no way out.

I suspect that Major-General Deng in Shijiazhuang obtained the collaboration of his nearest colleague commanding a similar large Army Unit. This colleague was probably based in Anyang, an old Capital City originally called the **Great Shang** (the Shang dynasty, c1650-1027, BC) in Henan Province just south of the border, on the same railway line to Beijing and not too far away from Shijiazhuang (125 km or so).

> Thus, within a week perhaps 100,000 soldiers, mostly young adults (18-24 years old) plus perhaps a couple of dozen tanks were rushed to Beijing. Those mostly young troops had no preparation for the horrible and specific task that was awaiting them. They were confronted by irate students of their own age whom many admired having seen them on television during the past few weeks. Many had relations or friends who were University/College students, not necessarily in Beijing. They were asked to fire their weapons and incapacitate them.

Few people at that time understood the **Culture of Young Adults:**

Young adults are in a very precarious situation in every country, but <u>more so in China with its one boy-per-family regulation</u>. They have to chose a job, leave home, establish relationships, earn money; what job: University, Technical School, the Armed Forces, working in the Family Business such as farming? In China, families now consist of just a married couple with one male child, unlike their own parents and grandparents. These children are less docile, unprepared for a struggle. Unlike their parents when they were young they can change jobs to try various experiences. They travel around.

Many soldiers presumably join the Army for a limited time. Young adults everywhere need a lot of support, but they are so often unwilling to seek advice or help: they want to prove their independence. They ignore simple safety precautions, such as wearing ear-muffs to protect their hearing, or protective clothing when they drive motor-bikes, or orders to fire and disable other young adults; instead, they could fire in the air or into the ground when confronted with such a ghastly order.

Many soldiers had sisters, relatives, acquaintances who were collegiate or university students in Beijing or elsewhere. They would never have thought they might be sent to Beijing to settle that kind of problem. That was not why they had joined the Army. So, how would they behave? What did they do? The whole of the future of the People's Liberation Army was at stake. The PLA had never been in such a disastrous situation. <u>Chairman Mao had always pledged compensation for physical losses caused by the PLA.</u> What about human injuries or deaths?

The following relates to events occurring from 10:30pm on June 3rd 1989 to 1.00 am June 4th:

> *The chaos was such that the Colonel himself never knew exactly what was going on, yet he had officially to try and explain the situation. He felt he had totally failed to do his job and felt so badly about it.* **He had the most horrible and impossible job in the world at that particular moment.**
>
> *His wife, a Nurse, described the consequences, the dead with fractured skulls/severe injuries with* **very few bullet wounds,** *people with severe injuries caused by having been beaten up by sticks, bricks, knives or thrown missiles, with fractures, multiple cuts and bruises; lots of people with more minor injuries needed care too. The dead were piled up on one side: most were younger young adults 18-20 years old. There*

definitely were more soldiers than civilians amongst them. It was more like a medieval skirmish before the existence of gun-powder.

They both felt that, although many shots were fired, few injuries/deaths were caused by bullets; the shots that were heard were mostly directed to the ground or the sky.

Within ten minutes or so the four of us were sobbing; the whole experience was so emotional. It was a very touching. We did not talk about the numbers of the sick and wounded.

Our young driver came back and explained to us in his car that in the early hours of the day after the firing had stopped he had driven around to see what had gone on particularly in the various similar small hospitals surrounding the Square; these small hospitals seemed to be more like our first-aid posts during WWII plus a few beds. The situation was the same as what is described above: bodies piled in a corner. He took as around along the same route showing us the small hospitals. At around 3pm, we felt tired and hungry; I felt grateful for what he had done for us and asked what I could do for him:

'take me out for lunch: there is a nice new Japanese restaurant around the corner; I have never been there; that is where I would like to go'.

The food was very good but it cost me $70.00, an unheard of price in China. But it had been worth it. He then drove us to the station for the trip back to Shijiazhuang.

After thinking about this for twenty years I now feel that no one in the world should carry guns or knives under the age of 25; that includes the Police and the Armed Forces: young members of those forces can do all the other jobs required in those professions.

I will always remember **my wife's Joan's father (Pop Campbell)'s story: during WWI,** he was a soldier in the Black Watch with his kilt; he had to bayonet a German soldier who had suddenly confronted him while he was patrolling in a trench in Northern France; his opponent appeared younger: he waited to be attacked first as the army manual suggested; he parried and he carried scars on both thumbs the rest of his life. His opponent was put off-balance and dear Pop stuck his bayonet in the poor boy's guts; Pop remembers trembling like a leaf observing his opponent dying: it affected him all his life. Killing somebody is no joke.

Huichen and I caught our train back home on time. Huichen, then 33 years old, had always wanted to study ophthalmology like his dad: he was directed to his present career. But then my father, a doctor, had always directed me since the age of five towards following his foot-steps. I was a kid, whereas Huichen was a grown man.

The 40th Anniversary of the Chinese Peoples' Republic, Shijiazuang, the Capital of Hebei Province, Saturday 31st September and Sunday October 1st, 1989.

Security was increased: soldiers with helmets and rifles were stopping cars on the main road right outside the BIPH, the first time I had ever seen that. Only cars and trucks with special large stickers stuck on the windshield were allowed on the streets for those two days.

There was a dinner reception on **Saturday** by the Provincial Government for foreign experts: a total of about 150 people from around the world with their Chinese counterparts, three or four Canadians including one originally from Czechoslovakia. I could just about see Dr Lu Ruling from the BIPH about twenty meters away; at the head-table, four Chinese and five guests, with Vice-Governor Wang to my right. I was at the end of the row. I could only talk with Mr Wang. It was an excellent help-yourself meal with full service only at the head-table. There was another Canadian at the head-table, furious to be sitting there as he wanted to celebrate with his colleagues. The reception started at 5.30, with food from 6 to 7, all the Chinese leaving at 7pm sharp and the whole reception ending at 7:30 sharp. It worked like clock-work. The TV cameras seemed to never stop.

I met a charming Frenchman at the reception, a TV expert for a year at the provincial TV organization. One of his cousins taught at Laval University. I talked quite a bit with my neighbor, Vice-Governor Wang, who was an economist.

We talked mostly about each others' family and our children: he stressed that his own children worked like most other children, teaching, agriculture; it was a mistake to believe that they would have 'capitalist' jobs because he worked as a senior official in Government as is so common in the west.

I never contradicted Mr Wang, talked about my own four children (teaching ESL, secretarial work, medicine/teaching and journalism), Joan, a TESL teacher, and myself, a 65 year old full-time salaried University Professor at the University of Montreal, stressing that the University had always encouraged me to participate in

International projects. I doubt very much whether the BIPH had told him anything about the details of our project. We never mentioned the word 'army', nor Dr Bethune nor the BIPH. We had a very agreeable hour together. It was not up to me to mention anything about our project. He seemed to be a very nice, honest and straight-forward person.

But I doubt whether any other Provincial Capital (63 million people in the whole province) would have dealt with such a celebration in such a somewhat simplistic way. I cannot remember any toasts. It seemed like a first attempt at such an event. It was so different from our congenial celebration in Changchun just two weeks before. The political problems in those two provinces were so different and those in Hebei so much more profound and ancient.

On **Sunday,** I was invited to <u>a picnic in the hills</u> about twenty Km from Shijiazhuang, by two young couples (22-30 years of age) plus our usual funny driver. It was a beautiful day and it kept me out of harm's way. The young have a special ability in China regarding their relationship with older people: frankness, a natural relationship that I have not observed anywhere else. The 22 year-old lady knew all about Stendhal and his best known novel *'Le Rouge et le Noir'*, one of the first popular ones to be written in French (1830).

One of the men then mentioned Balzac (1799-1850). I mentioned that one of the first Chinese novels was written during the mid-eighteenth century, *'A Dream of Red Mansions'*, a good deal earlier. I had just received a copy from Dr Zhao!

A delicious picnic was set on a white table-cloth on mossy ground surrounded by persimmon trees. Their more orange-colored tomato-like fruit was the last food that Dr Bethune had enjoyed just fifty years ago and not that far from where we were. Personally, I do not like persimmons.

That same **<u>Sunday evening</u>** there was a fantastic variety show with acrobats and musicians at the City Auditorium: members of government and foreign experts were there, but the audience included only military personnel in uniform. Civilians were no where to be seen.

On September the 25th, I received two Honorary Letters of Appointment, and was asked to give a speech:

> *It's Our Great Pleasure to Engage Professor Delva as the Honorary Adviser of the* Bethune International Peace Hospital of the Chinese People's Liberation Army.
> *It's Our Great Pleasure to Engage Professor Delva as the Professor of the Centre for Children Health Care and Family Medicine.*

Each printed on a card (8"×11") with nice edging in a lovely material-covered folder half that size, Chinese Script with the translation underneath. I felt the second one was suggested by Dr Li Xifa, head of the department of pediatrics.

What follows is my shortened speech:

> Thank you for all the kindness you have shown me in the past and for the honor you have bestowed me this afternoon; I am very grateful and only wish my dearest Joan could have been here to-day.
>
> Yesterday, I happened to come across a speech by our own Dr Bethune when he opened the model hospital not far from here on September 15th 1938. It later became our BIPH in Shijiazhuang. He talked about **technique.**
>
> Now, it is very dangerous to speak about technology in China: after all, you invented it. Nearly two thousand years ago in Sichuan Province, following improvements in the manufacture of iron and steel, bamboo tubes fitted with valves were lowered to a depth of nearly one thousand meters in the ground in order to extract brine which could be evaporated to produce salt: think of it, bamboo pipes nearly one km deep into the earth two thousand years ago. Most of my Chinese friends lead me to think that technology was a Western invention: we are so behind they say.

Bethune brought to China the **three** world-important techniques developed by the Medical Services of the Spanish Republican Army:

= Blood transfusions at the Front itself: Colonel Bethune, a Canadian in the Spanish Republican Army, was the first to use his own mobile blood transfusion unit at the front in Madrid in **December 1936.** He had given at least seven blood transfusions (one to one) at *l'hopital du Sacre-Coeur* in **1933.** He was the highest foreign officer in the Spanish Republican Army.

- = <u>The Open Treatment of Wounds</u> as suggested by Trueta in Barcelona. Until then, wounds were all stitched up thus ensuring suppuration.
- = <u>The Mobile Hospital</u>, a complete portable one in a three-ton truck, was developed by a New Zealander for the Spanish Republican Army during that same period. It later developed into the MASH type organization so popular on TV.

Now, remember that Dr Bethune was only in Spain for six months: yet he was able to understand these three techniques, export the ideas to China, sell them to Chairman Mao, General Nieh, and to everybody else, and, so much more important, <u>put them into operation himself</u>: here lies his genius. He was not just a **hero** (great deeds), he was a **genius** (powerful good influence) and there are not many of those around; he did all this in the space of only three years, from Spain (December 1936) to his death in China (November 1939). Here is what he said that September 15th 1938:

> *"technique is the term used, in general, to describe the mastery of materials and processes. It is the most efficient way of doing things. It means that, instead of being controlled by nature, we control her. So we talk about the technique of cleaning the floor and the technique of organizing a hospital. The correct way is called 'good technique', the wrong way 'bad technique'.*

> <u>**We must learn the good technique.**</u>"

<u>This applies to everything one does</u>, including Medicine, interviewing, investigating (examination with the help of laboratory, radiology, consultants as needed), diagnosing, then treating and supporting, at the level of the individual, his family, his community and his province/country.

It is an arduous task best coped with when working as a member of a multi-professional team, remunerated by salary. Bonuses for excellence would be awarded according to the recommendations of colleagues.

<u>Unforeseeable events occur within the walls of the BIPH:</u>

For instance, about <u>twenty Mexicans spent three weeks there learning Acupuncture</u>. They loved Mexican Music and rarely went to bed before 2am: the evening of their departure they gave a party and invited everyone to dance. Their 'leader' was a charming and attractive 72 year old lady, and she personally invited the Chinese seniors present to join in. All this 'joy de vivre' was so unusual. It totally upset the calm and apparent usual serenity of the BIPH.

A Chinese teacher of English had a scholarship study at a Canadian university but had been unable to obtain a visa from the Embassy. I had to telephone Marilyn Colette several times at the Embassy to settle the problem at the last minute.

My Teaching Medical English (!):

Dr Lu Ruling had made arrangements that people from Singapore would come and teach English for six weeks to a group of 24 younger doctors from the Beijing Military Area (Hebei Province, Shanxi Province and eastern Mongolia). The Singaporeans had cancelled their assignment at the last minute and Lu Ruling, by now a good friend, had no other option than to ask me to take over, 3 times a week for three hours. He had always been so helpful and he was passing through a sticky patch himself particularly as far as our program was concerned, so I accepted. My course was entitled

'On Reading Medical Journals'.

Those young doctors were a very nice bunch: luckily for me, Wei Jey Ling, (alias Sister Jacqueline) took over after her arrival on October 15th. So my load lasted just three weeks. I had my series of five articles from the New England Medical Journal written by a group from the Hamilton (Ontario) Medical School mostly on Epidemiology and Statistics, basic reading for all future doctors anywhere in the world: the students got a copy of an article to keep every week. I would read it slowly one week, and discuss it next time before reading another article.

I felt totally exhausted after those three-hour spells. I think it was a useful endeavor. At any rate, the number of attendants increased, and at the end there were several older attendees.

We had a little party at the end of the course: we sat around a large table. One was beating a drum. We had to pass a bunch of flowers to our neighbor, and when the drum stopped, the person with the flowers had to perform. The Canadians had decided to sing 'Alouette', an easy task. One of the students might sing an aria from a Chinese opera, another recite a poem, in English as much as possible. After an hour they started to dance to cassettes of American Music. It was quite a pleasant if unexpected evening.

All day Thursday and Friday morning November 2nd/3rd we were in Beijing with a colleague from Montreal, Dr Marcel Provost and Jacqueline Villemure: we visited the Chinese Friendship Association with Foreign Countries which now had a new Oceania/Canada desk with its director, Mr Wang, and Ms Marilyn Colette at the Canadian Embassy whom I had met before. Mr Wang had spent seven years at the Chinese Embassy in Ottawa from its beginning in 1973.

Neither of them knew anything about the commemoration of Dr Bethune on the 50th anniversary of his death on November 11th. Ms Colette telephoned the office of the Ambassador: the Ambassador had just received a message that there would be a ceremony.

Ms Colette then asked me to inform Mr Wang that the Ambassador would be happy to attend provided he received an official invitation from the Friendship Association.

I did not even know the Ambassador's name, whereas the three ambassadors before him had always been so personal, cooperative and pleasant. I only recently realized that the Ambassador did not approve of Dr Bethune and had requested that his name should not be mentioned in his presence.

I telephoned Mr Wang; the official invitation arrived in due course on the afternoon of November the 10th. The Ambassador was nowhere to be seen at the Commemoration. Nor was he in Shijiazhuang the following day at Dr Bethune's burial site.

The First Congress of General Medicine in China, [*] Beijing.
(Friday afternoon November 3rd-Tuesday 7th).

WONCA [**] was implicated in the organization of the Congress from the start. About three hundred people attended, 150 from around the world mostly

---

[*] *en Francais, Medecine Generale*; in English, General Practice, now called Family Medicine in Canada. A Society of General Medicine was founded in Beijing on January 23rd 1989. Dr Li Shichuo was its President.

[**] World Organization of National Colleges and Academies of General Practice/ Family Medicine, founded largely by Canadians in Montreal in April 1964; thirty countries were represented. I was at the well-attended and well-organized 10th conference in Singapore in May 1983.

from the Far-East, and 150 Chinese from around the country. The Chinese never had the opportunity of meeting anybody: they arrived by bus at 8.59am and left at 12.01pm for lunch, returning at 1.59pm and leaving at 5.01pm. We never talked or ate together. The Chinese Federal Minister of Health, Chen Minzhang, attended the first and the last cessions.

At the introductory luncheon, my allotted seat was next to that of an Editor in Beijing of the Chinese Medical Journals. I asked him how they coped with regular meetings of all the different branches of Medicine in such a large country: there are yearly provincial meetings of each specialty, and the National meetings occur every three years in Beijing again for each specialty.

I presented a paper on the Epidemiology of Primary Care (the Kerr-White Square[***]) plus the paragraph below, and Marcel Provost talked about the training of Family Physicians/General Practitioners at the University of Montreal.

A large public health problem is looming in China: In Beijing, the three leading causes of death are cerebro-vascular accidents, heart attacks, and cancer; in China there are only 150 million people over the age of 50: by 2030, they will number 550 million. The idea of a general practitioner, working within a team of health workers and volunteers, seems a logical practical solution for providing health care to that older group.

I met a senior Public Health doctor from Shanghai. 80% of young Children in China are anemic: he reassured me that the cause was entirely nutritional. He also answered my question regarding pay: a general Practitioner in Shanghai might earn 4,000 US$ a year, whereas a surgeon would earn three or four times more. In Taiwan, a general Practitioner might earn $100,000/year. One of the attendees from Hong-Kong told me he drove a Bentley.

At the concluding dinner, my neighbor was the Senior Public Health person from the North-West of the country, probably Urumqui.

The Fiftieth Anniversary of the Death of Dr Norman Bethune on November 11th 1989:

The three of us were guests of the Chinese Government from Friday November 10th to Tuesday November 14th.

Our base was the old Residence of General Chiang Kai Shek, very comfortable. A tall wall with a guarded gate surrounded a beautiful not too large residence with a lovely garden and a pond. I shared a room with Marcel. We were delighted to see Dr Wendell McLeod, 84 years old. Wendell had

---

[***] **Kerr-White** considered 1000 working adults for one month: 750 don't feel well during that month, 250 consult a physician, seven see a specialist/consultant and one is admitted to hospital. The figures originate from a US National Census.

been asked to say a few words the next morning. He had met Dr Bethune while he was a medical student at McGill (1928) and worked with him in the thirties on the famous report on the future of Health Services in Quebec. He knew him at least as well as any other Canadian.

The Reception and the Meeting at the Great Hall of the People on Tiananmen Square:

> The Great Hall of the People is the home of the National People's Congress: every March, the Great Hall plays host to the *liang hui* (two meetings): the Chinese People's Political Consultative Conference (SCPCC) and the National People's Congress (NPC). The Communist Party of China (CPC) holds its' National Congress there every five years. The lower auditorium seats 3,693, the balcony 3,515 and the gallery 2,518.
>
> Our three hosts were **Han Xu,** President of the Society of Friendship of China with Foreign Countries (ex Chinese Ambassador in the USA), **Jiang Zenmin,** President of China, and **Li Ruihuan,** ex-mayor of Tianjin, a Standing Committee member of the Political Bureau of the CPC Central Committee, thought by many at the time as the new Chinese Gorbatchev.

The **Reception** was so simple: such informality can only occur in China. In addition to the three top leaders already mentioned, there were the two previous Ministers of Health whom I had met in Changchun earlier in the year. We all shook hands. Also there, Dr Mueller, an old German Physician in a wheel-chair with his nurse; he had worked at the BIPH from 1939 onwards. I had heard about him, and was delighted to meet him: I asked him whether he would object to my taking a photo and replied that he would be delighted. Dr Lu Ruling from the BIPH was there.

The **Meeting** in the Great Hall of the People followed: we all walked there just a few steps away.

We were sitting on chairs on the stage, looking at about two thousand young soldiers in uniform crowded on the left side of the balcony and gallery, perhaps one third of the space available on those two floors: there was not one civilian in sight in the audience. On the stage itself there were not more than 30 people. The television crew was there, concentrating on the left side of the balcony/gallery. At the back of the stage there were chairs for attendees.

About ten people were in the front, including Dr McLeod and myself, plus the Chinese leaders and Lu Ruling. The speeches were all so innocuous.

Wendell got up and talked for perhaps two or three minutes without a text concerning the Tiananmen episode:

> *"I felt sick to my stomach and was unable to sleep: I thought the whole thing was a disaster, never believing it could be possible. I could'nt imagine what Dr Bethune would have said!"*

That was the message: it was repeated two or three times. Then he turned round and looked at me anxiously; I put my thumb up and he smiled. He looked so tired. He told me he had written three texts during the night that he had torn up. He decided not to have a text. Unfortunately, few understood colloquial English. How could a Chinese interpreter cope without a text?

The tragedy is that no one was present from the Embassy.

That evening, we had an absolutely delicious dinner in one of the best restaurants in town. There were ten Canadians and ten Chinese. I sat between Lu Wanru and Dr/Mrs Kotnis.

Her husband was the Indian Physician who had trained at Grant University in Bombay (one of the best in India) and had succeeded Dr Bethune at the BIPH in 1939. She was then a young nurse who later became a pediatrician. Her husband died within a couple of years from epilepsy caused by a tape-worm settling in the brain creating a cyst, cysticercosis. Dr Kotnis had kept the long tape-worm that he had passed in his stools in a jar; he used it for teaching. They had a little boy who was killed during the Cultural Revolution in his twenties. His wife still worked in Changchun at the BMU and I had met her there.

I was so happy to meet Lu Wanru who had escorted us during our first three-week visit to China in 1980. She understood the problems we were going through. She knew Wendell and had attended the Bethune Conference in Montreal in 1979. We had lots of things to talk about.

On Sunday November the 12th, we returned to Shijiazhuang on the 9am express: two extra high-grade carriages had been added to the train, one with a table surrounded by comfortable arm-chairs; one could so easily walk around. Two old Chinese Generals were on board, General Liu and General Weichuantong. Six people on that train had worked with Dr Bethune, two Canadians and four Chinese.

In the evening, the **Hebei Government** invited us all to dinner: there were about fifty of us, but only two from the BIPH, the Commissar and Lu Ruling, sitting as far from us as possible. I was sitting between the Provincial Minister of Public Health,

Wang Chunran, and the Director of Foreign Affairs of the City of Shijiazhuang, with a senior interpreter close-by. They never asked me a question; it soon became clear that they expected me to talk about our project about which they knew nothing at all.

I did just that, talked about the history of the project, stressing that Dr Bethune and the BIPH was an important link between Canada and China. I had first visited Shijiazhuang when the BIPH was its most important hospital nine years before. The BIPH was the first PLA Hospital in Shijiazhuang in September 1949, thus playing an important role in the development of the new China. The town had grown so fast subsequently. We parted full of good intentions for the future.

On Monday morning, November 13th, twelve hundred places were allotted in the Hospital Meeting Hall, fifty of them to the hospital: **not one of those fifty seats had been allotted to the Hospital Clinicians,** and not one of them accompanied us to <u>Bethune's</u> there; it was quite a moving experience. Thus, our dear friends who had come over as our guests and spent four weeks in Canada, had visited Gravenhurst where Dr Bethune was born and the hospitals where he had worked in Montreal, were not there on the fiftieth anniversary of his death not too far away from where we were. Dr Zhao had worked at that hospital for forty years.

That same evening, there was a final dinner at the hospital. Again, there were no clinicians present amongst the fifty or so guests, from administration, logistics, medical affairs and political affairs.

On Tuesday November 14th, four senior officers including the Commissar and Li Ruling came to see us off, with gifts for Joan (a wooly coat) and me (a leather jacket). Sun Huichen and Jin Hede, then head of Foreign Affairs at the Hospital, drove us to the airport. They asked me what I felt about the celebrations: I expressed my sorrow at the isolation of my Chinese Friends who had come to Canada: **"things have changed in China since we went to Xi Baipo last March"** said Jin Hede.

It was nice to return home.

Postscript:

I never saw **Li Ruling** again: he was transferred to administer a small 200 bed hospital in Beijing. His successor was a Colonel who bullied people around. Our project ended satisfactorily on time and on budget at the end of 1993. **Li Ruling was a great guy.**

The next step the **leaders of the country** should take to settle finally the Tiananmen tragedy is to **build a memorial** on the square with the names of all the dead and **compensate** the relatives of those young people that lost their lives so stupidly.

What pushed me to write this final chapter was the issue of **Granta 105!**

The most important contribution of **Jacqueline Villemure** to our program was her offering to take over the training in Montreal of the **future nursing director of the BIPH: Wang Yali** was an exceptionally bright young lady who spent a whole year at the Montreal Children's Hospital spending time in activities that covered every possible aspect of modern nursing. At the BIPH, Nursing had only recently become a Department. That contribution was providential.

Half of our students eventually became Heads of Department.